REDUPLICATION

This groundbreaking new study takes a novel approach to reduplication, a phenomenon whereby languages use repetition to create new words. Sharon Inkelas and Cheryl Zoll argue that the driving force in reduplication is identity at the morphosyntactic, not the phonological, level and present a new model of reduplication – Morphological Doubling Theory – that derives the full range of reduplication patterns. This approach shifts the focus away from the relatively small number of cases of phonological overapplication and underapplication, which have played a major role in earlier studies, to the larger class of cases where base and reduplicant diverge phonologically. The authors conclude by arguing for a theoretical shift in phonology, which entails more attention to word structure. As well as presenting the authors' pioneering work, this book also provides a much-needed overview of reduplication, the study of which has become one of the most contentious in modern phonological theory.

SHARON INKELAS is Professor in the Department of Linguistics, University of California at Berkeley. She has over fifteen years' research and teaching experience and has been in the Department of Linguistics at the University of California, Berkeley since 1992. She is the author of a wide variety of articles in phonology and morphology.

CHERYL ZOLL is Associate Professor in the Department of Linguistics and Philosophy, Massachusetts Institute of Technology, with research interests in phonology and morphology, particularly in relation to African languages. She is the author of *Parsing Below the Segment* (1998) as well as numerous articles on a variety of topics in phonology and morphology.

In this series

CAMBRIDGE STUDIES IN LINGUISTICS

General editors: P. AUSTIN, J. BRESNAN, B. COMRIE,
S. CRAIN, W. DRESSLER, C. J. EWEN, R. LASS,
D. LIGHTFOOT, K. RICE, I. ROBERTS, S. ROMAINE
N. V. SMITH

Reduplication

REDUPLICATION

DOUBLING IN MORPHOLOGY

SHARON INKELAS

University of California, Berkeley

and

CHERYL ZOLL

Massachusetts Institute of Technology

CAMBRIDGE
UNIVERSITY PRESS

PUBLISHED BY THE PRESS SYNDICATE OF THE UNIVERSITY OF CAMBRIDGE
The Pitt Building, Trumpington Street, Cambridge, United Kingdom

CAMBRIDGE UNIVERSITY PRESS
The Edinburgh Building, Cambridge, CB2 2RU, UK
40 West 20th Street, New York, NY 10011–4211, USA
477 Williamstown Road, Port Melbourne, VIC 3207, Australia
Ruiz de Alarcón 13, 28014 Madrid, Spain
Dock House, The Waterfront, Cape Town 8001, South Africa

http://www.cambridge.org

First published 2005

Printed in the United Kingdom at the University Press, Cambridge

Typeface Times 10/13 pt.   *System* LATEX 2ε   [TB]

A catalogue record for this book is available from the British Library

ISBN 0 521 80649 6 hardback

Contents

Acknowledgments

The broad focus of this book has given us the opportunity to benefit from the expertise of a multitude of linguists whose interest and insightful input have contributed immeasurably to the construction of a morphological theory of reduplication. Orhan Orgun and Larry Hyman challenged and inspired us throughout. Juliette Blevins, Andrew Garrett, Michael Kenstowicz, Teresa McFarland, Anne Pycha, Richard Rhodes, Ronald Sprouse, and Donca Steriade all read the manuscript in various stages and facilitated the development of our ideas with their penetrating critiques. We owe a debt of gratitude as well to Terry Crowley, Laura Downing, Danny Fox, Claire Lefebvre, Frank Lichtenberk, Johanna Nichols, Nick Sherrard, Galen Sibanda, Rajendra Singh, Ken VanBik, and many others who generously provided us with useful materials and shared their knowledge about languages, phenomena, and theories once unfamiliar to us. We also thank our students, east and west, for their stimulating interest and willingness to participate in the development of MDT. The work benefited significantly from the feedback of audiences at a number of colloquia and conferences, including Phonology 2000 (MIT/Harvard), NAPhC (Concordia University, Montreal), the 1999 Linguistics Society of America Meeting, and the 2002 Graz Reduplication Conference (Graz, Austria), and from discussions at UC Berkeley and MIT during various less formal presentations. Much of this book was written with the generous support of the Radcliffe Institute for Advanced Study at Harvard University, which assisted one of the authors with a fellowship in 2001–2002. We are grateful also to the Linguistics Department at UC Davis for providing office space and a library card during one crucial summer. Anne Nesbet, Nancy Katz, Klara Moricz, and David Schneider provided unending encouragement. Vineeta Chand sustained us with her expert and cool-headed copy-editing, and Anne Pycha took time in a busy semester to research the language table. We thank, finally, our families: the children we raise on our laps while we type, Jem, Eli, and Lydia, and our spouses, Orhan Orgun and Eric Sawyer, who remove them at crucial moments for their occasional bath or hot meal, and who provide boundless moral and logistical support. This book is dedicated to our children, and to Curry Sawyer, whose inspiration, practical assistance, and unparalleled ability to get things done make everything possible.

Table of languages

This table of languages is a compilation of information from the sources consulted in this work and the SIL Ethnologue, available from SIL International at http://www.ethnologue.com.

Language	Primary country	Regions within primary country	Secondary countries	Special note
Abkhaz	Georgia	Abkhazia	Turkey, Ukraine	
Amele	Papua New Guinea	Madang Province		
Amuesha	Peru	Central and eastern Pasco region		
Apma	Vanuatu	Central Pentecost (Raga)		
Arapesh	Papua New Guinea	North coast		
Armenian	Armenia		29 others	
Arosi	Solomon Islands	Northwest Makira (San Cristobal) Island		
Arrernte	Australia	Northern Territory, Alice Springs area		
Axininca Campa	Peru	Pichis and Sheshea tributaries of the Pachitea River		
Babine	Canada	West central British Columbia		
Banoni	Papua New Guinea	North Solomons Province, southwestern Bougainville		
Bella Coola	Canada	Central British Columbia coast		
Bellonese	Solomon Islands	Rennell and Bellona Islands		
Bierebo	Vanuatu	West Epi		

(*cont.*)

Language	Primary country	Regions within primary country	Secondary countries	Special note
Boumaa Fijian	Fiji		Nauru, New Zealand, Vanuatu	
Burmese	Myanmar	South, central, and adjacent areas	Bangladesh, Malaysia, Thailand, USA	
Chaha	Ethiopia	West Gurage Region		
Chamorro	Guam		Northern Mariana Islands	
Chechen	Russia	Chechnya, north Caucasus	Georgia, Germany, Jordan, Kazakhstan, Kyrgyzstan, Syria, Turkey, Uzbekistan	
Chichêwa	Malawi	West central and southwestern	Botswana, Mozambique, Zambia, Zimbabwe	
Chinese, Mandarin	China	Northern and southwestern China	Brunei, Cambodia, Indonesia, Laos, Malaysia, Mauritius, Mongolia, Philippines, Russia, Singapore, Taiwan, Thailand, United Kingdom, USA, Vietnam	
Chukchee	Russia	Northeastern Siberia		
Chumash	USA	Southern California coast		Extinct
Dakota	USA	Northern Nebraska, southern Minnesota, North and South Dakota, northeastern Montana	Canada	
Diyari	Australia	South Australia, Leigh Creek		Extinct
Dyirbal	Australia	Northeast Queensland		
Eastern Kadazan	Malaysia	Northeast Sabah, Sandakan, Labuk-Sugut, and Kinabatangan districts		
Emai	Vanuatu	Emae		
English	United Kingdom, USA		104 others	

Language	Country	Region	Also spoken in
Fongbe	Benin	South central	Togo
Fox	USA	Eastern Kansas-Nebraska border and central Oklahoma	
Fula	Guinea	Northwest, Fouta Djallon area	Gambia, Guinea-Bissau, Mali, Senegal, Sierra Leone
Gapapaiwa	Papua New Guinea	Milne Bay Province	
German	Germany		40 others
Hausa	Nigeria	Throughout northern Nigeria	Benin, Burkina Faso, Cameroon, CAR, Chad, Congo, Eritrea, Germany, Ghana, Niger, Sudan, Togo
(Modern) Hebrew	Israel		Australia, Canada, Germany, Palestinian West Bank and Gaza, Panama, United Kingdom, USA
Hindi	India	Throughout northern India	Bangladesh, Belize, Botswana, Germany, Kenya, Nepal, New Zealand, Philippines, Singapore, South Africa, Uganda, UAE, United Kingdom, USA, Yemen, Zambia
Hopi	USA	Northeastern Arizona, southeastern Utah, northwestern New Mexico	
Hua	Papua New Guinea	Eastern Highlands Province, Goroka District	
Hungarian	Hungary		Australia, Austria, Canada, Israel, Romania, Slovakia, Slovenia, Ukraine, USA, Yugoslavia
Ilokano	Philippines	Northern Luzon	USA
Indonesian	Indonesia		Netherlands, Philippines, Saudi Arabia, Singapore, USA

(cont.)

Language	Primary country	Regions within primary country	Secondary countries	Special note
Japanese	Japan		26 others	
Jaqaru	Peru	Lima Department, Yauyos Province		
Javanese	Indonesia	Java and resettlements in Irian Jaya, Sulawesi, Maluku, Kalimantan, and Sumatra	Malaysia (Sabah), Netherlands, Singapore	
Kashaya	USA	Northern California		Nearly extinct
Kawaiisu	USA	California; Mojave Desert		Possibly extinct
Khasi	India	Assam; Meghalaya, Khasi-Jaintia hills; Manipur; West Benga	Bangladesh	
Khmer	Cambodia			
Kikerewe	Tanzania	Northwestern Ukerewe Island, southern Lake Victoria, Kibara	China, France, Laos, USA, Vietnam	
Kinande	Democratic Republic of Congo	Nord-Kivu Province		
Klamath	USA	South central Oregon		Nearly extinct
Kolami	India	Northwestern Kolami: Maharashtra, Yavatmal, Wardha, and Nanded districts; Andhra Pradesh; Madhya Pradesh Southeastern Kolami: Andhra Pradesh, Adilabad District; Maharashtra, Chandrapur, and Nanded districts		

Language	Country	Region	Other locations	Status
Lango	Uganda	Lango province, north of Lake Kyoga		
Lushootseed	USA	Washington, Puget Sound area		Nearly extinct
Madurese	Indonesia	Island of Madura, Sapudi Islands, northern coastal area of eastern Java	Singapore	
Malay	Malaysia	Peninsular Malaysia, Sabah, and Sarawak		
Johore Malay	Malaysia	Johor state		
Ulu Muar Malay	Malaysia	Southeast of Kuala Lumpur, Ulu Muar District		
Malayalam	India	Kerala, Laccadive Islands, and neighboring state	Bahrain, Fiji, Israel, Malaysia, Qatar, Singapore, UAE, United Kingdom	
Mangarayi	Australia	Mataranka and Elsey stations, Northern Territory		
Marathi	India	Maharashtra and adjacent states	Mauritius	
Marquesan	French Polynesia	Marquesas Islands: Hatutu, Nuku Hiva, Ua Huka, Ua Pou islands South Marquesan: Marquesas Islands: Hiva Oa, Tahuta, Fatu Hiva islands		
Mende	Sierra Leone	South central	Liberia	
Miya	Nigeria	Bauchi State, Ganjuwa LGA, Miya town		
Mongolian	Mongolia	Buryat ASSR of Russia and Issyk-Kul Oblast of Kyrgyzstan	Kyrgyzstan, Russia, Taiwan	
Nadrogā	Fiji	Fiji Islands, western half of Viti Levu, Waya Islands		
Nakanamanga	Vanuatu	Efate, Shepherd islands		
Namakir	Vanuatu	Efate, Shepherd islands		

(cont.)

Language	Primary country	Regions within primary country	Secondary countries	Special note
Nāti	Vanuatu	Malakula		
Navajo	USA	Northeastern Arizona, northwestern New Mexico, southeastern Utah, southwestern Colorado		
Ndebele	Zimbabwe	Matabeleland, around Bulawayo	Botswana	
Nez Perce	USA	Northern Idaho		
Niuafo'ou	Tonga	Niuafo'ou and 'Eua islands		
Orokaiva	Papua New Guinea	Oro Province Popondetta District		
Oykangand	Australia	Wrotham Park, Kowanyama, Edward River, Queensland		
Paamese	Vanuatu	Paama, east Epi, Vila		
Pacoh	Vietnam	Bl'nh Tri Thien Province	Laos	
Pali	India	(literary language of Buddhist scriptures)	Myanmar, Sri Lanka	Extinct
Piro (Yine)	Peru	East central Urubamba River area		
Ponapean	Micronesia	Pohnpei Island, Caroline Islands		
Quechua	Peru	Northeast Huánuco Department		
Raga	Vanuatu	Pentecost island		
Rotuman	Fiji	Rotuma Island		
Roviana	Solomon Islands	North central New Georgia, Roviana Lagoon, Vonavona Lagoon; Western Province		
Sahaptin	USA	North central Oregon		
Sanskrit	India			
Sekani	Canada	North central British Columbia		

Language	Country	Region	Also spoken in
Serbo-Croatian	Yugoslavia		Albania, Australia, Austria, Bosnia-Herzegovina, Bulgaria, Canada, Croatia, Germany, Greece, Hungary, Italy, Macedonia, Romania, Russia, Slovakia, Slovenia, Sweden, Switzerland, Turkey
Sereer	Senegal	West central Senegal and the Sine and Saloum River valleys	Gambia
Siroi	Papua New Guinea	Madang Province, Saidor District	
Siswati	Swaziland		Mozambique, South Africa
Slave	Canada	Northwest Territories, northern Alberta	
Southeast Ambrym	Vanuatu	Southeast Ambrym Island	
Spokane	USA	Northeastern Washington	
Sundanese	Indonesia	Western third of Java Island	
Sye	Vanuatu	Erromango Island	
Tagalog	Philippines	Manila, most of Luzon, and Mindoro	Canada, Guam, Midway Islands, Saudi Arabia, UAE, United Kingdom, USA
Tamil	India	Tamil Nadu and neighboring states	Bahrain, Fiji, Germany, Malaysia (Peninsular), Mauritius, Netherlands, Qatar, Réunion, Singapore, South Africa, Sri Lanka, Thailand, UAE, United Kingdom
Tarok	Nigeria	Plateau State, Kanam, Wase, and Langtang LGAs; Gongola State, Wukari LGA	
Tawala	Papua New Guinea	Milne Bay Province	
Telugu	India	Andhra Pradesh and neighboring states	Bahrain, Fiji, Malaysia, Mauritius, Singapore, UAE

(cont.)

Language	Primary country	Regions within primary country	Secondary countries	Special note
Tohono O'odham	USA	South central Arizona	Mexico	
Trukese	Micronesia	Chuuk Lagoon, Caroline Islands, some on Ponape	Guam	
Turkish	Turkey		35 other countries	
Ulithian	Micronesia	Ulithi, Ngulu, Sorol, Fais islands, eastern Caroline Islands		
Umpila	Australia	Cape York Peninsula, north of Cairns		
Urdu	Pakistan			
Vietnamese	Vietnam		Afghanistan, Bahrain, Bangladesh, Botswana, Fiji, Germany, Guyana, India, Malawi, Mauritius, Nepal, Norway, Oman, Qatar, Saudi Arabia, South Africa, Thailand, UAE, United Kingdom, Zambia	
Warlpiri	Australia	Northern Territory, Yuendumu, Ali Curung Willowra, Alice Springs, Katherine, Darwin, and Lajamanu		
Yoruba	Nigeria	Oyo, Ogun, Ondo Osun, Kwara, and Lagos states; and western LGAs of Kogi State	Benin, Togo, United Kingdom, USA	
Yupik, Central Alaskan	USA	Nunivak Island, Alaska coast from Bristol Bay to Unalakleet on Norton Sound and inland along Nushagak, Kuskokwim, and Yukon rivers		

Abbreviations used in morpheme glosses

3SG	3rd person singular	INF	infinitive
ABS	absolutive	INTR	intransitive
ADJ	adjective	LOC	locative
AF	actor focus	MID	middle
AOR	aorist	MULREC	multiple reciprocal
ASS.COL	associate collective	MULSER	multiple serial distribution
AUG	augmentative	n.	noun
CAUS	causative	NEG	negative
CL	classifier	N.INTEN	non-intentive
COMP	completive	N.SER	non-serious
COMPR	comprehensive	NML	nominal(izer)
CONT	continuative	NONFUT	non-future
CTR	control	NONPRES	non-present
DEF	definite	NPAST	non-past
DES	desiderative	OBJ	object
DIM	diminutive	OBV	obviative
DISS	dissimulation	OP	operator
DIST	distributive	PERF	perfective
DOM	dominant	PL	plural
DU	dual	POSS	possessive
DUR	durative	PP	past participle
DX	deictic	PRES/PRS	present
ERG	ergative	PRO	pronoun
EXAS	exasperation	REC	recent completive (E. Kadazan)
EXCL	exclusive		
FUT	future	REC	recessive
IMP	imperative	REP	repetitive
IMPERF/IMPF	imperfective	RF	referent focus
INCL	inclusive		

s.o.	someone	T rs	transitive subject
s.t.	something	U F	undergoer focus
S F X	suffix	U N . D I S T	unequal distribution
S G	singular		
sp	species	V	verb
S U B J	subject	V B L	verbalizer
T R / T R A N S	transitive	W P	witnessed past

1 *Introduction*

Repetition is encountered in every language and affects all types of linguistic units. One finds reiteration of phrases, as in the Quechua example in (1a), of words, as in the Amele example in (1b), and even of single segments, as in the onomatopœtic ideophone from English (1c):

(1)   a. Chawra mishi alpurhapita **[horqorkur kutirkUchir] [horqorkur kutirkUchir]** huk umallantashi chunka ishkayta yupaykun.

        'Then the cat, **repeatedly removing** the head from the saddlebag and **returning** it, counts the one head twelve times.' (Weber 1989:323)[1]

    b. Odeceb **fojen**. Rum oso eu **fojen**. Ihoc leceb haun rum oso na li **fojen**. Ihoc leceb haun rum oso na li **fojen**. Ihoc leceb oso na ha li ihoc leceb haun jo oso na toni nu lena. **Fojen**. Ihoc leceb jo oso na toni nu len eu na **fojen** ihoc len. Rum cunug ca **foji** hedon. Odimei madon, "Quila qa ihoc," don.

        'Then she **vomited**. She **vomited** in that room. Then after she had filled that room with **vomit** she went to another room and filled that with **vomit** and then filled another room with **vomit**. Then she went down and went to another house. She **vomited** there. She filled all those rooms with **vomit**. Then she finished **vomiting** and said to him, "Now that is enough."' (Roberts 1987:255–56)

    c. English: [ʃ-ʃ-ʃ-ʃ-ʃ-ʃ . . .] 'be quiet!'

This book concerns itself with a select subtype of repetition, namely grammatical doubling or duplication effects within words, illustrated by the forms in (2). Word-internal reduplication may be partial (a) or total (b, c); it may involve perfect identity between copies (c) or exhibit imperfect identity (a, b).[2]

(2)   a. Hausa   kiraː   'call'   kik-kiraː   (pluractional)
        b. Amele   bala-doʔ 'to tear' bala-bulu-doʔ (irregular iterative)
        c. Warlpiri kamina 'girl'   kamina-kamina (plural)

The mechanism of reduplication and manner in which copies can differ from each other have been a foundational concern in theoretical and descriptive linguistics over the past twenty-five years. They constitute the central interest of this book.

1.1   Two approaches to duplication

Speaking broadly, two general approaches to duplication are possible: *phono-logical copying* and *morpho-semantic (MS) feature duplication*. Phonological copying is an essentially phonological process that duplicates features, seg-ments, or metrical constituents, as in the example of 'eat' in (3a). Under MS feature duplication, two identical sets of abstract syntactic/semantic features ('EAT', in (3b)) are provided by the grammar and spelled out independently (3b).

(3)   a. [EAT]   →   [eat]   →   [eat-eat]
                         Spellout   **Phonological copying**
         b. [EAT]   →   [EAT] [EAT]   →   [eat-eat]
               MS feature duplication   ***Spellout***

While theories of morphological reduplication have focused on the duplica-tion mechanism of phonological copying, it is the thesis of the present work that both mechanisms are needed and that their empirical domains of application are nearly complementary. In introducing this vision it is useful first to consider cases which clearly instantiate the two poles of duplication.

The clearest examples of phonological copying are those in which small pieces of phonological structure are copied to satisfy a phonological well-formedness constraint. In Hausa (Chadic), for example, the most productive noun pluralization suffix is *-oːCiː*, whose medial consonant is a copy of the final consonant of the noun stem (Newman 2000:431–32). As noted by Newman, who calls this phenomenon "pseudoreduplication" (p. 511), copying is driven by the need to flesh out an underspecified suffixal consonant (or, on another view, to provide an onset to the final syllable of the suffix). The data shown here are taken from Newman 2000:432:

(4)   a. bindigàː   bindig-oːgiː   'gun/guns'
         b. fannìː   fann-oːniː   'category/categories'
         c. hùkuːmàː   hukuːm-oːmiː   'governmental body/bodies'

The well-known Yoruba gerundive construction constitutes another instance of phonologically driven copying (Akinlabi 1985, Pulleyblank 1988, Kawu 1998).[3] Gerunds are formed by prefixation of a high front vowel marked with a high tone (*í-*), preceded by a copy consonant whose presence Akinlabi and Kawu attribute to the need for Yoruba syllables to begin with a consonantal onset. Although Alderete et al. (1999) treat Yoruba gerunds as resulting from morphological reduplication, Akinlabi and Kawu instead view them as an instance of what Newman (2000) calls "pseudoreduplication" or what Urbanczyk (1998) calls "non-reduplicative copying." The data below are taken from Kawu 1998:3:

(5) Verb   Gerund

gbé	**gb-í**-gbé	'take; taking'
jɛ	**j-í**-jɛ	'eat; eating'
wɔ	**w-í**-wɔ	'enter; entering'
wã	**w-í**-wã	'measure; measuring'
bú	**b-í**-bú	'insult; insulting'

In contrast to phonologically driven local duplication of phonological material are clear cases of MS feature duplication. Such cases typically have morphological or syntactic, rather than phonological, motivation; they duplicate more than a single phonological element; and they may not even result in phonological identity. Consider, for example, Modern Hebrew VP-fronting, a construction in which the verb is spelled out in two positions (Landau 2003:7):[4]

(6)   lirkod,   Gil lo   yirkod   ba-xayim
       to-dance, Gil not will-dance in-the-life
       'Dance, Gil never will'

The source of MS feature duplication will vary across theoretical frameworks; on Landau's analysis, verb doubling results from the pronunciation of two links of a chain (i.e. copies of identical feature bundles in the terms of Chomsky 1995; 2000). What is relevant is that the duplication in (6) cannot be analyzed as phonological copying. It is not motivated by phonological well-formedness and the two copies are not even phonologically (or morphologically) identical. While there is full inflection on the lower copy of the verb, the higher verb is an infinitive. Divergent spellout of this sort is a clear sign that what is being copied is an abstract syntactic or semantic aspect of the representation, rather than phonological material.

Despite the existence of these two very different mechanisms for duplicating grammatical material, virtually no attention has been given in the reduplication literature to arguing for one over the other. Instead, theoretical approaches to morphological reduplication have focused nearly exclusively on the idea that phonological copying occurs to flesh out a skeletal reduplicative morpheme (see, for example, Marantz & Wiltshire 2000 for a recent overview).[5] The example in (7), using the Warlpiri form for 'girls' (Nash 1986:130), illustrates total reduplication under the dominant derivational approach taken in the 1980s (Marantz 1982; Clements 1985; Kiparsky 1986; Mester 1986; Steriade 1988). RED, a skeletal Prosodic Word affix marking the plural, is fleshed out by copying the base segments and associating the copies by rule to the RED template.

(7)　　Morphological reduplication by phonological copying

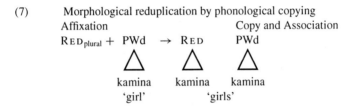

The more recent Base-Reduplication Correspondence Theory (BRCT) approach to reduplication in the Optimality Theory literature makes the same assumptions, with the additional proposal that copying into the RED morpheme is coerced by violable constraints that compel RED to be identical to the base (McCarthy & Prince 1993; 1995a; for an overview, see Kager 1999). In the Chumash example in (8) (Applegate 1976), RED is required, by the output constraint $RED = \sigma_{\mu\mu}$, to instantiate a bimoraic syllable and, by BR-FAITH, to correspond segmentally to the material in the base. IO-FAITH » $RED = \sigma_{\mu\mu}$ prevents the base from truncating:

(8)　　Morphological reduplication by BR correspondence

	RED,čʰumaš	IO-FAITH	RED=$\sigma_{\mu\mu}$	BR-FAITH
☞ a.	čʰum-čʰumaš			aš
b.	čʰumaš-čʰumaš		aš!	
c.	čʰum-čʰum	aš!		

A definitive rationale for providing a phonological copying analysis, rather than a MS feature duplication analysis, of phenomena of this type has not been provided in the literature.[6] One likely motivation for the focus on phonological copying is the variety of phonological modifications that often accompany morphological reduplication.[7] However, as is argued at length in Chapters 3 and 4 of this book, phonological modification is not restricted to morphological reduplication and cannot be used as a criterion to determine the doubling mechanism. Truncation is found not only in morphological constructions which are not reduplicative (see, for example, Weeda 1992; McCarthy & Prince 1999b and Chapter 3), but is found even in clearly "syntactic" reduplication constructions where MS feature duplication is unequivocally at work.

Consider, for example, the phenomenon in Fongbe (Kwa) which Lefebvre and Brousseau (2002) analyze as syntactic doubling of the verb. Verb doubling occurs in four syntactic constructions: temporal adverbials (9a), causal adverbials (9b), factives (9c), and predicate clefts (9d). In each case, an extra copy of the verb appears initially in the verb phrase. The fronted copy of the verb can be identical to the main verb; crucially, for some speakers, it can also be truncated to its first syllable (Collins 1994, cited in Lefebvre & Brousseau 2002:505):

(9)   a. **sísɔ́ ~ sí** Kɔ́kú **sísɔ́**   tlóló   bɔ̀   xɛ̀sí ɖì Bàyí
             tremble Koku **tremble** as.soon.as and fear get Bayi
             'As soon as Koku trembled, Bayi got frightened'
    b. **sísɔ́ ~ sí** Kɔ́kú **sísɔ́**   útú   xɛ̀sí ɖì Bàyí
             tremble Koku **tremble** cause fear get Bayi
             'Because Koku trembled, Bayi got frightened'
    c. **sísɔ́ ~ sí** ɖé-è   Bàyí **sísɔ́**   ɔ́,   vɛ́   nú mi
             tremble OP-RES Bayi **tremble**, DEF bother for me
             'The fact that Bayi trembled bothered me'
    d. **sísɔ́ ~ sí** wɛ̀, Kɔ́kú **sísɔ́**
             tremble it.is Koku **tremble**
             'It is tremble that Koku did'

In Fongbe, the only difference between the main verb and its fronted copy is the optional truncation; both copies can be assumed to have phonologically and semantically identical inputs.

A second likely motivation for the lack of attention to the issue of whether phonological copying or MS feature duplication underlies reduplication is simply that so many cases of canonical morphological reduplication appear amenable to either approach. By way of illustration, consider again the case of total pluralizing reduplication in Warlpiri, for which a standard phonological copying analysis was presented in (7). Suppose, instead, that plural formation in Warlpiri is governed by a morphological construction, such as the one shown in (10), which dictates double insertion of the singular form of the noun. In this case, there would be no phonological copying. Such an analysis differs from the account of Hebrew argued for by Landau only in that it is the morphology rather than the syntax that provides multiple instantiation of identical features.

(10)   Morphological reduplication by MS feature duplication:

Spellout

[GIRL +GIRL] plural   →   [GIRL   +GIRL] plural

△ △   △ △

kamina kamina

While the analysis in (10) is logically possible, the prevailing intuition that word reduplication should be treated as phonological copying (as in (7)) has precluded the development of a detailed theory of word reduplication based on MS feature duplication.

This book addresses this asymmetry in previous approaches to morphological reduplication, surveying a wide range of duplication effects and developing numerous arguments to support the use of MS feature duplication, formalized as Morphological Doubling Theory, for morphological reduplication, while reserving phonological copying as the correct analysis of purely phonologically driven duplication.

1.2   Morphological Doubling Theory

The essential claim of Morphological Doubling Theory (MDT) is that reduplication results when the morphology calls twice for a constituent of a given semantic description, with possible phonological modification of either or both constituents. MDT has roots in proposals by Hyman, Inkelas, and Sibanda (to appear) and also resonates in important respects with Yip's (1997; 1998) REPEAT(Stem) constraint, with the large body of work on Bantu reduplication by Downing (1997; 1998a; 1998b; 1998c; 1998d; 1998e; 1999a; 1999b; 1999c; 2000a; 2000b), with the Reduplicative Blending Theory of Sherrard (2001) and with the word-and-paradigm approach of Saperstein (1997), who also argues for a type of double stem selection and eschews the use of a morpheme "RED" which phonologically copies a base. MDT also has points of contact with Steriade's Lexical Conservatism approach to allomorphy; see, for example, Steriade 1997; 1999. Arguments supporting elements of the MDT approach to reduplication can be found in Pulleyblank (to appear).

Any morphological analysis requires an explicit morphological framework. In this book, MDT is couched within Sign-Based Morphology (SBM; Orgun 1996; 1997; 1999; Orgun & Inkelas 2002), a flexible morphological framework which can incorporate many different approaches to morphology. SBM, discussed more fully in §1.2.2, is compatible both with item-based and with realizational morphology; it is compatible with Optimality Theory and with rule-based theories of phonology. The SBM framework makes it easy to discuss and depict morphological constructions, a centerpiece of the approach to reduplication developed here.

1.2.1   The morphology of reduplication

MDT assumes the basic structure in (11) for morphological reduplication. A reduplicated stem (or "reduplication construction," to use a theory-neutral descriptive term) has two daughters that are featurally identical, i.e., mean the same thing:

(11)

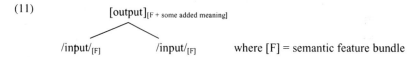

$[\text{output}]_{[F + \text{some added meaning}]}$

$/\text{input}/_{[F]}$ $/\text{input}/_{[F]}$ where [F] = semantic feature bundle

By requiring the two sisters to be identical only semantically, MDT makes a prediction which sets it apart from all phonological copying theories: other kinds of deviation, whether morphotactic or phonological, between the two copies are expected to be possible.

A theory much like MDT is anticipated by Moravcsik (1978), who writes:

> Constituents to be reduplicated may in principle be definable . . . either by their meaning properties only, or by their sound properties only, or in reference to both. They may, in other words, be either semantic-syntactic constituents, such as one or more semantic-syntactic features, or morphemes, or words, or phrases, or sentences, or discourses; or they may be phonetic-phonological terms, such as one or more phonetic-phonological features, or segments, or syllables; or they may be morphemes of a particular phonetic shape, or sentences of a particular number of phonetic segments; etc.   (pp. 303–304)

Moravcsik wrote this passage at a time when it was thought that the first type of reduplication did not exist; she states (p. 305) that no language possesses a reduplicative construction "which involves the reduplication of a syntactic constituent regardless of its form . . . in reduplication reference is always made both to the meaning and to the sound form of the constituent to be reduplicated." Similar statements are made on p. 315, fn. 8.

Our subsequent research has revealed some of the missing data that supports Moravcsik's original hypothesis that reduplication does not necessarily involve phonological identity. A number of morphological constructions require semantic identity, semantic similarity or (in some cases) semantic dissimilarity between their daughters. Among the cases of this sort, discussed in Chapter 2, are languages exhibiting "synonym compounding," in which the two members of the compound are phonologically distinct, perhaps etymologically distinct synonyms (e.g. Khmer *peel-weeliə* 'time,' from Sanskrit *peel* 'time' + Pali *weeliə* 'time'; Ourn & Haiman 2000:485). In the Khmer and Vietnamese examples below, the meanings of these constructions can be lexicalized but frequently are the same as the meaning of the individual parts. Page numbers for Khmer and Vietnamese refer to Ourn and Haiman 2000 and Nguyen 1997, respectively:

(12)   a.   Khmer synonym compounds

cah-tum	'old + mature'	'village elder'	485
kee-mɔrdɔk	'heritage + heritage'	'legacy'	501
camnəj-ʔahaa(r)	'food + food'	'food'	485
ʔaar-kɑmbaŋ	'secret + secret'	'secret'	500
cbah-prakɑt	'exact + exact'	'exact'	500

       b.   Vietnamese synonym compounds

mạnh-khoẻ	'strong + strong'	'well in health'	67
dơ bẩn	'dirty + dirty'	'filthy'	67
lười-biếng	'lazy + lazy'	'slothful'	67
tội-lỗi	'offense + fault'	'sin'	70
kêu-gọi	'to call + to call'	'to call upon, appeal'	70

It is argued in Chapter 2 that any theory with the ability to model these constructions already has the ability to model reduplication and does not need recourse to extra mechanisms like a RED morpheme or base-reduplication correspondence. Some related arguments against a morphemic approach to reduplication can be found in Saperstein 1997.

Another type of case discussed in Chapter 2 is divergent allomorphy, in which the two copies – "base" and "reduplicant," to use traditional terminology – differ in their morphological makeup. Divergent allomorphy provides striking evidence for the MS feature duplication approach because it clearly shows that the two copies can have different morphological inputs, as long as they are semantically matched. Recall that in Hebrew VP-fronting, alluded to in (6), the two copies of the verb appear in different forms. Chechen (North Caucasian) likewise illustrates the possibility of divergent allomorphy when a construction calls for only semantic identity between independent copies. Chechen exhibits syntactic reduplication to satisfy the requirements of a second position clitic (Conathan & Good 2000; see also Peterson 2001 on the closely related language Ingush). As shown in (13), from Conathan and Good (2000:50), chained clauses are marked by an enclitic particle *ʔa*, which immediately precedes the inflected, phrase-final, main verb. The enclitic must be preceded by another element in the same clause. Two types of constituent may occur before the verb (and enclitic particle) in the clause: an object (13a), or a deictic proclitic or preverb (13b).

If neither of these elements is present in a chained clause, then the obligatory pre-clitic position is filled by reduplicating the verb (13c):[8]

(13)   a. Cickuo, [chʔaara =ʔa gina]$_{VP}$,   ʔi   buʔu
          cat.ERG [fish   =& see.PP]$_{VP}$ 3S.ABS B.eat.PRS
          'The cat, having seen a fish, eats it.'
       b. Ahmada, [kiekhat jaaz =ʔa dina]$_{VP}$,   zhejna dueshu
          Ahmad.ERG [letter   write =& D.do.PP]$_{VP}$ book   D.read.PRS
          'Ahmad, having written a letter, reads a book.'
       c. Ahmad, [ʕa   =ʔa ʕiina]$_{VP}$,   dʕa-vaghara
          Ahmad [stay.INF =& stay.PP]$_{VP}$ DX.V.go.WP
          'Ahmad stayed (for a while) and left.'

The Chechen reduplicant occurs in infinitive form, while the main verb is inflected. Inflected verbs require a different form of the verb stem from that used in the infinitive; in some cases the stem allomorphy is clearly suppletive, e.g. *Dala* 'to give' vs. *lwo* 'gives,' or *Dagha* 'to go' vs. *Duedu* 'goes.' As Conathan and Good (2000:54) observe, the result is that Chechen can exhibit suppletive allomorphy differences between base and reduplicant; they cite as one example the reduplicated verb phrase *Dagha 'a Duedu*, based on 'go.'

What is going on in Chechen is the use of two verbs with (almost) the same meaning. MS feature duplication allows for divergent allomorphy of this sort, since there is no requirement that multiple tokens of concurring feature bundles be expressed identically. Divergent allomorphy in reduplication is, however, impossible to generate with phonological copying, since the normal base-to-reduplicant copying process cannot introduce an allomorph into the reduplicant that is not present in the base. Therefore, evidence that morphological reduplication exhibited divergent allomorphy would provide strong support that MS feature duplication, rather than phonological copying, is the driving force in reduplication.

Divergent allomorphy does indeed occur in morphological reduplication. Consider, for example, a fragment of data from Sye (Central-Eastern Oceanic; Crowley 1998; 2002d).[9] Sye presents the type of morphological divergence in which reduplicant and base contain different suppletive allomorphs of the same morpheme. The main points of Sye reduplication are these:

(14)   a. Most verb roots in Sye appear in two different shapes: Stem1 and Stem2
       b. Each affixation construction selects for one of the two stem shapes
       c. Reduplication in morphological contexts calling for Stem1 yields two
          copies of Stem1
       d. Reduplication in contexts that call for Stem2 surfaces as Stem2-Stem1

Examples of some stems showing this allomorphy are shown below:

(15)   Stem1   Stem2   Gloss

evcah	ampcah	'defecate'	Crowley 2002d:704
ocep	agkep	'fly'	Crowley 1998:84
omol	amol	'fall'	Crowley 1998:79

Reduplication in Sye, which is total and has an intensifying meaning, is illustrated in (16). As seen, the verb 'fall' is reduplicated and combined with the third person future prefix, which conditions the Stem2 form of a verb. The two copies of 'fall' assume different stem shapes: *amol* is Stem2 and *omol* is Stem1:

(16)   cw-**amol-omol**   '3.F U T-fall$_2$-fall$_1$ = they will fall all over'

Because the phonological relationship between Stem1 and Stem2 is not fully predictable, the "reduplicant" in a Sye reduplicated verb cannot always be described as a phonological copy of the "base," as phonological theories of reduplication would require. Rather, in at least some cases the reduplicant and base consist of different suppletive allomorphs of the same morpheme.

Ndebele (Nguni; Bantu) presents a different kind of divergent allomorphy in reduplication: the reduplicant contains semantically empty morphs not present in the base (Downing 1999a; 2001; Sibanda 2004; Hyman, Inkelas & Sibanda to appear). One such morph is the stem-forming *-a* (see Chapter 2 for a fuller discussion). Reduplication, which targets the verb stem and contributes the meaning that "the action is done for a short while before it stops or is done from time to time, perhaps not very well" (Sibanda 2004:282), truncates the first copy of the verb stem to two syllables. When the root is itself disyllabic or longer, the reduplicant consists of its initial two syllables. The outputs of reduplication here and throughout are shown with the final vowel in place, the standard citation form for verb stems. Data are taken from Hyman, Inkelas, and Sibanda to appear (HIS) and Sibanda 2004 (S):

(17)

nambith-a	nambi+nambith-a	'taste'	HIS
thembuz-a	thembu+thembuz-a	'go from wife to wife'	HIS
hlikihl-a	hliki+hlikihl-a	'wipe'	S:289
dlubulund-a	dlubu+dlubulund-a	'break free of control	S:289
tshombuluk-a	tshombu-tshombuluk-a	'become unrolled'	S:289

There are some conditions, however, under which empty morphs can appear in the reduplicant which are not present, because nothing motivates their presence, in the base. One condition is when the verb root is monosyllabic. As illustrated by the cases in (18), based on example (6) from Hyman, Inkelas, and Sibanda to appear (see also Downing 2001; Sibanda 2004:284), subjunctive and perfective suffixes are not in the domain of reduplication; they cannot be duplicated. The disyllabicity requirement on the reduplicant must be satisfied, however, and in Ndebele compels the insertion of the semantically empty stem-forming morpheme -*a*:

(18)   lim-e   lima-lime   'cultivate (subjunctive)'
        lim-ile   lima-limile   'cultivate (perfective)'
        thum-e   thuma-thume   'send (subjunctive)'
        thum-ile   thuma-thumile 'send (perfective)'

Example (19) illustrates the MDT approach to reduplication of the stem *lim-* in Ndebele. Both the left-hand stem ("reduplicant") and the right-hand stem ("base") have the same semantic description, i.e. 'CULTIVATE.' This morphosyntactic agreement is not disrupted by the fact that the reduplicant has an input morph, semantically empty -*a*, that the base does not.

(19)   [lima-lim-]$_{[F + \text{'here and there'}]}$

        / lim-a/$_{[F]}$ /lim/$_{[F]}$ where F = [CULTIVATE]

Suppletive allomorphy in Sye reduplication is illustrated in (20). Both stems have the meaning of 'fall' and are thus semantically identical, even though they differ in their phonology.

(20)   [amol-omol]$_{[F + \text{'random'}]}$

        /amol/$_{[F]}$ /omol/$_{[F]}$ where F = [FALL]

In summary, morphological reduplication in MDT is double selection (insertion) of a morphological constituent such as stem or root. There is no inherent morphological asymmetry between the daughters; there is no morpheme RED. The terms "base" and "reduplicant" in fact have no formal status, despite being descriptively handy in some cases.

1.2.2   *Constructions in morphology*
MDT makes heavy use of the concept of a morphological construction to handle reduplicative semantics and phonology, the latter being the primary focus of Chapters 3–6. A few words of explanation are in order here, especially in light of the great variety of morphological frameworks in use in the literature.

A "construction," broadly speaking, is any morphological rule or pattern that combines sisters into a single constituent. Each individual affix, compounding rule, truncation construction, and/or reduplication process is a unique morphological construction. Constructions can be related to each other under the rubric of more general "meta-constructions," which capture commonalities in the morphological component of the grammar.

The formalization of constructions and meta-constructions varies across morphological theories, some of which explicitly use the term "construction" and some of which do not. For Bochner (1992), the equivalent of a morphological construction would be a "pattern" relating words in the same inflectional or derivational paradigm, e.g. for English nouns, the rule in (21a). In a realizational morphological theory like that of Anderson (1992), the comparable affixation construction would take the form of a phonological rule conditioned by the features [Noun, plural] (21b). In an item-based morphological theory like that of Lieber (1980) or Selkirk (1982), affixation constructions take the form of subcategorization frames specifying features of each affix and the stem it combines with (21c):

(21)   a. $<[X]_{\text{Noun, singular}} \leftrightarrow [Xz]_{\text{Noun, plural}}>$
         b. [Noun, plural]
              $/X/ \rightarrow /Xz/$
         c. $[[\quad]_{\text{Noun, singular}} z]_{\text{Noun, plural}}$

The implementation of morphological construction used here draws heavily on Sign-Based Morphology (SBM; Orgun 1996; 1997; 1999; 2002; Orgun & Inkelas 2002), a versatile framework capable of capturing the insights of all three frameworks sketched in (21). Readers with attachments to particular morphological frameworks may freely translate the MDT constructions into the framework of their choice, as long as two crucial aspects of constructions are respected: the ability to encode idiomatic semantics and the ability to encode morphologically conditioned phonology.

In SBM constructions (and meta-constructions) are grammatical primitives, elaborated versions of phrase-structure rules which encode the semantic, syntactic, and phonological mappings between daughters and mothers. The morphological grammar of any language consists of a set of constructions, which combine with roots or with each other to form complex words. The English noun plural construction is sketched in (22), temporarily omitting phonological details. Like all of the statements in (21), it specifies that the noun plural construction has two daughters – a nonplural noun and the suffix /z/ – and that its mother is a plural noun.

(22) Affixation construction: Example:

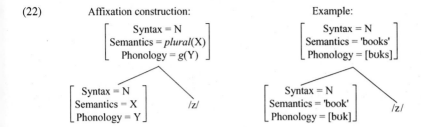

As mentioned earlier, the constructional approach to morphology permits a unified approach to the wide range of morphological construction types. Shown below are SBM constructions for compounding (using noun-noun compounding in English as an example) and for truncation (using nickname formation in English as an example):

(23) Compounding schema: Example:

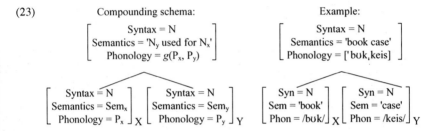

1.2.3 Constructional semantics

The constructional schemata in (22–23) differ in a couple of ways from the subcategorization frames or realizational rules with which readers may be more familiar. One difference is that the semantics of the mother node is specified, in each construction, as a particular function of the semantics of the daughters. This function could be a simple percolation function, as in Lieber (1980); percolation is appropriate for constructions in which meaning is entirely compositional, and no aspect of the meaning of the whole needs to be stipulated. However, the semantic function could also involve some information not derivable from either daughter. This is appropriate for cases of idiomaticity or exocentricity. The semantics of reduplication, at least from a naïve descriptive point of view, vary from the iconic to the potentially quite idiomatic, supporting a constructional approach to morphology.

A natural null hypothesis as to the meaning of reduplication constructions might be that the meaning of a given reduplication construction is a purely iconic function of the meaning of its daughters: for nouns, plurality; for verbs, iterativity or pluractionality; for adjectives and adverbs, intensity, and so forth.

Many examples of reduplication do indeed meet this description. In Rotuman (Central-Eastern Oceanic), for example, partial verb reduplication marks "repetition, frequency, continuance or spatial extension of a state or action" (Schmidt 2002:825); "The progressive tense or continuous aspect is formed by reduplicating the verb (which can also signify repetition or frequency) and/or adding a pronominal suffix" (ibid. p. 827). The prevalence of semantically iconic reduplication can readily be seen, for example, in the brief survey conducted by Moravcsik (1978) and the more extensive ones by Niepokuj (1997) and Kiyomi (1993); the latter catalogs a very wide range of reduplication constructions in the Bantu, Papuan, Austroasiatic, and Malayo-Polynesian language families.

Iconic semantics is not, however, the general rule. Reduplication, especially partial reduplication, is associated cross-linguistically with all sorts of meanings, both inflectional and derivational, whose degree of iconicity is often negligible. In Tarok (Benue-Congo), for example, partial reduplication marks third person singular possessive (Robinson 1976). In Arosi (Central-Eastern Oceanic; Lynch & Horoi 2002), partial reduplication serves as one of four possessive classifiers, used for different semantic subclasses of possessive constructions. For those possessive constructions involving "food or drink," "things done to or intended for the possessor," or "things closely attached to the possessor" when the possessor is first or second person, the possessor pronoun, which precedes the possessed noun, is subject to CV prefixing reduplication, e.g. *mu-murua bwaa* 'CL-2DU taro = your (dual) taro' (Lynch & Horoi 2002:567). (In apparent free variation with reduplication, a prefix *ʔa-* can be used instead, with different word order, e.g. *bwaa ʔa-murua* 'taro CL-2DU = your (dual) taro' [p. 567].) Though no longer productive, reduplication in another Central-Eastern Oceanic language, Marquesan, "marks dual and plural subject with some verbs," e.g. *ʔua moe ia* 'PERF sleep 3SG=he slept', *ʔu mo-moe ʔaua* 'PERF REDUP-sleep 3DU=the two of them slept together' (Lynch 2002a:872). Triplication likewise illustrates the non-iconic nature of reduplicative semantics. In Emai (Edoid; Benue-Congo), for example, the number of iterations of an ideophone is a function of the size of the base: monosyllabic ideophones triplicate (*rí-rí-rí* 'red'), disyllabic ideophones reduplicate (*kútú-kútú* 'boiling (water)," trisyllabic ideophones occur as singletons (Egbokhare 2001:88). The number of iterations is, in principle, orthogonal to the semantics of the construction.[10]

Reduplication can also serve seemingly arbitrary derivational functions, marking changes in syntactic category or verbal argument structure. In Rotuman, "adjectives are formed from nouns by reduplication," e.g. *rosi* 'fraud,' *ros-rosi* 'cunning,' *hafu* 'stone,' *haf-hafu* 'stony, rocky' (Schmidt 2002:822). In Banoni (Western Oceanic), partial reduplication derives instrumental nouns from verbs (e.g. *resi* 'grate coconut,' *re-resi* 'coconut grater'; Lynch & Ross 2002:442). In Ulithian (Micronesian; Lynch 2002b), reduplication derives intransitive verbs from nouns, e.g. *sifu* 'grass skirt,' *sif-sifu* 'wear a grass skirt'; *yaŋi* 'wind,' *yaŋi-yaŋi* 'blow' (p. 799). The same is true in the Central-Eastern Oceanic language Niuafo'ou, e.g. *maka* 'stone,' *maka-maka* 'to be stony' (Early 2002:856). In Marquesan (Lynch 2002a), "[s]ome verbs are derived from nouns by reduplication," e.g. *ivi* 'bone,' *ivi-ivi* 'be thin,' *niho* 'tooth,' *niho-niho* 'be notched' (p. 872). In Siroi (Trans-New Guinea; Wells 1979), noun reduplication yields an intransitive verb meaning 'act like N', in the *-k-* class (all Siroi verb stems fall into one of four classes), e.g. *zon* 'John,' *zon-zon-k-ate* 'John-John-k-3SG.PRES = he is acting (like) John'; *ragitap* 'turtle,' *ragitap-ragitap-k-ate* 'he is acting like a turtle,' *gua* 'young child,' *gua-gua-k-ina* 'young_child-young_child-k-3S.PAST = she acted childishly' (p. 35; hyphenation has been modified from the original). A similar pattern in which the first copy of the verb also possesses a class marker connotes pretence, e.g. *malmbi-k-et-malmbi-k-et-ng-ate* 'cry-k-1SG.PRES-cry-k-1SG.PRES-ng-3SG.PRES = he is pretending to cry' (p. 36). In Nadrogā (Central-Eastern Oceanic; Geraghty 2002:841), reduplication is used "to form intransitives of patient-oriented verbs," thus *vuli* '[to be] turned over,' *vuli-vuli* 'turn over'. (Agent-oriented verbs form frequentatives when reduplicated, e.g. *tola-vi-a* 'look at it,' *tola-tola-vi-a* 'look repeatedly at it.')

Idiomatic reduplicative constructions are similar to exocentric compounds, like *pick-pocket*, *blue-hair*, etc. The meaning of the whole is not the result of adding together the meanings of the parts; rather, it must be stipulated as a property of the construction as a whole. The difference between *pick-pocket* and e.g. the Banoni form *re-resi* 'coconut grater' is that the meaning of *pick-pocket* is lexicalized, whereas in Banoni there is a semantic generalization over all instances of this reduplication construction. The instrumental noun semantics of Banoni verb reduplication is listed, in MDT, as a property of the mother node of the schematic reduplication construction, as shown below:

(24)   Banoni reduplication construction

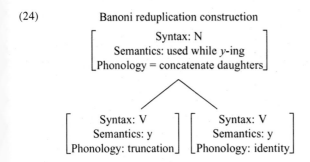

Example (*resi* → *re-resi*)

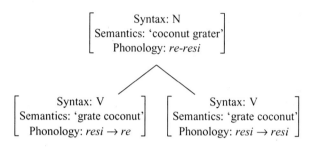

The advantage of a constructional approach is that semantically regular, partially idiomatic, and totally idiomatic, constructions are all handled in the same way, the difference being in how general or specific a particular construction is. The same motivation drives the use of consructions in syntax (see, for example, Fillmore, Kay & O'Connor 1988; Koenig 1992; Nunberg, Sag & Wasow 1994; Goldberg 1995; Sag & Wasow 1999; Riehemann 2001; Kay 2002 for extensive discussion).

This section is intended only as an illustration of how semantics would be handled in MDT; reduplicative semantics is not used in this work to argue for MDT over other theories. Certainly theories in which reduplication results from the presence of a RED morpheme would be equally well-equipped to handle the range of observed effects.

1.2.4   Constructional phonology

Of greater import than semantics in the choice of a constructional approach to reduplication is reduplicative phonology, one of the main focus areas of this book. Constructions in SBM are equipped with phonological functions computing the phonology of the mother node (the "output") from the phonology of its daughters (the "inputs"). These mappings, termed "cophonologies" in Inkelas, Orgun, and Zoll 1997, are necessary in order to describe morphologically conditioned phonology. A language in which all cophonologies are identical has no morphological conditioning; a language in which many constructions have different cophonologies has a lot of morphologically conditioned phonology. As argued extensively in work by Orgun (1996, 1997; see also Inkelas 1998; Yu 2000), cophonologies also intrinsically give rise to cyclic, or layering, effects. Cophonologies figure prominently in Chapters 3–5, where they are used to account for the attested range of phonological effects in reduplication.

In the affixation and compounding constructions illustrated thus far, cophonologies do only moderate work. The cophonology of the plural construction includes the voicing assimilation and epenthesis alternations, general to the language, that drive pural suffix allomorphy; the cophonology of the compounding construction assigns compound stress.

Cophonologies play a highly important role in nonconcatenative morphology, such as truncation, zero-derivation and ablaut constructions. These phenomena have traditionally fallen outside the scope of phrase-structure rules or subcategorization frames (see, for example, Lieber 1980), yet they are centrally important in the morphology of many languages. Constructions for truncation, zero-derivation and ablaut are illustrated below. English nickname formation exemplifies truncation, in (25a), whose cophonology (ϕ_k) deletes all but the initial syllable (loosely speaking) of the input name. Zero-derivation is exemplified in (25b) by English noun-to-verb conversion of the sort Kiparsky (1982c) located in Level 1 of the morphology (e.g. *pérmit* (n.), *permít* (v.)). Since English noun-to-verb conversion potentially results in stress shift, stress assignment must be part of Cophonology ϕ_q. Ablaut is illustrated by the German umlaut-only plural formation (e.g. *Vater* 'father.sg', *Väter* 'father.pl'). In German, the relevant cophonology (ϕ_r) requires back stressed vowels to front:

(25) a.   Truncation Schema:

$$\begin{bmatrix} \text{Syntax} = g(\text{Syn}_x) \\ \text{Semantics} = f(\text{Sem}_x) \\ \text{Phonology} = \phi_k(\text{P}_x) \end{bmatrix}$$

|

$$\begin{bmatrix} \text{Syntax} = \text{Syn}_x \\ \text{Semantics} = \text{Sem}_x \\ \text{Phonology} = \text{P}_x \end{bmatrix}_x$$

Example (*Daniel* → *Dan*):

$$\begin{bmatrix} \text{Syn} = \text{masculine N} \\ \text{Sem} = \text{'nickname of Daniel'} \\ \text{Phonology} = /\text{dæn}/ \end{bmatrix}$$

|

$$\begin{bmatrix} \text{Syn} = \text{masculine N} \\ \text{Sem} = \text{'Daniel'} \\ \text{Phonology} = /\text{dænjəl}/ \end{bmatrix}_x$$

b.   Zero-derivation Schema:

$$\begin{bmatrix} \text{Syntax} = \text{V} \\ \text{Semantics} = \text{do something} \\ \text{involving X} \\ \text{Phonology} = \phi_q(\text{P}_x) \end{bmatrix}$$

|

$$\begin{bmatrix} \text{Syntax} = \text{Syn}_x \\ \text{Semantics} = \text{Sem}_x \\ \text{Phonology} = \text{P}_x \end{bmatrix}_x$$

Example (*pèrmit* → *permìt*):

$$\begin{bmatrix} \text{Syn} = \text{N} \\ \text{Sem} = \text{'permit'} \\ \text{Phonology} = [\text{'pɚm'}] \end{bmatrix}$$

|

$$\begin{bmatrix} \text{Syn} = \text{V} \\ \text{Sem} = \text{'permit'} \\ \text{Phonology} = /\text{pərmit}/ \end{bmatrix}_x$$

c.   Ablaut schema:

$$\begin{bmatrix} \text{Syntax} = \text{Plural N} \\ \text{Semantics} = \text{Plural of (Sem}_x) \\ \text{Phonology} = \phi_r(\text{P}_x) \end{bmatrix}$$

|

$$\begin{bmatrix} \text{Syntax} = \text{Singular N} \\ \text{Semantics} = \text{Sem}_x \\ \text{Phonology} = \text{P}_x \end{bmatrix}_x$$

Example (*Vater* → *Väter*):

$$\begin{bmatrix} \text{Syn} = \text{Plural N} \\ \text{Sem} = \text{'fathers'} \\ \text{Phonology} = \phi_q(/\text{fatɛɪ}/) = [\text{fetɛɪ}] \end{bmatrix}$$

|

$$\begin{bmatrix} \text{Syn} = \text{N} \\ \text{Sem} = \text{'father'} \\ \text{Phonology} = /\text{fatɛɪ}/ \end{bmatrix}_x$$

As discussed by Orgun (1996), an interesting consequence of using constructional schemata like these, rather than phrase-structure rules or subcategorization frames, is the free choice it allows between an item-based approach to affixation, as shown in (22), or the realizational approach argued for by morphologists such as Anderson (1992). In a realizational constructional approach the cophonology would be responsible not only for any morphologically conditioned phonology associated with a particular affix, but also for realizing overt affixes themselves. A realizational approach to the English noun plural suffix, comparable to that in (21b), is provided below:

(26)   Noun pluralization in English   Example:

$$
\begin{bmatrix}
\text{Syntax} = \text{N} \\
\text{Semantics} = plural\ of\ \text{X} \\
\text{Phonology} = \phi_2(\text{P}_x,\ /\text{z}/)
\end{bmatrix}
\begin{bmatrix}
\text{Syntax} = \text{N} \\
\text{Semantics} = \text{'books'} \\
\text{Phonology} = \phi_2(/\text{bʊk}/,\ /\text{z}/) = [\text{bʊks}]
\end{bmatrix}
$$

$$
\begin{bmatrix}
\text{Syntax} = \text{N} \\
\text{Semantics} = \text{Sem}_x \\
\text{Phonology} = \text{P}_x
\end{bmatrix}_x
\qquad
\begin{bmatrix}
\text{Syntax} = \text{N} \\
\text{Semantics} = \text{'book'} \\
\text{Phonology} = /\text{bʊk}/
\end{bmatrix}_x
$$

The cophonology of this construction adds the plural /z/ ending as well as performing voicing assimilation.

1.2.5   The phonology of reduplication

The primary phonological issues arising in reduplication are these: (a) how, if at all, are the copies in reduplication phonologically modified relative to how they would appear in isolation? (b) is surface phonological identity an extrinsic requirement on reduplication?

In MDT, the essential identity in reduplication is semantic. This sets MDT apart from what can be termed Coerced Identity theories (Wilbur 1973; McCarthy & Prince 1995a), in which phonological identity between the copies in reduplication is an explicit surface requirement of the grammar. MDT is, by contrast, a Native Identity theory, in the sense that surface phonological identity between the two copies occurs only as a side effect of semantic identity; often the simplest, or only, way to assure semantic identity is to select exactly the same morphological entity for the two daughters. Surface phonological identity is not, however – and cannot be – required.

Beyond not requiring phonological identity, MDT also makes strong, distinguishing predictions about the potential for phonological modification of the morphological elements involved in reduplication. The principal way in which MDT differs from other theories of reduplication is in allowing the daughters of reduplication, as well as the mother, to be associated with potentially distinct cophonologies.

Much of the reduplication literature has focused on certain kinds of reduplication constructions in developing theories of what is phonologically possible. Of primary focus have been partial reduplication constructions in which one copy assumes the same form that it would in isolation, while the other is simplified in some manner – truncated, subjected to contrast neutralization, or both. Our extensive surveys of reduplicative phonology, presented in Chapters 3 to 6, have shown that the range of phenomena goes far beyond this sort of case. Reduplicative phonology does not always privilege one copy (the "base") while shrinking the other (the "reduplicant"); in some constructions, both daughters are modified, even in different ways.

In MDT, phonological modification in reduplication results from the interactions of three cophonologies: one for each daughter, and one for the mother.

(27)

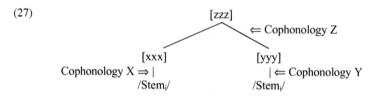

Some reduplication constructions have active phonological effects only in one or the other daughter; some have active effects only at the mother node; others have active alternations in all three cophonologies.

In Hausa pluractional reduplication, for example, the first stem is reduced to its initial CVC string, while the second is maintained intact (28). In addition, the final C of the first copy geminates with the base initial consonant, a process whose obligatoriness is specific to this construction (see Newman 1989a; 2000:424–25, as well as Chapter 4 of the present work). Examples are taken from Newman 2000:424:

(28)   a. kiraː   kik-kiraː   'call'
       b. bugàː   bub-bùga   'beat'
       c. kaːwoː kak-kaːwoː 'bring'

The construction in (29) illustrates the essential elements of an MDT analysis of the pluractional data in (28). The construction calls twice for two semantically agreeing stems, in this case *kira:* 'call.' Each daughter is subject to an independent cophonology, an approach to the phonology of reduplication pioneered by Steriade (1988). In this case, the cophonology of the first daughter is a truncating one, and outputs a CVC syllable. The second daughter is subject to an identity-preserving cophonology whose output matches its input. Together the two pieces are subject to the cophonology of the mother node, which imposes gemination of the consonant cluster at the juncture between the two copies.

(29)

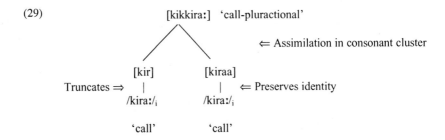

         [kikkiraː] 'call-pluractional'

                ⇐ Assimilation in consonant cluster

     [kir]   [kiraa]

Truncates ⇒ | | ⇐ Preserves identity

    /kiraː/$_i$ /kiraː/$_i$

     'call'   'call'

The precise formalization of each cophonology depends largely upon one's choice of phonological model. The framework used in this work is Optimality Theory (OT; McCarthy & Prince 1993; Prince & Smolensky 1993), in which each cophonology consists of a hierarchy of ranked and violable markedness, faithfulness, and alignment constraints.[11]

A crucial aspect of the use of cophonologies in handling reduplicative phonology is the layering intrinsic to the construction. Because Cophonologies X and Y are associated with the daughters and Cophonology Z is associated with the mother, there is an intrinsic cyclic effect: the outputs of Cophonologies X and Y are the inputs to Cophonology Z. This chaining of cophonologies is, as argued in Chapter 5, a crucial component of the phonological opacity which has put reduplication in the forefront of phonological theory construction.

1.3   Phonological copying

As discussed above, the primary motivation for MDT comes from cases (e.g. Sye and Ndebele) in which phonological copying cannot explain the different morphotactics of the two copies or their morphological complexity. MS feature duplication is clearly necessary in these cases, as will be argued throughout the book. The question is whether there is still a role for phonological copying. It is argued in Chapters 5 and 7 that MS feature duplication cannot replace phonological copying, but that the scope of phonological copying is limited to a narrow set of contexts. These include some phenomena that previously have been classified as reduplication but which are not amenable to a morphological doubling analysis, in part because the doubled element is something very small, like a single consonant or vowel, and in part because the doubling has a purely phonological purpose, rather than being associated with a change in meaning. Restricting the use of phonological constituent copying to cases motivated by phonological necessity, resonates with recent arguments by Gafos (1998b), Hendricks (1999) and, to some extent, Zuraw (2002) that a theory should provide only one type of analysis to single-segment copying within a word, not two. It is argued in this work that the proper analysis of such cases is phonological copying, not morphological reduplication; although Gafos and Zuraw adopt the seemingly opposite view that the unified analysis should be reduplication (though without templates), their analyses, which use reduplicative morphemes (Gafos) or the constraint R E D U P L I C A T E (Zuraw), are conceptually more consistent with phonological copying or assimilation than with morphological reduplication.

The Hausa and Yoruba onset copying cases discussed above, for example, are unequivocal examples of phonological copying. In both Hausa and Yoruba, the duplication of the consonant is driven purely phonologically, by the need for a syllable onset. Spokane (Interior Salish) provides another such example, differing from Hausa and Yoruba in that phonological copying occurs in only one allomorph of an otherwise nonreduplicative affix. The repetitive form of a verb is formed by infixing /e/ into what would (due to unstressed schwa deletion) be an initial consonant cluster (30a). For stems beginning with only a single consonant, however, the stem-initial consonant is doubled, with /e/ appearing between the two copies (30b) (Black 1996:210ff., Bates & Carlson 1998: 655).

(30)   a. Repetitive *e-* infixes into initial consonant cluster:[12]
        i. /-e-, šl'-n'-t-ən'/   → š-e-l'n'tén'
            REP, chop-CTR-TR-IsGTrS   'I cut it up repeatedly'
        ii. /-e-, lč'-n'-t-ən'/   → l'-e-č'n'tén'
            REP, tie-CTR-TR-IsGTrS   'I tied it over and over'
        b. Phonological copying provides onset for repetitive prefix *e-*
        i. /-e-, šəl'/   → še- šil'
            /REP, chop/   'I cut it up repeatedly'
        ii. /-e-, nič'-n'-t-əxʷ/   → n'-e-n'íč'n'txʷ
            REP, cut-CTR-TR-2sGTrS   'you kept cutting'

In all such cases, phonological copying is at work. Autosegmental phonology would spread a consonant to the onset position; in Optimality Theory the ONSET constraint compels the insertion of a consonant that agrees featurally with a nearby consonant (on string-internal segmental agreement, see, for example, Walker 2000a; Hansson 2001; Rose & Walker 2001).

1.4   Distinguishing the two types of duplication

This book focuses on morphological reduplication and the arguments for analyzing it as morphological doubling. In order to assess this argument, it is important to have criteria for classifying a given duplication phenomenon as morphological, in which case MS feature doubling is the correct analysis, or phonological, in which phonological copying is called for.

One criterion distinguishing the two duplication effects is that phonological copying serves a phonological purpose, while morphological reduplication serves a morphological purpose, either by being a word-formation process itself or by enabling another word-formation process to take place. Chapter 7 discusses several cases (from Chukchee, Kinande, and Nancowry) in which an affix or stem-forming construction imposes a prosodic requirement that can be satisfied only through semantically null morphological reduplication. All three languages independently possess the relevant morphological reduplication construction, which is simply recruited, minus its semantics, to serve in these cases.

The second criterion is proximity. Phonological duplication is proximal, meaning that it targets the closest eligible element (a copied consonant is a copy of the closest appropriate consonant, for example), while this is not necessarily true of morphological reduplication. Sections 1.1 and 12.1 of this chapter discuss several cases of syntactic reduplication in which the two copies are separated by other words; many parallel examples, in which base and reduplicant are nonadjacent, exist in morphology as well, e.g. the opposite-edge reduplication in Chukchee *nute-nut* 'earth (absolute singular)' (Krause 1980), Umpila *maka* 'die, go out' → *maka-l-ma* 'die, go out (progressive)' (Harris & O'Grady 1976; Levin 1985b), or Madurese *wā-mõwā* 'faces' (McCarthy & Prince 1995a and references therein), all discussed in Chapter 7.

The third criterion is structural. Each instance of phonological copying involves a single phonological segment, as in Hausa, Yoruba, or Spokane onset-driven consonant copying; morphological reduplication involves an entire morphological constituent (affix, root, stem, word), potentially truncated to a prosodic constituent (mora, syllable, foot). This property of morphological reduplication is discussed in Chapter 2, under the rubric of the Thesis of Morphological Targets.

The fourth criterion involves phonological identity. Phonological copying by definition involves phonological identity, while morphological reduplication involves semantic identity. Phonological identity may occur in morphological reduplication, but as a side effect of the fact that semantic identity requirements result in identical inputs. Chapters 3 to 6 all discuss, in various ways, the evidence that morphological reduplication does not presuppose or enforce phonological identity between its daughters. Chapter 7 presents an argument that phonological copying not only presupposes identity but actively enforces it, solidly distinguishing the two types of process.

1.5   Wrapup and outline of book

MDT is a novel theory of reduplication which situates reduplication within a solid morphological and phonological context. MDT differs from previous phonological copying theories of reduplication in a number of important ways, listed in (31):

(31)   a. Most phonological theories of reduplication posit a RED morpheme, while in MDT the reduplicant is a potentially morphologically complex stem.

b. MDT posits separate, and potentially distinct, inputs for base and reduplicant, while phonological copying theories posit a single, shared input for the two output strings.

c. MDT draws no fundamental asymmetry between base and reduplicant; neither is logically prior to the other. In most phonological copying models, the base and reduplicant have an asymmetrical relationship to the input.

d. MDT accepts phonological identity, insofar as it exists, between its daughters as an epiphenomenon resulting from their semantic identity but does not actively enforce it; by contrast, all phonological copying theories minimally presuppose phonological identity as a starting point in reduplication, and Coerced Identity theories like BRCT actively require it in output.

The various chapters of this book demonstrate that MDT is more descriptively adequate and at the same time more constrained in its predictions than existing phonological approaches to reduplication. Chapter 2 presents the basic morphological evidence for MDT, focusing on data new to the theoretical literature on reduplication that demonstrate the need for a theory in which the two daughters in a reduplication construction are morphologically independent. Chapters 3, 4, and 5 closely investigate the phonology of reduplication. Chapter 3 covers languages which motivate the phonological independence of the two daughters and begins to make the case that reduplication-specific phonology is part of a general phenomenon of morphologically conditioned phonology. This broader context reveals that Coerced Identity theories are too narrow; by giving reduplicative phonology a special status, such theories are unable to account for the disposition of reduplicative phonology in the context of a language's full morphological system. Chapter 4 continues the argument that reduplication must be understood in context, and presents evidence for the layered cophonologies central to MDT's conception of morphophonology. Case studies of underapplication and sandhi phenomena in reduplication demonstrate the futility of trying to account for reduplicative phonology with reduplication-specific devices such as BR correspondence (McCarthy & Prince 1995a) or Existential Faithfulness (Struijke 2000a). Chapter 5 tackles the issue of phonological opacity in reduplication, focusing on the so-called "overapplication" and "underapplication" effects in reduplication which have long been of special interest to phonologists. Case studies of Fox, Javanese, and a number of other languages show that reduplicative opacity effects result from the input–output chaining of the cophonologies associated with the nodes in the morphological constituent structure of a reduplication construction. One important result of this organic approach to morphologically conditioned phonology, in which no reduplication-specific technology is used, is that MDT can correctly account for the grouping of alternations in a language with respect to overapplication and normal application, patterns that appear random or arbitrary in Coerced Identity accounts of reduplicative opacity. Building on the results of Chapter 5, Chapter 6 looks at two cases of ostensible backcopying, in Tagalog and Chumash, which have been cited in the literature in support of Coerced Identity theories. For both cases, however, morphological structure and cophonologies are sufficient not only to describe but also to explain the effects. Opacity in particular, and reduplicative phonology in general, can properly be understood only in the context of the entire morphological system of a language. Finally, Chapter 7 reviews the results of our investigation and stresses again the distinction between morphological reduplication and phonological copying.

2 Evidence for morphological doubling

Morphological Doubling Theory views reduplication as a morphological construction containing some number of daughters – prototypically two – which are identical in their semantic and syntactic features.

(1)   Mother: [   ]$_{g([F])}$

       Daughters: [   ]$_{[F]}$ [   ]$_{[F]}$

One or both of the daughters in a given reduplication construction may be the product of a stem-forming construction which modifies them phonologically by the phonological rules or constraints associated with the construction. In addition, the reduplication construction itself may be associated with phonological rules or constraints which apply to the construction as a whole. The nature of reduplicative phonology is the particular subject of Chapters 3 and 4, and will not be discussed further in this chapter. It is, however, essential to recognize that the two daughters have morphologically and phonologically independent inputs. This is what allows them to diverge in the morphotactic and phonological ways demonstrated in this chapter.

This chapter focuses on two essential morphological insights of MDT. One is that the targets of reduplication – the types of thing that reduplication constructions propagate – are morphological constituents. The other is that the foundational identity in reduplication is semantic. In MDT, reduplication couples morphological constituents which agree in their semantic (and syntactic) specifications. These constituents are not required to match phonologically or even in their internal morphotactic makeup; and as shown later in this chapter, there are cases of reduplication in which the two constituents do differ in both respects. The two central theses of this chapter are formulated below:

(2)   **The Thesis of Morphological Targets**: a reduplication construction calls for morphological constituents (affix, root, stem, or word), not phonological constituents (mora, syllable, or foot)

       The Thesis of Semantic Identity: reduplication calls for semantic identity of its daughters, not phonological identity

This chapter marshals a variety of evidence supporting these two components of MDT. The theses in (2) contrast fundamentally with the precepts of the Phonological Copying view which has dominated the literature for thirty years. The Phonological Copying perspective on reduplication, as represented here by Base-Reduplicant Correspondence Theory (BRCT; McCarthy & Prince 1995a), is very different: reduplication is driven by the presence of an affixal morpheme, "RED," which is associated with the grammatical requirement that it phonologically copy material in the phonological string to which it is adjacent.

(3)   Counterparts of (2) in BRCT:
       The target of reduplication is phonological (e.g. mora, syllable, foot)
       The strings that reduplication doubles are identical phonologically

This chapter shows that a theory that hews to the theses in (2) is the right way to approach reduplication; the main insights of MDT correspond to the data better than do the main insights of phonological copying theories like BRCT. The additions to phonological theory which BRCT embodies are, therefore, unnecessary.

We begin with the demonstration that there are clear cases of reduplication in which the essential identity between the copies is semantic, rather than phonological. These cases support the Thesis of Semantic Identity.

It is common for the two copies in reduplication to differ phonologically. This asymmetry could have two causes: (a) the copies are identical in input but differ in output because of normal or special reduplicative phonology, or (b) the copies are different in input. These two scenarios are contrasted, below:

(4)   a. Copies are identical in morphological input

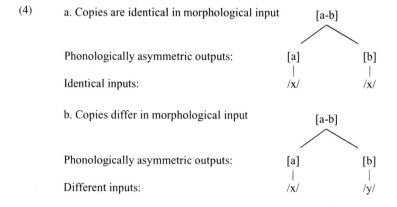

Any existing theory – MDT, Full Copy, BRCT – can describe scenario (4a). Scenario (4b) is the one that is unique to MDT: base and reduplicant have different inputs, although the aggregate semantics of the inputs is identical. This situation can arise in several ways. As discussed in §2.1, semantically empty morphs occur in one copy but not the other, such that semantic identity occurs without phonological identity. A special case of this is the phenomenon famously known, since McCarthy and Prince 1999b [1986], as "Melodic Overwriting," discussed in §2.2.4. An alternative source of scenario (4b) occurs when the two daughters in reduplication contain morphemes or morphological constituents which are identical in their semantic content but differ phonologically – i.e., they are synonyms of each other. Synonym constructions are discussed in §2.3.

Before turning to evidence for the Thesis of Semantic Identity, however, we address evidence bearing more directly on the Thesis of Morphological Targets, namely affix reduplication.

2.1 Morphological targets: affix reduplication

The literature is full of examples of reduplication which are sensitive to the morphological root or stem. This is not surprising on any view of reduplication. Under most existing phonological copying theories, for example, reduplicants are treated as affixes (Marantz 1982), and it is well known that affixes select for certain types of roots or stems and can be sensitive to where their edges are.

Data which better show how the Thesis of Morphological Targets sets MDT apart from other theories come from affix reduplication, the situation in which reduplication targets a specific affix or type of affix, regardless of its phonological shape. For example, in Dyirbal (Pama-Nyungan), the nominal suffix -*ŋaŋgay* 'without' can reduplicate, intensifying the semantic contribution of 'really/absolutely without' that it normally carries (Dixon 1972:242):

(5)   bana   'water'
        bana-ŋaŋgay   'without water'
        bana-ŋaŋgay-ŋaŋgay 'with absolutely no water at all'

This construction is semantically iconic: the affix appears twice, and its semantic contribution is reflected twice (by increasing the degree of absence of the property designated by the noun with which the affix combines), and could even be represented as multiple affixation rather than as reduplication per se.

In the following cases of affix reduplication, however, the meaning of reduplication is not at all related to the meanings of the individual affixes being doubled. Rather, the meaning is an arbitrary property of the reduplication construction itself.

2.1.1   Preverb reduplication: Hungarian

Tauli (1966):182 states that reduplication of the Hungarian preverb – analyzed variously in the literature as a prefix or proclitic – occurs "to express iterativeness or frequentativeness," citing these examples: *el-el-fújita* 'blow out many times,' vs. *el-fúj* 'blow out'; *vissza-vissza-vágyom* 'I frequently long to be back.' Moravcsik (1978:306) also adds the form *bele-bele-néz* 'he occasionally looks into it.' Many more examples are provided by Piñon (1991), in a more extensive discussion based in part on Soltész 1959.

Although the roughly 60–70 preverbs that Piñon estimates exist in Hungarian do tend to have their own meanings (e.g. *el-* means 'away'), preverb reduplication does not intensify this particular component of the meaning of the constituent consisting of verb plus preverb. Rather, preverb reduplication adds a fixed meaning component to any combination of preverb plus verb. Piñon characterizes preverb reduplication as denoting "an irregular iteration of the event denoted by the verb." The fact that the meaning of preverb reduplication is not derivable from the meaning of the preverb itself supports the constructional approach Morphological Doubling Theory takes to reduplication, in which any semantic idiosyncrasies or noncompositionality can be listed as properties of the mother node of the construction.[1]

2.1.2   Reduplication within the derivational stem

In Dyirbal, nominals reduplicate to mark plurality (Dixon 1972). A bare nominal simply undergoes total reduplication, as shown in (6a). If, however, the nominal is derived by a stem-forming nominal suffix, then there are two options for marking plurality: root reduplication or suffix reduplication. Dixon is quite clear that the two options are semantically equivalent (p. 272):

(6)	a. **midi-midi**		'lots of little ones'
	gulgiṛi-gulgiṛi		'lots of prettily painted men'
	b. **midi-midi**-baḍun	~ midi-**baḍun-baḍun**	'lots of very small ones'
	bayi **yaṛa-yaṛa**-gabun	~ bayi yaṛa-**gabun-gabun**	'lots of other men/ strangers'

From the perspective of Morphological Doubling Theory, what unites affix and root doubling is the generalization that *some* morphological element in the affixed stem occurs twice. Meaning is associated with the act of reduplicating something, not with the reduplicated thing itself. This same generalization holds in several other languages that permit affix reduplication.

In Gapapaiwa (Papuan Tip cluster, Western Oceanic), reduplication within the (potentially complex) verb stem marks imperfective aspect (McGuckin 2002). According to McGuckin (p. 308), if the verb stem contains a derivational prefix, such as causative *vi-* or 'with the hands' *vo-*, the derivational prefix reduplicates, as shown in (7a). Otherwise, the verb root reduplicates, as shown in (7b); according to McGuckin, root reduplication follows phonologically conditioned patterns, which unfortunately are not described.

(7) a. a-**vi-vi**-sisiya   '1SG-IMPF-CAUS.PAST-speak = I was speaking' 308
        i-**vi-vi**-tete   '3.NONPRES-IMPF-CAUS.PAST-come.and.go'   309

     b. i-**kam-kam**   '3.NONPRES-IMPF-eat'   318
        a-ta-**kita-kita**   '1SG-SUBJ-IMPF-see = that I was seeing'   309
        ko-na-**yeba-**   '2PL-FUT-IMPF-fish = you [will be] fishing' 318
          yebagha
        i-**ne-nae**   '3.NONPRES-IMPF-go'   320
        a-na-vo-**yu-yuna** '1SG-FUT-with.hands-IMPF-gather'   319

Amele (Gum, Trans-New Guinea) has several constructions reduplicating inflectional affixes within the verb. To express iterative aspect in Amele, "the whole stem is normally reduplicated if the verb does not have an object marker, otherwise the object marker is reduplicated either in place of or in addition to the reduplication of the verb stem" (Roberts 1991 [R91], pp. 130–31; see also Roberts 1987 [R87], p. 252).[2] Example ((8a) illustrates root reduplication, and (8b) illustrates object reduplication:[3]

(8) a. qu-qu   'hit'   R87:252
        ji-ji   'eat'   R87:253
        budu-budu-eʔ   'to thud repeatedly'   R91:131
        g͡batan-g͡batan-eʔ 'split-INF'   R91:131

     b. hawa-du-du   'ignore-3s-3s'   R87:254
        gobil-du-du   'stir-3s-3s = stir and stir it' R87:254
        guduc-du-du   'run-3s-3s'   R87:254

Simultaneous action reduplication, which is partial, exhibits almost the same pattern; if there is an object suffix, it reduplicates, e.g. *mele-do-do-n* 'as he examined' (Roberts 1991:129); otherwise, the root partially reduplicates, e.g. *g͡ba-g͡batan-en* 'as he split' (Roberts 1991:128).

2.1.2.1 Double reduplication within the stem
In Boumaa Fijian (Central-Eastern Oceanic), stems formed by spontaneous or adversative prefixes reduplicate both the prefix and the root in order to mark plurality (Dixon 1988:226):

(9)	ta-lo'i	'bent'	ta-ta-lo'i-lo'i	'bent in many places'
	ca-lidi	'explode'	ca-ca-lidi-lidi	'many things explode'
	'a-musu	'broken'	'a-'a-musu-musu	'broken in many places'

In some of the other affix reduplicating languages, as seen, double reduplication is an option, though not required as it seems to be in Boumaa Fijian. Gapapaiwa and Amele both permit root doubling in stems that also have affix doubling. In Gapapaiwa (10a), doubling of both results in an intensified semantic contribution; double reduplication indicates "a long time-frame for the imperfective action" (McGuckin 2002:308). In Amele (10b), root doubling in words with object suffixes simply appears to be an option, without any particular additional semantic contribution:

(10)	a. i-**vo-vo-koi-koi**	'3.NONPRES-with.	(McGuckin 2002:306)
		hands-weed'	
	b. **bala-bala-du-du**-e?	'tear-3s-INF=to tear	(Roberts 1991:131)
		it repeatedly'	

In Dyirbal, by contrast, double root-affix reduplication is prohibited; Dixon (1972) says explicitly that words like *midi-midi-baḏun-baḏun* are ungrammatical (p. 242).[4]

2.1.2.2   Discussion of reduplication within the stem

If one assumes that root + stem-forming suffix in Dyirbal, root + object marker in Amele, root + derivational prefix in Gapapaiwa, and root + nominalizing suffix in Boumaa Fijian form morphological constituents that we can call "stems," then the generalization is the same in all four languages: reduplication doubles some morphological constituent *within the stem*, irrespective of phonological size or linear position. Without going into the details of the morphological construction that handles affix doubling, it is clear that these languages strongly support the Thesis of Morphological Targets (2).

2.1.3   *Further implications*

The existence of affix reduplication, as distinct from root reduplication, requires reconsideration of the root vs. affix distinction among reduplicants postulated in McCarthy and Prince's Generalized Template Theory (GTT; McCarthy & Prince 1994c; d; Urbanczyk 1996). According to GTT, there are two kinds of reduplicative morphemes: roots and affixes. The only consequence of this distinction is phonological.[5] Roots are subject to constraints requiring them to be minimally foot-sized, while affixes are subject to constraints requiring them to be less than a foot (i.e. no larger than a syllable). The existence of affix doubling shows, however, that the relevant distinction between reduplicated roots and reduplicated affixes is not phonological, but morphological. In Dyirbal, Amele, and the other languages discussed in §2.1, reduplicated affixes can be of any size, as can reduplicated roots.[6]

Although somewhat of a side issue, it is worth noting that the existence of affix doubling, especially in conjunction with root doubling, appears to support theories of morphology which treat affixes as morphological constituents. In realizational theories in which affixed stems lack internal constituent structure, e.g. the A-morphous theory of morphology developed by Anderson (1992), it is difficult to express affix doubling and root doubling as instances of the same phenomenon.

2.2 Morphotactic asymmetries: empty morphs

A major prediction of MDT, following from the Thesis of Semantic Identity, is that there should be reduplication constructions in which the two daughters are identical in their meanings but differ phonologically because their internal structural makeup is different. This section examines a variety of cases in which phonological identity is negated by the existence of empty morphs in one of the copies. For example, in Ndebele (Nguni; Downing 2001; Sibanda 2004; Hyman, Inkelas, and Sibanda to appear), to be discussed in greater detail below, reduplication of a verb stem involves a preposed, disyllabic version of the verb stem, as shown in (11a).[7] When the base itself is not disyllabic, however, the reduplicant must contain a morph not present in the base, simply in order to satisfy disyllabicity. The only way to do this and still maintain semantic identity is to use a semantically vacuous morph. This is illustrated in (11b), where the reduplicant, *dlayi*, contains the root 'eat' (*dl-*) plus the semantically empty morph *-yi*. Data are taken from examples (2) and (27) of Hyman, Inkelas, and Sibanda to appear; see also Sibanda 2004:289–300:

(11)   a. 'taste' /nambith-a/ nambitha nambi-nambitha
          b. 'eat'   /dl-a/   dla   dlayi-dla

The presence of *yi* in the reduplicant is tolerated because it does not affect the semantic identity between *dlayi* and *dla*. Cases of this sort prove that the identity in reduplication is essentially semantic, not phonological.

2.2.1 *Empty morphs in morphology*
To have a proper context for understanding the role of empty morphs in reduplication, it is useful first to survey the use of empty morphs in morphology

generally. There is, in fact, nothing unique morphologically about the empty morphs that occur in reduplication. The factors that motivate the presence of empty morphs in reduplication are the same factors that motivate their presence in nonreduplicative constructions. These factors can be either phonological or morphological.

Many morphological constructions require the presence of a morphological formative which has no clearly isolable meaning but plays a structural role. Final vowels in Bantu are a good example. Verb stems in many Bantu languages are required to end in one of a small set of "Final Vowel" (FV) suffixes, so called because they close off a verb stem to further suffixation. Some FV suffixes do make a semantic contribution; for example, in Ndebele, the FV suffix *-e* marks subjunctive mood, and the FV suffix *-ile* markes perfective aspect (12). But there is usually one FV suffix which is semantically vacuous, serving only the structural role of closing off the verb. In Ndebele the FV suffix *-a* meets this description. It is simply the "elsewhere" FV (see, e.g., Sibanda 2004):

(12)   lim- 'cultivate'   Subjunctive: lim-e
                              Perfective: lim-ile
                              Elsewhere: lim-a

Wise (1986) proposes empty morph status for the /t/ formative which appears in the PreAndine languages of Peru (which include the Campa, Amuesha, and Piro-Apurinã languages). Although in Axininca Campa and other Campa languages the distribution of /t/ appears wholly governed by phonology (Wise 1986:579; see also, for example, Payne 1981; Spring 1990; McCarthy & Prince 1993), Wise cites examples from Piro and Amuesha (p. 578) where the cognate formative "is not necessary on phonological grounds; it occurs simply because certain verb roots and suffixes . . . cannot occur word or stem finally and no other potentially closing suffix . . . occurs" (p. 581). In this description, /t/ has a function similar to the final vowel in Bantu; it is a semantically empty element which serves to close off a stem morphologically.

The elements Hockett (1954) termed "markers" of constructions are also pro-totypical empty morphs. Hockett's example was the English conjunction *and*, but many examples occur in morphology proper. Aronoff (1994) points to theme vowels in European languages, particularly those of Latin, as being "[a]mong the best-known examples of empty morphs" (p. 45); the *bindungs*-elements commonly found in compounding constructions constitute another. English has this to only a limited degree, e.g. *huntsman, batsman, swordsman, clans-man*; but many compounding constructions in other languages illustrate the phe-nomenon more clearly, e.g. Serbo-Croatian *vod-o-paad* 'water-MARKER-fall =

waterfall,' *plaav-o-zelen* 'blue-MARKER-green = blue green,' etc. Turkish (see, for example, Lewis 1967; Kornfilt 1997) marks one of its compounding constructions with a final suffix, which, though homophonous with the third person possessive suffix, does not contribute any independent meaning to the construction, e.g. *bebek-hastane-si* 'baby-hospital-MARKER = baby hospital,' *okul kitab-ı* 'school-book-MARKER.'[8]

2.2.2 *Phonologically beneficial empty morphs*

Some empty morphs are not part of particular constructions in the sense discussed above but are used when they serve a phonological purpose, e.g. aiding in the satisfaction of prosodic minimality. Many Bantu languages impose minimality requirements on verbs or verb stems. For example, Chichêwa and Ndebele require their verbs to be minimally disyllabic (on Chichêwa, see, for example, Mtenje 1988; Kanerva 1989; Hyman & Mtenje 1999; on Ndebele, see Downing 2001; Sibanda 2004; Hyman, Inkelas & Sibanda to appear). When verbal prefixes are present, disyllabicity is guaranteed; no stem is smaller than a syllable and all prefixes are monosyllabic. But in the imperative, which consists of a bare stem, a verb whose stem is monosyllabic falls short of minimal size. Chichêwa augments monosyllabic verbs with the formative *i-* (13a) (see, for example, Hyman & Mtenje 1999:108), while Ndebele augments with *yi* (13b) (example (24) from Hyman, Inkelas & Sibanda to appear; see also Downing 2001; Sibanda 2004):

(13)

		Infinitive	Imperative	Gloss
a.	i.	ku-fótókozera	fotokozera	'explain'
	ii.	ku-dyá	**i**-dya	'eat'
b.	i.	uku-lima	lima	'cultivate'
		uku-bamba	bamba	'catch'
		uku-nambitha	nambitha	'taste'
	ii.	uku-dla	**yi**-dla	'eat'
		uku-lwa	**yi**-lwa	'fight'
		uku-ma	**yi**-ma	'stand'
		uku-za	**yi**-za	'come'

To take one other example, the Athapaskan languages Slave and Navajo use *(h)e-* (Rice 1989:149, 132–35, 426) and *yi-* (McDonough 1990:138ff.), respectively, to augment verb roots which lack prefixes. According to McDonough, verb prefixes belong to a constituent (the I-stem) which is obligatory in every verb and which cannot be empty.[9]

The analysis of empty morphs adopted here is as follows. Some empty morphs are associated with particular constructions, in which they are obligatory. These are the kind seen in §2.2.1. Others, however, are listed in the lexicon without being mentioned in any particular constructions; these include the phonologically beneficial morphs in §2.2.2. Their distribution in inputs is regulated by the grammar, in a way that we model here by building on existing proposals in Optimality Theory for determining the lexical representation of morphemes (Lexicon Optimization) and, in cases of allomorphy, for selecting among the different lexical allomorphs of a morpheme.[10] Lexicon Optimization (Prince & Smolensky 1993; see also Inkelas 1995; Itô, Mester & Padgett 1995; Yip 1996, among others) is a deterministic method for establishing underlying representations by considering all of the possible inputs that would generate a given output, and selecting the most harmonic. In some cases, more than one underlying allomorph for a given morpheme must be memorized, in a form determined by Lexicon Optimization. We follow Dolbey 1996; Kager 1996; Sprouse 1997; Steriade 1997; 1999; Sprouse in preparation in assuming that these listed allomorphs compete for position in words calling for the semantic content that they share. The grammar selects that allomorph which phonologically optimizes the word containing it.

Combining these two proposals yields the following approach to determining morphological inputs: the input candidates considered for a word with meaning (M) are those sets of lexically listed morphological formatives whose meanings add up to M. These combinations can differ from each other in several ways. They can vary by lexical allomorph (as in the cases considered by Dolbey and Kager); they can vary by including, or not including, semantically empty morphemes, the case in question here. The presence or absence of a semantically empty morph has no effect on the meaning (M) of any given candidate.

The tableaus in (14) evaluate competing possible morphological inputs for the Chichêwa words meaning 'eat (imperative)' and 'explain (imperative).' These tableaus mirror those used for Lexicon Optimization by Inkelas 1995; Itô, Mester & Padgett 1995 and for allomorph selection by Dolbey 1996; Sprouse 1997; in preparation. In each case the optimal input is the one judged most harmonic by standards of output well-formedness and input–output faithfulness; each input is compared, separately, to the full range of possible output strings. In the first tableau, for 'eat (imperative),' the competing inputs are /dy-/, dy-a/, and /i-dy-a/. By virtue of containing the same root, /dy/, all mean 'eat'; the absence of other semantically contentful morphemes results (by means that cannot be fully explored here) in the default interpretation of imperative. The input /dy-a/

has one empty morph; the input /i-dy-a/ has two. Each input is compared with three reasonable outputs, [dy], [dya], [idya], which are evaluated for well-formedness. Constraints on syllabification (not formalized here, but abbreviated as SYLL) eliminate the output [dy] from consideration, as it is not a well-formed syllable. DISYLL favors the disyllabic output [idya], while *STRUC (arbitrarily evaluated in terms of syllable count) favors the more compact outputs. IO-FAITH favors those input–output pairs which are faithful over those which exhibit epenthesis or deletion. Because DISYLL outranks *STRUC, the output [idya] is favored over the other two outputs; because IO-FAITH is high-ranked, the input /i-dy-a/ is optimal for the output [idya], and this input–output pairing is therefore selected as optimal overall. The presence of empty morphs in the input for 'eat (imperative)' is optimal because the morphs contribute to the well-formedness of the output without disrupting faithfulness (as epenthesis, for example, would). The second tableau, for 'explain (imperative),' exhibits a parallel set of candidate inputs and outputs. The difference between 'eat' and 'explain' is phonological size; the root – *fotokozer-* is already polysyllabic, meaning that DISYLL is satisfied by all of the input–output pairs under consideration. The input /i-fotokozer-a/, with two empty morphs, violates *STRUC to a greater degree than does the input without the /i-/ empty morph, which wins the overall competition.

(14)

			'eat (imperative)'		IO-FAITH	SYLL	DISYLL	*STRUC
			input candidates	*output candidates*				
	a.	i.	/dy-/	[dy]		*!	*	*
		ii.		[dya]	*!		*	*
		iii.		[idya]	*!*			**
	b.	i.	/dy-a/	[dy]	*!	*	*	*
		ii.		[dya]			*!	*
		iii.		[idya]	*!			**
	c.	i.	/i-dy-a/	[dy]	*!*	*	*	*
		ii.		[dya]	*!		*	*
☞		iii.		[idya]				**

			'explain (imperative)'		IO-FAITH	SYLL	DISYLL	*STRUC
			input candidates	*output candidates*				
	a.	i.	/fotokozer/	[fotokozer]		*!		****
				[fotokozera]	*!			*****
				[ifotokozera]	*!*			******
	b.	i.	/fotokozer-a/	[fotokozer]	*!	*		****
☞		ii.		[fotokozera]				*****
				[ifotokozera]	*!			******
	c.	i.	/i-fotokozer-a/	[fotokozer]	*!*	*		****
		ii.		[fotokozera]	*!			*****
				[ifotokozera]				******!

From here forward we will assume that an approach of this kind regulates the distribution of empty morphs in inputs, without providing similarly lengthy justifications for every case.

2.2.3 *Empty morphs in reduplication*

The presence of empty morphs in one or both daughters in reduplication can disrupt phonological identity while still preserving semantic identity between them.

One type of empty morph commonly found in reduplication constructions is the so-called "linker morph," which comes between the two copies in the same way that *bindungs*-elements join the two members of compounds. For example, Khasi iterative verb reduplication separates the two copies of the verb by the linker *ši* (Abbi 1991:130), e.g. *iaid-ši-iaid* 'to go on walking,' *leh-ši-leh* 'keep repeating,' *kren-ši-kren* 'keep talking' (Abbi 1991:128). Tamil "discontinuous" reduplication partially reduplicates a numeral (X) to mean 'X and only X;' separating the two copies is a linker element -*e*-, as in: *o-e-oṇṇu* 'only one' or *na:l-e-na:lu* 'only four' (Abbi 1991:65). In Huallago (Huánuco) Quechua (Weber 1989), the first of two reduplicated verbs is followed by -*r*. Many languages with more than one reduplication construction use different linkers for each; in Arrernte (Arandic; Central Australia), frequentative reduplication uses the linker *-ep*, e.g. *akemir-em* 'is getting up' vs. *akemir-ep-ir-em* 'keeps getting up,' while attenuative reduplication uses the linker *-elp*, e.g. *itir-em* 'thinking' vs. *it-elp-itir-em* 'half-thinking' (Breen & Pensalfini 1999:6–7). In Jaqaru, a Jaqi language of Peru (Hardman 2000), two total reduplication constructions are distinguished *only* by the linker consonant separating the two copies. Intensive adjective reduplication separates the two copies with the palatal glide *y*; intensive verbs use the palatal affricate linker *ch*. Hardman presents the following minimal pair, based on *t'usqi* 'dust': *t'usqi-y-t'usqi* 'very like smoke' (the intensive adjective) vs. *t'usqi-ch-t'usqi* 'to be causing a lot of dust' (the intensive verb) (p. 54). For some additional examples of linker constructions, see Moravcsik 1978. Linker morphs may be assumed to be semantically empty when there is no positive evidence that they, as opposed to the reduplication they co-occur with, distinctively contribute any specific meaning to the construction. What is clear is that they are concomitants of reduplication whose presence could not be predicted based on other knowledge of the language.

The constituent structure of reduplication constructions with linker morphs is not always determinate. If the so-called "linker" forms a morphological constituent with one of the daughters (15b), then its presence disrupts phonological identity. If, on the other hand, the linker is a third daughter of the construction (15a), then identity is not disturbed.

(15)   (a)   t'usqicht'usqi   (b)   t'usqicht'usqi

       t'usqi   *ch*   t'usqi   t'usqi   *ch*   t'usqi

Only in the presence of evidence for a structure like (15b) (or its mirror image) do linker morphs support the claims of MDT. Unfortunately, the morphological constituency of linker morphs is difficult to determine in many cases; a similar problem is presented by *bindungs*-elements in compounding. The claims of MDT are more clearly illustrated by cases in which the empty morph unambiguously belongs to one daughter or the other.

In the Mon-Khmer language Pacoh, for example, an empty morph can occur, under certain conditions, in the base of reduplication. Verb reduplication expresses the meaning of simulation; reduplicating 'laugh' yields a meaning of 'pretend to laugh' (Watson 1966:95). Both copies – base and reduplicant – are subject to prosodic size conditions. The second copy must be monosyllabic; the first must be disyllabic. If the input root is disyllabic, then the first copy is intact, while the second is truncated to the final (main) syllable of the input verb

(16a). If the input root is monosyllabic, then the second copy is intact, while the first is augmented with the semantically empty morph *qâN-* (16b). All of the reduplicated forms cited in (16) are preceded by the verb *táq* 'to do':

(16)   a. kacháng   'to laugh'   táq kacháng-cháng   'to pretend to laugh'
           qaqay   'sick'   táq qaqay-qay   'to act sick'

        b. cha   'to eat'   táq **qân**-cha-cha   'to pretend to eat'
           bíq   'to sleep'   táq **qâm**-bíq-bíq   'to pretend to sleep'
           pôk   'to go'   táq **qâm**-pôk-pôk   'to pretend to go'

We may assume, building on the discussion in §2.2.2, that the Pacoh lexicon includes the empty morph *qâN-*. Though normally absent from inputs because its presence would gratuitously violate *STRUC, *qâN* is available to inputs that would not otherwise produce stems meeting the prosodic minimality conditions. It is needed in the input to the first copy in reduplication to satisfy the disyllabicity requirement; it is not needed in the second copy.

(17)

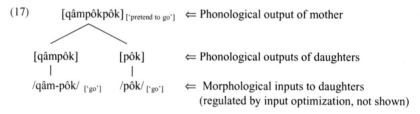

On this analysis of Pacoh, the inputs of the daughters can differ morphotactically but are still identical semantically. Cases of this sort, in which the base is more complex than the reduplicant, do not necessarily distinguish among theories of reduplication; however, cases in which the reduplicant is more complex than the base provide strong support for MDT.

Empty morphs in the reduplicant play a significant role in Bantu reduplication, as discussed, for example, in the significant bodies of insightful work on Kinande (Mutaka & Hyman 1990; Downing 1998b; 2000a), Chichêwa (Hyman & Mtenje 1999), Siswati and Kikerewe (Downing 1997a; b; 1999a; c). Here the focus will be on Ndebele, drawing on work by Downing 1999a; 2001, Sibanda 2004, and Hyman, Inkelas & Sibanda to appear. Ndebele has two empty morphs: *yi*, which augments subminimal words, and *-a*, which is the default final suffix in verb stems (see below). Both also aid in achieving reduplicant disyllabicity in verb stem reduplication.

As noted above, Ndebele exhibits a common Bantu verb stem reduplication pattern: the first copy of the verb stem is restricted to the CVCV prosodic shape, while the second is not phonologically restricted. Standard practice is to refer to the first copy as the "reduplicant" and the second as the "base"; of course, in MDT the two copies have equal morphological status. Reduplication adds the meaning of 'do here and there, a little bit.' As shown below, a cursory look at the phenomenon suggests that the reduplicant consists simply of the initial CVCV portion of the base. Verbs are shown in the infinitive, marked by the prefix *uku-*:

(18)

	Unreduplicated stem		Reduplicated counterpart
'taste'	/uku-nambith-a/	uku-nambitha	uku-nambi-nambitha
'go from wife to wife'	/uku-thembuz-a/	uku-thembuza	uku-thembu-thembuza

When the verb stem is sufficiently short, however, empty morphs can appear in the reduplicant which are not present in the base. If the verb stem is disyllabic only by virtue of containing an inflectional suffix, then the reduplicant must end in the empty morph -*a*:

(19) a. 'cultivate' SUBJUNCTIVE /lim-e/ lime lima-lime
    PERFECTIVE /lim-ile/ limile lima-limile
  b. 'send' SUBJUNCTIVE /thum-e/ thume thuma-thume
    PERFECTIVE /thum-ile/ thumile thuma-thumile

According to Downing (see, for example, Downing 1999a for an overview), *a*-final reduplicants are common in the Bantu family; the pattern arises when morphological factors prevent the morphological material making the base disyllabic (or larger) from appearing in the reduplicant.

As observed by Hyman, Inkelas, and Sibanda (to appear) and Sibanda (2004), the domain of reduplication in Ndebele is what Downing has called, for Bantu languages generally, the Derivational Stem (DStem), consisting of root plus any derivational suffixes (see, for example, Downing 1997; 1998a; 1999a; c; 2000a; 2001). The DStem combines with an inflectional suffix, which could be the semantically empty final vowel (FV) -*a*, to produce the Inflectional Stem (IStem), which is normally what Bantuists mean by the term "verb stem." Many Bantu languages, including Kinande, reduplicate the IStem. However, as proposed in Hyman, Inkelas, and Sibanda (to appear) and Sibanda 2004, Ndebele reduplication targets Dstems. It produces another Dstem, with the added meaning of 'do here and there, a little bit,' which then must obligatorily combine with a FV (not shown).

(20)

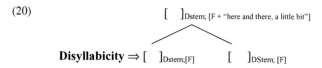

If the Dstem is smaller than two syllables, the disyllabicity requirement on the reduplicant can be satisifed only if a semantically empty morph is present in input. The example below shows what the construction generating the reduplicative constituent [lima-lim], within the subjunctive verb stem *lima-lime*, would look like:

(21)

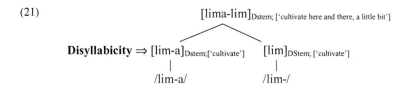

Empty *a* is needed in the reduplicant, and hence the input containing it is preferred to the input not containing it; *a* is not needed in the base, and hence the more economical input is preferred.

What is important here is that the morphotactic discrepancy observed in Ndebele clearly requires the kind of semantic equivalence central to MDT and cannot be accounted for in theories where reduplication consists exclusively of phonological copying.

Some Ndebele reduplicants are so far from achieving disyllabic minimality that they need more help than empty -*a* can provide. As shown below, Dstems consisting only of a consonantal root need help not only from -*a* but also from the other semantically empty morph in Ndebele, namely -*yi*, introduced earlier in a discussion of subminimal verb augmentation. Both -*a* and -*yi* are needed to make the reduplicants of consonantal DStems disyllabic. -*a* alone would be insufficient (*dl-a*, for example, would still be only monosyllabic), as would -*yi*; *yi-dl* is still only monosyllabic and has an illegal coda, while *dl-yi* is monosyllabic and has an impermissible onset cluster. Data are taken from example (29) of Hyman, Inkelas, and Sibanda to appear:

(22)

	Infinitive (no reduplication)		Reduplicated counterpart
a. 'eat'	/uku-dl-a/	uku-dla	uku+dl-a-yi+dla
b. 'stand'	/uku-m-a/	uku-ma	uku+m-a-yi+ma
c. 'fight'	/uku-lw-a/	uku-lwa	uku+lw-a-yi+lwa
d. 'come'	/uku-z-a/	uku-za	uku+z-a-yi+za

For the Dstem meaning 'eat,' based on the consonantal root *dl-*, the optimal input for the reduplicant is /dl-a-yi/, which can faithfully achieve a disyllabic output; the optimal input for the base is /dl-/, which is both faithful and structurally minimal (since no size conditions constrain it).

(23)

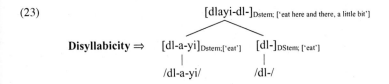

$$[\text{dlayi-dl-}]_{\text{Dstem; ['eat here and there, a little bit']}}$$

Disyllabicity $\Rightarrow$ $[\text{dl-a-yi}]_{\text{Dstem;['eat']}}$ $[\text{dl-}]_{\text{DStem; ['eat']}}$

/dl-a-yi/   /dl-/

Ndebele reduplication is striking in the degree of phonological discrepancy that can result between reduplicant and base. Forms like *dlayi-dla* or *lima-limile* are clearly more consistent with the precepts of MDT than with the precepts of BRCT; *lima* cannot be derived from *limile*, nor *dlayi* from *dla*, by phonological copying. The equivalence is not phonological. It is semantic.

These facts are amply discussed by Sibanda (2004) and Hyman, Inkelas, and Sibanda (to appear), who adopt a morphological analysis of the sort taken here; suffice it to say here that the data in (22) confirm the degree of morphotactic autonomy of the two copies in reduplication.

2.2.4   Simple melodic overwriting
In Ndebele, the empty morphs *a* and *yi* supplement consonantal roots. Sometimes, however, empty morphs compete for surface position with some of the material from the semantically contentful morphemes in the input. Particularly interesting is the fact that semantically empty *-a* and *-yi* are in free variation, in the reduplicant, with material from derivational suffixes, as illustrated below (data from example (3) of Hyman, Inkelas, & Sibanda to appear):

(24)   a. lim-el-a lim-e+lim-el-a 'cultivate for/at' (applicative -el-)
               lim-a+lim-el-a
        b. lim-is-a lim-i+lim-is-a 'make cultivate' (causative -is-)
               lim-a+lim-is-a

The variation is even more extreme with consonantal roots, as discussed by Sibanda (2004) and Hyman, Inkelas and Sibanda (to appear), who take an MDT approach to the data. The important point is, however, sufficiently illustrated by the CVC roots in (24). The grammar has a choice between using the empty morph *-a* or the input derivational suffix vowel in the second syllable in the reduplicant; the two choices are equally preferred, resulting in the observed variation.

The interested reader is encouraged to consult Downing 2001, Sibanda 2004, and Hyman, Inkelas, and Sibanda (to appear) for further information on the rich reduplication system of Ndebele. The main point here is that an empty input morph can, under conditions like the disyllabic size condition in Ndebele reduplication, surface at the expense of (part of) a semantically contentful input morph.

It is competition of this sort that underlies the phenomenon commonly known as Melodic Overwriting. "Melodic Overwriting" is the term given by McCarthy and Prince 1986, Alderete et al. 1999, and others to the situation in which one of the two copies in reduplication exhibits phonological material not present in the other, material which appears to be replacing segments that would otherwise be expected to be present in a way that cannot be accounted for by natural phonological alternations. In parade examples of Melodic Overwriting, like the Yiddish-English ironic construction exemplified by *fancy-shmancy*, the replacive material is a segmental string which targets a syllable constituent at a fixed edge of the copy designated as the reduplicant. Initial onset replacement, as in *fancy-shmancy*, is probably the most common type of case discussed in the literature; it also occurs, for instance, in the well-known, virtually pan-Asian "X and the like" construction manifested as *m-* replacement in Turkish *kitap-mitap* 'books and the like' (see Lewis 1967 for discussion), Armenian *pətuʁ-mətuʁ* 'fruit and stuff' (Vaux 1998:246), and Abkhaz *gaʒák'-maʒák'* 'fool and the like' (Vaux 1996, Bruening 1997; Vaux forthcoming), and as *gi*-replacement in Kolami *kota-gita* 'bring it if you want to' and Telugu *aːku giːku* 'leaf, etc.' (Emeneau 1955:101–102; Bhaskararao 1977:7ff.).

Just as initial onset replacement can be seen as affixation, final rime or coda replacement can be seen as suffixation. One example of final rime replacement occurs in Vietnamese; the "iếc-hoá" construction, which "supplies some emotional coloring (disinterest, irony, etc.) to the meaning of any base," reduplicates a base of any size, and replaces the rime of the final syllable of the second copy the formative *-iếc*, e.g. *hát* → *hát.hiếc* 'to sing,' *cà.phê* 'coffee and the like' → *cà.phê cà.phiếc*, *câu.lạc.bộ* 'clubs and the like' → *câu.lạc.bộ câu.lạc.biếc* (Nguyen 1997:53–54).[11] Apparent coda overwriting occurs, for example, in the emphatic adjective reduplication construction, found throughout Turkic (see, for example, Johanson & Csato 1998) as well as in Armenian (Vaux 1998:242–45), which reduplicates the first CV of the adjective and interposes a fixed consonant between reduplicant and base. This interposed consonant is normally interpreted in descriptions as part of the reduplicant; it syllabifies as a coda except when the adjective is vowel-initial, in which case it syllabifies rightward as an onset. Turkic languages vary in the precise details of this construction; one of the simpler manifestations occurs in Mongolian, where the fixed consonant is always /v/, e.g. *khav-khar* 'coal black,' *chiv-chimeegüi* 'completely silent,' *uv-ulaan* 'bright red' (Bosson 1964:110).[12]

Alderete et al. (1999) have argued for treating Melodic Overwriting as affixation; in MDT, the affix in question is generated within one of the copies, the one traditionally termed the reduplicant. The affix is a semantically empty morph required by the construction, parallel to the empty linker morphs discussed in §2.2.1 except in the one respect that it supplants, instead of coexisting with, input material. (Thus, in retrospect, the Ndebele data discussed in §2.2.1 could be analyzed in terms of Melodic Overwriting, insofar as the empty -*yi* and -*a* in the reduplicant potentially supplant input affixes.) Based on a proposal made for comparable data in Inkelas 1998, we assume that the competition between empty affix and input material is driven by faithfulness: the output must be faithful prosodically, e.g. in syllable count, to the input size of the base of affixation. In a case like Vietnamese *càphê+càph-iếc*, the input base of the affixed copy is *càphê*; faithfulness to its syllable count forces the suffix *iếc* to replace *ê*:

(25)   càphêcàphiếc

      [càphê]   [càph-iếc]   ⇐ output has 2 syllables
        | ∧
      /càphê/   /càphê-iếc/   ⇐ input root has 2 syllables

Melodic Overwriting is thus distinguished from ordinary cases of morphologically required linker morphs, discussed in §2.2.3, in just one respect: in cases of Melodic Overwriting, a prosodic size faithfulness condition is imposed on the subconstituent containing the linker morph. The ensuing competition between affix and base of affixation is what provides evidence that the linker morph belongs to one of the two daughters, and this fact is what makes Melodic Overwriting particularly relevant to MDT. Any case of Melodic Overwriting is evidence that one daughter in reduplication contains an empty morph that the other does not, with the result that the two daughters are different phonologically – but identical semantically. Melodic Overwriting is a prototypical case of what MDT predicts in reduplication.

2.2.5   Double melodic overwriting

By the same token that one daughter can contain an empty morph not found in the other, the MDT approach to reduplication leads one to expect constructions in which both daughters contain empty morphs not found in the other. This pattern is indeed attested. One well-known case, described in Yip 1982, occurs in Chinese secret languages. Another, from Hua, is presented here.

In the Papuan language Hua (Haiman 1980), verbs are intensified through total reduplication, followed (in most caes) by the helping verb *hu*. One subpattern of reduplication replaces the final V with /u/ in the first copy and final V with /e/ in the second copy: this is Melodic Overwriting in both copies (data from Haiman 1980:126):

(26)   kveki   'crumple'   kveku kveke hu   'crumple'
        ebsgi   'twist'   ebsgu ebsge hu   'twist and turn'
        ftgegi   'coil'   ftgegu ftgege hu   'all coiled up'
        ha-vari 'grow tall'   ha-varu ha-vare hu   'grow up'

Sticking with the affixation approach to Melodic Overwriting, the Hua reduplication construction can be analyzed as calling for two different stem types: a u-stem, formed by suffixing empy -*u*, and an e-stem, formed by replacing the final stem vowel with -*e*.[13]

(27)   kveku kveke

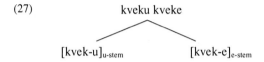

            [kvek-u]_{u-stem}   [kvek-e]_{e-stem}

The daughters of the Hua reduplication construction are formed by the stem-forming constructions illustrated below.

(28)   u-stem construction   e-stem construction

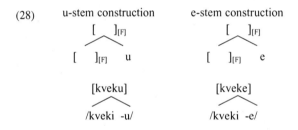

Both constructions in (28) are associated with a phonological requirement that the output and input contain the same number of syllables, which results in root-vowel deletion by standard means which it is not necessary to spell out here.

The Hua reduplication construction illustrated in (27) is like all other MDT reduplication constructions in calling for two daughters which are semantically identical; it adds the further specification that the daughters must be of different lexical types. Each has a semantically empty morph not present in the other, and as a result the two are not phonologically identical.

If Hua had called for two daughters of the same lexical type, the expected result would be phonological identity. Such a case occurs in Siroi, a non-Austronesian language of Papua New Guinea, in which adjective reduplication signifies plurality. According to Wells (1979:37), "[t]he infix -*g*- replaces the central consonant in two-syllable words and is added in one-syllable words," as shown below.[14] The digraph "ng" represents the prenasalized stop [$^{\eta}$g]:

(29)   a. tango maye → tango mage-mage
            'man' 'good'
            'a mature man'   'mature men'
    b. tango sungo → tango sugo-sugo
            'man' 'big'
            'a ruler'   'rulers'
    c. tango kuen → tango kugen-kugen
            'man' 'tall'
            'a tall man'   'tall men'

This pattern can be described in terms of *g*-infixation to the beginning of the final syllable; the intrusion of *g* causes the deletion of an input onset, plausibly due to a prohibition on the consonant clusters that would otherwise result. This analysis of Siroi thus parallels the analysis of Hua point for point, with the exception that only one stem-forming construction (*g*-infixation) is involved, rather than two.

This discussion of stem-forming constructions, and lexical stem types, draws on a growing literature, not about reduplication, which includes Aronoff 1994; Koenig & Jurafsky 1995; Orgun 1996; Blevins 2003. The reader is referred to these works for further discussion of the role of stem types in morphology generally.

2.2.6   *Tier replacement*

In the constructions examined thus far, a particular syllable constituent is targeted for replacement by an empty morph, making affixation (whether adfixation or infixation) a straightforward analysis. But reduplication constructions also admit the possibility of modifications that fall in the fuzzy area between affixation and morphologically conditioned phonology.

The Papuan language Amele has a construction which Roberts (1987; 1991) calls the "irregular iterative"; it reduplicates the verb stem and adds a meaning of haphazardness, spasmodicity, intermittency, etc. (p. 133). Morphologically the construction doubles the verb root (with suffixes being added at the right edge); phonologically, the vowels in the second copy are replaced. As shown in (30a), input /a/ vowels are replaced with /u/; the same is true of (b), whose stems have an input [-high]-i vocalism. In (c) are inputs whose input vowels are all /i/. In this case the vowels of the second copy are replaced by /o/.[15] The data in (a–b) are from Roberts 1991:135; those in (c) are from p. 136.

(30) a. bala-doʔ   'to tear'   bala-bulu-doʔ   'to tear and scatter'
         ʔaʔagan-eʔ   'to talk in sleep'   ʔaʔagan-ʔuʔugun-eʔ 'to talk sporadically
                                                                in sleep'
         fag-doʔ   'to pierce'   fag-fug-doʔ   'to stick all over'
      b. faliʔ-doʔ   'to turn'   faliʔ-fuluʔ-doʔ   'to revolve'
         lahi-doʔ   'to shake s.t.'   lahi-luhu-doʔ   'to shake s.t.
                                                                all over'
      c. ʔifiliʔ-doʔ   'to open s.t. out'   ʔifiliʔ-ʔofoloʔ-doʔ 'to open s.t. out
                                                                all over'
         gili-doʔ   'to move'   gili-golo-doʔ   'to move from side
                                                                to side'

A similar situation obtains in Siroi; when verb roots reduplicate to indicate "plurality and/or intensification and variableness of an action ... all vowels in the first form change to *i*," e.g. *kare* 'be hard', *kiri-kare* 'wither'; *kutuŋ* 'move', *kitiŋ-kutuŋ* 'wobble' (Wells 1979:36).[16] Tier replacement is not limited to vowels; it also commonly affects tone. In Hausa adverbial reduplication, for example, discussed in more detail in Chapter 3, input tones are completely replaced in both copies by a distinct melody specific to the reduplication construction (Newman 1989b). In Hausa, complete tonal tier replacement is also common in affixation; it is not specific to reduplication (see, for example, Newman 1986; 2000).

Tier replacement is difficult to describe in the standard terms of item-based morphology. Affixing /i/ to the Siroi stem *kare* is not going to produce *kiri* in any automatic way. The analysis offered here of tier replacement effects like these is completely parallel to the analysis of affixational Melodic Overwriting: *kiri* is derived from *kare*, in Siroi, by a stem-forming construction whose only effect is to replace all vowels with /i/. The replacement itself adds no semantics to the stem:

(31)
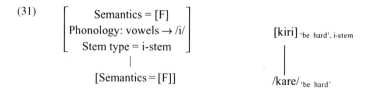

Although its manifestation is different phonologically, vowel replacement in Amele and Siroi is morphologically equivalent to the cases traditionally called Melodic Overwriting, which involve affixation of a more canonical, segmentally overt affix. In both types of cases, reduplication calls for daughters which are products of different stem-forming constructions. Since the stem-forming constructions in question are semantically null, the essential semantic identity is maintained. However, phonological identity is disrupted.

Chapter 3 goes into much more detail about how phonology is associated with stem-forming constructions. For now, discussion will focus on the fact that the phonology of the daughters can diverge, as a result of semantically null morphology, while their meanings stay the same. This is strong support for the Thesis of Semantic Identity.

2.3   Synonym and antonym constructions

This section presents a second major source of supporting evidence for the Thesis of Semantic Identity, namely cases in which the sets of semantically contentful morphemes in each daughter in reduplication are different. One type of case is typified by Sye, in which the two daughters in the reduplication construction may under certain specific circumstances be suppletive allomorphs of the same morpheme. In meaning and function the two are identical, but in phonological form they are lexically distinct.

Once the potential for selecting different lexical allomorphs of the same morpheme is recognized, it becomes clear that MDT correctly predicts the existence of a second, actually quite voluminous set of constructions which have been observed to be very similar in character to reduplication, namely juxtaposition constructions in which the two daughters are synonyms, or near-synonyms, or in some cases antonyms, of each other. These constructions have played little role in the development of phonological reduplication theories of reduplication (though are well known in the repetition literature; see, for example, Wierzbicka 1986; Haiman 1998; Ourn & Haiman 2000). Singh (1982) makes, to our knowledge, the first argument in the literature that these constructions are intimately related to reduplication and should be accounted for in the same way.

2.3.1   *Root allomorphy*
We begin with a discussion of root reduplication in languages from two different language families, both of which exhibit root allomorphy which is at least to some degree lexicalized, i.e. suppletive. In both families there are conditions under which root reduplication manifests both allomorphs, such that the two copies in reduplication are based on different lexical allomorphs of the same morpheme. Such constructions clearly revolve around semantic identity; the construction is drawing twice from the lexicon, with different results in each daughter.[17]

2.3.1.1   Kawaiisu

Root allomorphy interacts with reduplication in Kawaiisu (Numic, Uto-Aztecan; Zigmond, Booth & Munro 1990). Kawaiisu retains the remnants of historic alternations, primarily between p~v, p~b, t~r, t~d, k~g, kw~gw, which show up synchronically as allomorphy, e.g. for 'head,' *toci* ~ *roci*, or for 'taste,' *kama* ~ *gama*. Only some roots show allomorphy. This lack of predictability, coupled with the fact that for roots in /p/ and /t/ the nature of the allomorphy is unpredictable, requires the allomorphy to be treated as lexically suppletive.

For those roots exhibiting allomorphy, the voiced-initial allomorph is used in second position in compounding (32a) and in repetitive/inceptive aspectual reduplication (32b) (Zigmond, Booth & Munro 1990:8, 97):

(32)   a. Compounding

i. kama ~ gama	'taste (intr.)'	?owa-**gama**-	80, 211
		'to taste salty'	
ii. karɨ - ~ garɨ -	'sit'	kwinuurɨ-**garɨ-dɨ**	221
		(name of mountain	
		near Tehachapi)	
		cf. *kwinuurɨ -dɨ*	221
		'to prepare yucca'	
iii. toci ~ roci	'head'	cɨga-**roci**	199
		'rough-head = tangle-	
		haired'	

b. Reduplication

i. ka?a ~ ga?a	'eat'	**ka-ga?a**-na=ina ?iivi	8, 97
		'he's starting to eat now'	
ii. tono ~ dono	'hit, pierce, etc.'	**to-dono**-kwee-dɨ=ina	97, 284
		'he stabbed him repeatedly'	
iii. kiya ~ giya	'play, laugh'	**ki-giya**	214
iv. tahna ~ rahna	'put down/away'	**ta-rahna**	272
v. tɨniya ~ dɨniya	'to tell'	**tɨ-dɨniya**	280

The fact that the two daughters in reduplication can consist of different lexically listed allomorphs (potentially truncated) of the same morpheme strongly supports the prediction of MDT that the essential identity in reduplication is semantic but not phonological. No phonological copying theory of reduplication can account for this sort of effect.

The productivity of this particular construction in Kawaiisu is somewhat questionable; not all roots exhibiting allomorphy in general show different allomorphs in reduplication. However, Kawaiisu is by no means the only example of its kind.

2.3.1.2   Central Vanuatu

Verb root allomorphy, largely centering on the root-initial consonant, is widespread in the languages of Central Vanuatu, which also tend to have verb root reduplication. Useful discussions of Vanuatu verb root allomorphy can be found in Walsh 1982, Crowley 2002b:31ff., Lynch, Ross and Crowley 2002:44, and, especially, Crowley 1991. In numerous languages, represented by those in the table below, roots have two allomorphs, conditioned by morphological context. One, termed "primary" or "basic" in the literature and referred to here as Stem1, is generally the elsewhere case; the other, termed "secondary" or "modified" and referred to here as Stem2, is found in a more restricted set of morphological contexts. Root allomorphy is widely assumed to trace back historically to one or more prefixes which fused with the verb roots to form the Stem2 allomorphs. Crowley (1991) argues that this fusion may have occurred independently several times, rather than being a reconstructable property of Proto-Central Vanuatu. The following chart shows the differences in the initial consonant across root allomorphs in six languages representing the simplest type of root allomorphy in which there are only two variants. The Nāti, Nakanamanga, Namakir and Bierebo data come from Crowley 1991:198ff.; the Raga and Apma data come from Walsh 1982:

(33)

	Nāti	Nakanamanga	Namakir	Bierebo	Raga	Apma
Stem1	Stem2	Stem2	Stem2	Stem2	Stem2	Stem2
v-	mp-	p-	b-	p-	b-	b-
w-	mpw-	p^w-	b-	p^w-		bw-
vw-					bw-	
r-	ntr-	t-	d-	d-	d-	
t-	nt-	t-	d-	d-	nd-	
k-	ŋk-	ŋ-	ŋ-	ŋ-	ŋk-	g-
g-					ŋg-	
?-	ŋk-					
c-				nj-		

The morphological contexts calling for Stem2 vary across languages. In the Nāti language of Malakula, for example, Stem2 is used "when there is a preceding future tense prefix . . . or when the verb carries the negative prefix *sa-*" (Crowley 1991:198).[18] In Raga, Stem2 is used when the root "is directly preceded by the action-in-progress marker . . . by any verb-aspect marker ± *hav* 'negation' + *mom* 'still, yet' . . . [or when] preceded by *ba* 'verb ligature' when the verb preceding *ba* is in a context marked for action-in-progress" (Walsh 1982:237). In Nakanamanga, Stem1 is used when any of the following prefixes directly precede: conditional *pe-*, intentional *ŋa*, imperative *pʷa*; in nominalizations, marked by the prefix *na-* and suffix *-ana*; and when the verb serves "as a postmodifying adjective or adverb, or as the second part of a compound" (Crowley 1991:201); Stem2 is used elsewhere.

Though data showing reduplication in a context calling for Stem2 is not plentiful in the published sources, several examples suggest that when a reduplicated verb root appears in morphological contexts requiring Stem2, the first copy of the verb root assumes its Stem2 form while the second copy is Stem1. The reduplicated verb thus consists of two different allomorphs.

In Raga (Walsh 1982; Crowley 2002a), for example, one of the morphological contexts conditioning Stem2 is an immediately preceding "action-in-progress" prefix (*m-* ∼ *mwa-* ∼Ø) (Walsh 1982:237). Alternations in root shape driven by the presence or absence of this prefix are shown in (34a), below. Root allomorphy in reduplication is illustrated in (b):

(34)

		Stem1 context	Stem2 context
a.		no-ⁿgu vano-ana	na-m **b**ano
		'my going'	'I go'
b.	i.	ra-n **t**u-tunu	ra-m **d**u-tunu
		'they cooked on hot stones'	'they are cooking on hot stones'
	ii.	na-n **v**an-vano	na-m **b**an-vano
		'I used to keep on going'	'I keep on going'

Similar data is reported for Apma, spoken on the same island (Pentecost) as Raga; Walsh (1982:238) cites the following examples of reduplicated roots in Stem1 and Stem2 contexts:

(35)

	Stem1 context	Stem2 context
a.	te **w**iri-wiri	na-mwa **bw**iri-wiri
	'he/she splashed water on face repeatedly'	'I splash water on face repeatedly'
b.	te **k**aha-kahaabe	mwa **g**aha-kahaabe
	'it (=bird) went from branch to branch'	'it (=bird) goes from branch to branch'
c.	te **v**al-valtoo	na-m **b**al-valtoo
	'he/she/it walked with legs apart'	'I walk with legs apart'

In Apma, as in Raga, the "action-in-progress" prefix conditions Stem2 (Walsh 1982:238).

Crowley (1991) does not explicitly mention reduplication in his brief sketch of Nāti verb root allomorphy (pp. 198–200), but one example suggests behavior parallel to that of Raga and Apma. In (36a), the Nāti verb 'hold' appears to be reduplicated; both halves are identical. The reduplicated verb root occurs in a context where Stem1 is called for. In (b), however, where the future prefix *a*- calls for a Stem2 base, the first copy of the root assumes its Stem2 shape, while the second is Stem1 (Crowley 1991:198):

(36)   a. Reduplicated verb root in Stem1 context: both copies = Stem1
           ntar-vur-vur
           1DU.NONFUT-hold$_1$-hold$_1$ 'we hold/held'
    b. Reduplicated verb root in Stem2 context: first copy = Stem2,
           second copy = Stem1
           ntar-a-**mp**ur-vur
           2DU.INCL-FUT-hold$_2$-hold$_1$ 'we will hold'

In the cases seen thus far, root allomorphy is generally phonologically transparent. In Nāti, for example, Stem2 can easily be derived phonologically from Stem1 through the addition of an initial nasal element, which in turn stops the initial portion of a following continuant. Different analyses have been given to phonologically analyzable mutations of this kind in the literature; see, e.g., the extensive literature on consonant mutation in Celtic and in West African languages (Fula [Arnott 1970], Mende [Innes 1971; Conteh, Cowper & Rice 1985], Sereer [McLaughlin 2000], and many others). A morphological analysis would attribute the nasal to a semantically bleached morpheme occurring in the selected set of morphological contexts; alternatively, a more phonological approach would posit a stem-initial nasalization rule triggered in the same set of contexts. This issue need not be resolved here, since languages like Nāti do not provide a test case for MDT in any event. Since the modification is derived by the grammar, any theory of reduplication could give a cyclic account of the mutation effects, on the assumption that the mutation-triggering prefix combines with the output of verb root reduplication. As with any other stem in a mutation context, only the consonant immediately following the prefix is affected.

Although the languages in (33) do not distinguish MDT from other theories, the languages that do are only a small step away. Recall that the mutations which are apparently productive and clearly phonologically general in the languages in (33) derive historically from prefix-root fusion. Any language in which the reflexes of that fusion have been muddied by reanalysis or sound change will not yield to a cyclic anlysis in which reduplication logically precedes mutation. When a reduplicated verb root occurs in a mutation context, such languages will require the direct selection, from the lexicon, of different lexically listed allomorphs of the verb root in question.

The first such case to be examined here is Sye, which exhibits two-fold allomorphy but has lost the phonological generality of the mutation process. We then turn to another set of Vanuatu languages, Paamese and Southeast Ambrym, whose more complex verb root allomorphy also precludes a simple phonological account.

2.3.1.2.1 Sye   Sye, spoken on the island of Erromango, resembles other languages of Southern and Central Vanuatu in exhibiting both verb root allomorphy and reduplication. The discussion of Sye in this section draws heavily on the detailed description and insightful analysis of Crowley 1998; 2002d. Verb root reduplication, which is total, indicates that "an action takes place in a variety of locations at once, e.g. *avan* 'walk', *avan-avan* 'walk all over'" (Crowley 2002d:714). Sye has two series of verb allomorphs, termed here Stem1 and Stem2. Stem2 forms appear in a collection of seemingly unrelated morphological environments (e.g. in verbs inflected for present or future tense, or bearing conditional or past habitual prefixes; Crowley 2002d:704). Stem1 forms appear elsewhere and can be understood as the default stem type. The distribution of stem alternants is illustrated in (37) for the verb 'provoke'. Its Stem1 alternant, *arinova*, is given in (a); in examples (b) and (c), 'provoke' co-occurs with future tense prefixes, and thus appears in its Stem2 form, *narinowa*. Data are from Crowley 2002d: 711:

(37)   a. etw-arinowa-g
            2SG.IMP.NEG-provoke$_1$.1SG   'Don't provoke me!'
        b. co-narinowa-nt
            3SG.FUT-provoke$_2$.1PL.INCL   '(S)he will provoke us'
        c. kokwo-narinowa-nd
            1INC.DU.FUT-provoke$_2$.3PL   'We will provoke them'

The verb 'provoke' is an example of what Crowley calls a weak verb. A weak verb root exhibits a completely transparent relationship between its Stem1 and Stem2 allomorphs: Stem2 consists of Stem1 with the addition of an initial nasal. Data are taken from Crowley 2002d:

(38)   Stem1   Stem2

tovop	ntovop	'laugh'	704
avan	navan	'walk'	704
arinowa	narinowa	'provoke'	711

Strong verbs, on the other hand, exhibit a much less transparent relationship between their allomorphs. While historically the Stem2 verb alternants appear to derive from *a*-accretion and nasalization, synchronically they are arbitrary to a sufficient degree that at least some, if not all, root pairs must be lexically listed (Crowley 1998:84).[19]

(39)

Stem1	Stem2	Gloss	Crowley source
ehvoh	ahvoh	'white'	2002d:704
evcah	ampcah	'defecate'	2002d:704
evinte	avinte	'look after'	1998:83–84
evsor	amsor	'wake up'	1998:84
evtit	avtit	'meet'	1998:83–84
mah	amah	'die'	2002d:704
ocep	agkep	'fly'	1998:84
ochi	aghi	'see it'	1998:84; 2002d:704
okili	agkili	'know'	2002d:704
omol	amol	'fall'	1998:79
oruc	anduc	'bathe'	1998:84; 2002d:704
otvani	etvani	'split'	2002d:720
ovoli	ampoli	'turn it'	1998:84
ovyu-	avyu-	causative	1998:84
ovyu-	ampyu-	desiderative	1998:84
owi	awi	'leave'	1998:84; 2002d:704
pat	ampat	'blocked'	1998:84; 2002d:704
pelom	ampelom	'come'	2002d:712
vag	ampag	'eat'	1998:84; 2002d:704

Comparison of *evcah* → *ampcah* and *evtit* → *avtit*, for example, shows a lack of complete phonological regularity in the mapping between root allomorphs. Even where the mapping is systematic, e.g. replacement of absolute initial *o* with *a*, but prefixation of *am* to consonant-initial words, there is no unitary process that can be appealed to of the sort that makes a phonological account of weak roots possible. At least some Sye root alternants must be lexically listed; we make the simplifying assumption here, adopting Zuraw's (2000) approach to patterned exceptions, that the root alternants are all listed, although the argument would not change if the phonology of Sye were allowed to derive some of the allomorphy. The lexicon provides Stem1 and Stem2 alternants of each root; affixal constructions specify the stem type they combine with. As seen in (39), future tense prefixes select for a stem of type Stem2; the second person singular negative imperative prefix selects for a stem of type Stem1 (or simply does not specify a stem type, Stem1 being the default).

We turn next to reduplication, an arena in which Sye patterns much like the other Vanuatu languages seen thus far. In those morphological contexts calling for Stem1, a reduplicated verb consists of two copies of Stem1. In contexts calling for Stem2, by contrast, reduplication shows morphotactic divergence: the first copy is Stem2, while the second is Stem1. This situation is illustrated below using 'fall', whose Stem1 and Stem2 forms are *omol* and *amol*, respectively (Crowley 1998:79). In (40), 'fall' is shown, reduplicated, in a prefixal context calling for Stem2:

(40)   cw-amol$_2$-omol$_1$
        3PL.FUT-fall$_2$-fall$_1$
        'they will fall all over'

As these Sye data show, reduplicants are not always phonological copies of their bases, as phonological theories of reduplication would require. What is instead occurring in (37) is semantic agreement between suppletive allomorphs: it is morphological doubling, not phonological copying.

2.3.1.2.2 Paamese and Southeast Ambrym   Both Paamese and Southeast Ambrym exhibit a larger set of verb root alternants than what has been seen thus far in Sye and the other Central Vanuatu languages discussed. In Southeast Ambrym, roots have up to five allomorphs each, one default allomorph (Stem1) and up to four other allomorphs (Stem2–Stem5), each restricted to a unique subset of irrealis morphological contexts. Root allomorphs are distinguished in the initial consonant position. As Crowley (1991:185) states in his summary of the situation, "[v]erbs in Southeast Ambrym can be assigned to one of nine classes (or conjugations) according to the nature of the mutation pattern of the initial segment of the root." The classes exhibiting alternations are presented below (the ninth class, all consonant-initial roots, does not alternate):

(41)

Class	Stem1	Stem2	Stem3	Stem4	Stem5
I	t-		t-		d-
II	x-		x-		g-
III	Ø-	x-	m-	v-	g-
IV	h-	h-	m-	v-	g-
V	h-	x-	m-	v-	g-
VI	h-	h-	m-	v-	b-
VII	h-	v-	m-	v-	b-
VIII	v-		v-		b-

There is no immediate phonological generalization available. According to Crowley (1991:185), Stem2 is used after the negative prefixes *nā-* and *tā-*; Stem3, after the first person singular immediate irrealis prefix *na-*; Stem4, after the second person singular immediate irrealis prefix *o-* and all nonsingular immediate irrealis prefixes; and Stem5, after all realis prefixes unless followed by the past tense marker *te-*. Most of these contexts are illustrated below for the verb 'dig' (Crowley 2002c:665):

(42)　　a. va-hil　'(s)he is about to dig'　(Stem1)
　　　　b. na-mil　'I am about to dig'　　(Stem3)
　　　　c. o-vil　　'you are about to dig'　(Stem4)
　　　　d. Ø-gil　　'(s)he digs/dug'　　　(Stem5)

Nothing in the overt segmental phonology of the prefixes could explain the root allomorphy. Class III, whose Stem1 forms are apparently vowel-initial, suggests a morphological account on which the basic pattern is to prefix *x-* to Stem1 to form Stem2, prefix *m-* to form Stem3, prefix *v-* to form Stem4, and prefix *g-* to form Stem5. However, the existence of four different patterns for h-initial roots (classes IV-VIII) makes it impossible to derive Stem2 by any regular means from Stem1.

Though Crowley does not provide any examples of reduplication, he does state that Stem1, the default, is used "as the second of a pair of reduplicated syllables," strongly suggesting that Ambrym behaves like Sye and the other languages discussed above in potentially using different allomorphs of the same verb root in reduplication, the first conforming to the requirements of the higher affix and the second consisting of the default stem allomorph. Parker (1968) mentions reduplication only briefly, indicating that reduplication copies the first CV of the stem (e.g. *ka-kal* 'scratch,' *pi-pili* 'be red,' *mu-mun* 'drink,' etc.). He does not explicitly address the question of what happens when a reduplicated verb occurs in a mutation environment (which, if our understanding is correct, he calls "Aorist"). However, Parker does provide one suggestive example, namely the reduplicated verb *go-xoles* 'he exchanges.' The first (truncated to CV) copy of the root begins with *g*, while the second begins with *x*. This alternation would put 'exchange' into Stem class V in the table in (41).

For Paamese, which has a similar system, we are fortunate to have more data. The following discussion is based on Crowley 1982; 1991. The description in Crowley 1991, covering all dialects, revises that of Crowley 1982, primarily covering a southern dialect, in a number of minor respects, including the number of verb stem classes posited. Presented below is the classification of verbs from Crowley 1991:190, based on the types of allomorphy they show across different morphological contexts. Verbs have up to five allomorphs each, depending on class. The Northern (N), Central (C) and Southern (S) dialects of Paamese differ in the verb root allomorphs occurring in contexts C and D:

(43)

		A	B	C (N/C/S)	D (N/C=S)
		Stem1	Stem2	Stem3	Stem4	Stem5
I		t-	t-	r-	r-/d-/d-	r-/d-
II		t-	t-	r-	mur-/d-/d-	mur-/d-
III		r-	r-	r-	mur-/d-/d-	mur-/r-
IV		k-	k-	k-	k-/g-/g-	k-/g-
V		Ø-	k-	k-	k-/g-/g-	k-/g-
VI		Ø-	k-	k-	k-/g-/ŋ-	k-/ŋ-
VII		Ø-	k-	k-	muk-/g-/ŋ-	k-/ŋ-
VIII		h-	h-	v-	v-	h-
IX		Ø-	Ø-	mu-	mu-	mu-/Ø-
X		C-	C-	C-	muC-/C-/C-	C-
XI		C-	C-	C-	C-	C-

The allomorphs labeled "Secondary" each have a tightly restricted morphological distribution; the allomorph labeled "Primary" occurs in the greatest variety of morphological contexts and is arguably the default. Stem2 is used in "the second part of compound noun construction in which a noun is compounded with a verbal stem"; Stem3 is used for serialized verbs with no inflectional prefix; Stem 4 occurs after realis or negative prefixes; Stem5 is used in realis or negative verbs which are inflected and initial in a serial verb construction – or which are fully reduplicated (Crowley 1991:190–91). Stem1, or the "Primary" allomorph, occurs following distant irrealis prefixes, immediate irrealis prefixes, imperative prefixes, potential prefixes, the adjectival derivational prefix *ta-*, "when there is no preceding morpheme and the verb is nominalized by *-en*," and – crucially – "in the second of a pair of reduplicated syllables" (p. 190).

Thus in reduplication there are apparently two possibilities. There are two phonological patterns of verbal reduplication, CV- and CVCV-, both associated with the same set of meanings: detransitivizing, habitual, random. Following Crowley (1982), we will not attempt to distinguish the constructions here; they behave alike for purposes of stem allomorphy.[20] If the reduplicated verb stem is realis or negative, both copies are expected to appear in their Stem5 form. If, however, the reduplicated verb stem occurs in another context, the first copy exhibits the allomorph expected in that context, while the second appears in its Primary, or default, form, i.e. Stem1. Examples taken from Crowley 1982 (C82) and Crowley 1991 (C91) illustrate these generalizations, below:

(44)   a. na-ro-**ngani**-ani   [naronganian]   C82:164
          1SG.real-NEG-eat-eat   In 'I am not a big eater'
       b. na-**gulu**-ulu   [nagulūl]   C82:209
          1SG.real-shake-shake   'I rattled'
       c. ko-**galo**-kalo   [kogalokal]   C82:209
          2SG.real-move-move   'you moved'
       d. ro-**gu**-kulu-tei   [rogukulutei]   C82:141
          3SG.real.NEG-swim-swim-part '(they) don't swim'
       e. Ø-vi-**hiramu**   [vihiram]   C82:155
          3SG.real-flicker-flicker 'flickered'
       f. Ø-**mu**seh-seh (N)   C91:195
          ~ Ø-**mu**seh-a-seh (C/S)
          3sg.real-breathe-breathe 'he/she puffs/puffed'
       g. vane-**hane**   [vanehan]   C82:153
          3SG.real-copulate-copulate 'copulates all over =
                                    is promiscuous'
       h. vutu-**hutu**   [vutuhut]   C82:154
          3SG.real-abuse-abuse   'swore'
       i. gaa-**kaa**   [gāka]   C82:164
          3SG.real-travel-travel 'travels'
       j. a-**ga**-kani-e   [agekani]   C82:152
          3PL.real-eat-eat-3SG   in 'is this edible?'
       k. a-**muke**-kaa   [amukeka]   C82:153
          3PL.real-fly-fly   'flew in all directions'
       l. a-**da**-tangosaa   [adetangosa]   C82:153
          3PL.real-rise-rise   'went up'
       m. a-**laa**-laapoo   [alālāpo]   C82:153
          3PL.real-fall-fall   'they fell down all
                                    over the place'
       n. re-demi-ene   [redemien]   C82:227
          think-think-nom   'ideas'

2.3.1.2.3 Analysis

In Sye, Southeast Ambrym, and Paamese, selectional restrictions on the part of affixes and other morphological constructions, including serial verb constructions, compounding, and reduplication, determine which allomorph of the verb stem is selected. In Paamese, where for a given verb there may be as many as five stem types lexically listed, realis and negative prefixes, for example, as seen in (44), select for Stem4. The verb reduplication construction is less specific, lexically, about stem type; while the second daughter always assumes its Stem1 form, the construction does not stipulate a particular stem type for the first daughter which can be any of the stem types. Rather, the

construction stipulates only that the stem type of the first daughter determines
the stem type of the construction as a whole:

(45)   Reduplication construction (Paamese)

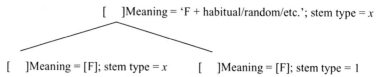

[   ]Meaning = 'F + habitual/random/etc.'; stem type = x

[   ]Meaning = [F]; stem type = x [   ]Meaning = [F]; stem type = 1

This permits Paamese reduplicated verbs to occur in a range of stem-selecting
contexts, as illustrated above.

An interesting exception to the generalization that the second stem in a reduplicated Paamese verb is always Stem1 is manifested in what Crowley terms
class V verbs (which in Crowley 1991 corresponds most closely to IX). In
this class, Stem1 and Stem2 have no prefix; Stem4 and Stem5 begin with *mu-*.
(Whether or not Stem3 begins with *mu-*is a little unclear; Crowley's verb classification chart on p. 190 indicates that it does, but his prose description of
the class on p. 195 indicates that it does not.) According to Crowley (1982),
verbs in this class behave differently under reduplication according to whether
their Stem1 form begins with a consonant or a vowel. "[C]onsonant-initial
roots reduplicate on the basis of their [Stem1] roots, while vowel-initial roots
reduplicate on the basis of their [Stem4] root" (p. 126). Example (46) shows
a vowel-initial class IX stem appearing in its Stem4 form in both copies in
reduplication:

(46)   Stem1 allomorph = *uasi*; Stem4 allomorph = *muasi*

na-ro-mu-muasi   [naromumuas]   Crowley 1982:141
1SG-real.NEG-hit4-hit4

The presumed reason that Stem4, rather than Stem1, appears as the second
daughter is that it is phonotactically superior, in possessing an onset. Crowley
(1982) points out (p. 126) that were a form like *uasi* to reduplicate as *u-uasi*,
"the regular phonological rules of the language would eliminate all trace of
[reduplication] having taken place." The fact that ONSET can outrank the preference for Stem1 supports the claim that the usual use of Stem1 form in the
second daughter position derives from its status as the default stem. In the terms
of Optimality Theory, the grammar would state a general preference for Stem1
allomorphs, which is overridable (a) by the specific requirements of higher
affixes or constructions or (b) by phonotactic constraints such as ONSET, as
illustrated schematically below:

(47)   Reduplication construction (Paamese, class IX)
          [   ]Meaning = 'F all over'; stem type = x

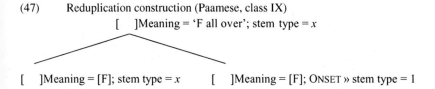

[   ]Meaning = [F]; stem type = x [   ]Meaning = [F]; ONSET » stem type = 1

2.3.1.3   Wrapup

This section has verified one of the most striking and unique predictions of MDT, namely that reduplication constructions are able to use distinct allomorphs of the same morpheme in the two daughters. This prediction follows from the thesis of MDT that the two copies in reduplication have independent inputs. We turn in the next section to a larger-scale instantiation of this same general phenomenon.

2.3.2   *Synonym constructions*

In exactly the same way that MDT predicts the existence of reduplication constructions in which the two daughters are different suppletive allomorphs of the same morpheme, MDT also predicts the existence of constructions whose two daughters are not the same morpheme at all but are semantically identical lexemes. Constructions of this sort abound; they are typically referred to not as reduplication but by terms like "redundant compounds" (Singh 1982), "semantically symmetrical compounds" (Ourn & Haiman 2000), or "synonym compounds" (Nguyen 1997). Here we will adopt the general term "synonym constructions" for these cases.

In what may be the first statement in the literature of the principal idea underlying MDT, Singh 1982 notes parallels between reduplication and a construction he refers to as "redundant compounds" in Hindi. These are noun-noun compounds in which the nouns are synonymous but differ etymologically: the first noun is native, while the second is of Perso-Arabic origin (p. 345). The overall meaning is 'noun, etc.'; the fact that echo-word reduplication with this same meaning is prevalent through Asia (e.g. *kota-gita* in Kolami, *kitap-mitap* in Turkish, etc.) supports Singh's characterization of the Hindi constructions as reduplicative. Examples from Singh 1982:346 are given below:

(48)   tan-badan   'body-body'   dharm-imān   'religion-religion'
          vivāh-šādi   'marriage-marriage'   sneh-muhabbat 'love-love'
          dhan-daulat   'money-money'   lāj-šarm   'deference-deference'
          šāk-sabji   'vegetable-vegetable' nāta-rista   'relation-relation'

Abbi (1991:24) provides similar examples in which the first word is native and the second comes from Urdu.

Synonym constructions are quite pervasive (for general discussion see Abbi 1991:24 and, especially, Ourn & Haiman 2000). To cite just two examples outside of Hindi, Li and Thompson (1981:68ff.) describe Chinese as having verbal compounds in which "[t]he two verbs that constitute a parallel verb either are synonymous or signal the same type of predicative notions," e.g. *gòu mǎi* 'buy-buy = buy,' *měi-lì* 'beautiful-beautiful = beautiful.' Ourn and Haiman (2000) discuss a similar construction in Vietnamese, examples of which, taken from Nguyen 1997, are provided below:

(49)   mạnh-khoẻ 'strong = strong = well in health'   67
    dơ bẩn 'dirty = dirty = filthy'   67
    lười-biếng 'lazy = lazy = slothful'   67
    tội-lỗi 'offense = fault = sin'   70
    kêu-gọi 'to call = to call = to call upon, appeal'   70

Clearly, these constructions cannot be derived by phonological copying. A phonological copying theory would have to declare them unrelated to reduplication. Yet this would be a mistake, as Singh argues; for one thing, they are semantically identical to another type of construction in Hindi, a productive process of echo-word reduplication in which the exact same stem is doubled.[21] As is definitional of echo-word constructions, the second copy is required to begin with a fixed segment, *v*, which replaces an existing onset. From p. 348:

(50)   roti   'bread'   roti-voti   'bread, etc.'
    namak   'salt'   namak-vamak   'salt, etc.'

Foreshadowing the theory of MDT, Singh argues for treating both constructions as reduplication:

> Reduplication is generally thought of as a morphological process that copies a word either as is or in some phonologically modified form. In order to regard our redundant "compounds" as outputs of a rule of . . . reduplication, we would have to modify the notion of reduplication to include reduplication of lexical items with or without certain morphological features such as [+Native]. We will, in other words, have to make a three-way distinction: reduplication with no modification whatsoever, reduplication with phonological modifications, and reduplication with morphological modifications.   (1982:349–350)

What Singh is suggesting here appears to be the same idea that MDT is built on: reduplication can (or according to MDT must) double a morphologically abstract entity, one defined essentially by semantic properties. The

MDT schemas for the two structurally similar constructions in (48) and (50) are given below:

(51)

Hindi synonym construction (= (48))   Hindi echo word construction (= (50))

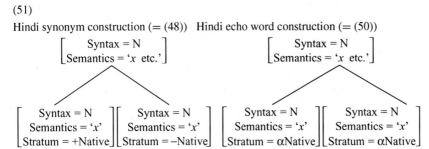

2.3.3 Beyond synonyms

By the same token that constructions have the ability to require daughters to be identical (or nearly so) semantically, we naturally expect other relationships to be possible as well, i.e. subset and opposite relationships. Their existence confirms the predictions of MDT.

Ourn and Haiman (2000) catalog four types of constructions which, like reduplication, juxtapose two morphological constituents with a fixed semantic relationship to one another: in addition to synonym constructions, which we have just seen, they discuss constructions which juxtapose near synonyms, as in "law and order"; members of the same semantic set, as in "field and stream"; and antonyms, as in "life and death." Similarly, Abbi (1991) describes a family of reduplication-like constructions as "compris[ing] lexical items of the same semantic field ranging from near-synonymous to polar terms" (p. 25).[22] To these arrays of existing juxtaposition constructions we can add semantic inclusion or classifier relationships, of the type often found in noun incorporation (see, for example, Mithun 1984; Gerdts 1998; Mithun 2000). Turkish, for example, has a number of noun-noun compounds in which the second member denotes a class of which the first is a member (often a prototypical member), e.g. *martı kuş* 'seagull bird = seagull,' *serçe kuş* 'sparrow bird = sparrow'; *çam ağacı* 'pine tree,' *meşe ağacı* 'oak tree'; *papatya çiçeği* 'daisy flower = daisy,' *gül çiçeği* 'rose flower = rose'; etc. (Orhan Orgun, p.c.).

MDT situates reduplication squarely within this family of construction types, whose members all obtain parallel analyses within MDT. In prototypical reduplication, the daughters agree in every morpho-semantic feature. In synonym constructions, the daughters may vary etymologically; in the case of near-synonym constructions, they must share most features but may differ in small ways. In the case of antonym constructions, the relationship between the two daughters is still defined semantically, but in terms of disagreement in certain features, rather than agreement.

(52)	Reduplication	all features agree
	Synonym constructions	all features agree except stratum/register/etc.
	Near-synonym constructions	most features agree
	Members of same semantic set	basic semantic category features agree
	Semantic inclusion	the features of one are a proper subset of the features of the other
	Antonyms	the two are specified with opposite values for certain features

The goal here is not to provide a comprehensive survey of all of the types of semantic relationship that constructions can mandate, or tolerate, among their daughters, but rather to show that pure reduplication is simply one point along the cline of semantic similarity. This is true cross-linguistically; it is also true within languages. Many languages have some subset of these construction types. Vietnamese, for example, has not only the near-synonym constructions seen above, but also antonym constructions. For case studies of languages with constructions at many points along the cline in (52), we turn to Khmer and Acehnese. Both illustrate the benefits of a uniform approach to these six construction types.

2.3.3.1 Khmer

Khmer is rife with coordinate or symmetrical compounds, including what Ourn and Haiman call "near-synonym" compounds like the following (Ourn & Haiman 2000:485, 500–502) (see also Gorgoniev 1976:318). With respect to semantics, Ourn and Haiman state that, "They seem to be simply semantically redundant and rhythmically elaborated ways of saying what could be said by a single word" (p. 491). Ourn and Haiman clearly characterize these synonym and near-synonym constructions as reduplication.

(53)	a. cah	+	tum	'village elder'	485
	'old'		'mature'		
	b. chap	+	rɔhah	'fast'	485
	'quick'		'fast'		
	c. clooh	+	prɑkaek	'quarrel'	485
	'squabble'		'argue'		
	d. ʔaar	+	kɑmbaŋ	'secret'	500
	'secret'		'secret'		
	e. cbah	+	prɑkɑt	'exact'	500
	'exact'		'exact'		
	f. kee	+	mɔrdɔk	'legacy'	501
	'heritage'		'heritage'		

Ourn and Haiman write that "[s]o strong is this tendency to compound near-synonyms that sometimes a verb will be conjoined with a doublet" (p. 485). The example in (54a), below, is one in which the two nouns are semantically identical but have different etymological origins, one coming from Sanskrit and the other from Pali. The example in (54b) exhibits not etymological but morphological divergence; the second daughter is a simple verb meaning 'step,' while the first is a morphological construction, termed by Ourn and Haiman a "cognate accusative," literally meaning 'take a step.'

(54) a. peel   + weeliə   'time'   485
          'time' (Sanskrit)   'time' (Pali)
       b. baoh cumhiən + chiən   'take steps' 485
          'take steps'   'step'

Khmer also has the next point on the scale, constructions in which both daughters are what Ourn and Haiman call "typical or representative members of a group," as follows:

(55) a. klaa   + damrəj   'big game'   485
          'tiger'   'elephant'
       b. cruuk   + kdaan   'hooved animals' 485
          'pig'   'deer'
       c. phuum   + phiək   'region'   485
          'village'   'plot of land'
       d. tək   + dəj   'country'   485
          'water'   'earth'

Ourn and Haiman note that some of the (near)-synonym compounds are semantically opaque, meaning (somewhat) exocentric (pp. 485, 503).

2.3.3.2 Acehnese

Acehnese provides phonological evidence for the structural parallel claimed in MDT to hold between reduplication and synonym/antonym constructions. Examples of total reduplication, which confers emphasis, include the following, from Durie 1985:

(56) tambô-tambô   'drum-drum'   39
      ma-ma   'mother-mother' 39
      tuleueng-tuleueng   'bone-bone'   40
      jamee-jamee   'guest-guest'   40

The two parts are usually identical in form but may vary slightly: sometimes the second copy differs in its vowel or final consonant, and sometimes unstressed syllables can differ (ibid. p. 43). Reduplication can also be partial, targeting the final syllable (ibid. p. 42):

(57)   singöh-ngöh   'sometime indefinite in the future' cf. singöh 'tomorrow'
        bubê-bê   'as big as'   cf. bubê 'size (classifier)'

Like Sye, Acehnese permits different, suppletive allomorphs of the same morpheme to be used in what appears to be the same construction (p. 43):

(58)   irang-irôt   'zig-zag'   cf. irang 'skew,' irôt 'skew'
        kreh = kroh   'rustling dry sound'   cf. kreh 'rustling dry sound,' kroh
                                               'rustling dry sound'

In what Durie calls "juxtaposition of opposites," "two words of contrasting meaning can be combined to give a meaning that encompasses both" (ibid. p. 44):

(59)   tuha-muda   'old and young'
        bloe-publoe   'buy and sell'
        uroe-malam   'day and night'
        beungöh-seupôt   'morning and evening'

Durie remarks that this construction is "phonologically identical with reduplication," meaning that it has the same unique double stress configuration. Thus with respect to stress, reduplication and juxtaposition of opposites form a natural class. Normally, in Acehnese, word stress falls on the final syllable, regardless of the morphological makeup of the word. (Durie 1985:9). However, precisely when a word is reduplicated – or when it is a juxtaposition of opposites construction – it has double word stress, with an equal degree of stress on each of the two salient parts. The examples below illustrate double stresses in total reduplication (60a), partial reduplication (b), and juxtaposition of opposites (c):

(60)   ureueng'-ureueng'   'people' (lit. 'person-person')   40, 42
        singöh'-ngöh'   'sometime indefinite in the future'   42
                             (lit. 'tomorrow-tomorrow')
        lakoe'-binoe'   'men and women'   44

Clearly, one would want to say about Acehnese that there is a meta-construction whose daughters are either synonyms or antonyms, and which assigns stress to each daughter. Treating double stress as the result of base-reduplicant identity would obscure the relationship between reduplication and juxtaposition of opposites; the allomorphy cases show that reduplication is not a matter of BR identity to start with.

2.3.4 Wrapup

Clearly there is a cline of semantic similarity on which total identity is an endpoint. As attested by the fact that descriptive grammarians standardly use the term "reduplication" for the kinds of constructions we have been looking at, reduplication includes cases in which the essential relation between the two daughters is one of semantic identity, similarity, or opposition.

2.4   Comparison of MDT with OO correspondence

In light of the facts discussed above, no theory could maintain that reduplication is a purely phonological copying process in which the reduplicant is derived entirely from the phonological material of the base. Indeed, recognizing some of the kinds of data we have talked about in this chapter, researchers working in BRCT have responded with some interesting theoretical modifications. One proposal, found in a series of illuminating studies of Bantu verb reduplication by Downing (see especially Downing 1998a; 1999a; 2000a), invokes output–output (OO) correspondence, i.e. analogy to other (related) words, to generate morphological material in the reduplicant which is not present in the base. In a form like Ndebele *lima-limile*, for example, although *lima* does not correspond perfectly with the base, it does correspond perfectly with the independently occurring stem *lima*.

Output–output correspondence was originally founded on the assumption that correspondence can occur between independently occurring words in the same language (Kenstowicz 1996; Benua 1997; Kenstowicz 1997). However, as Hyman, Inkelas, and Sibanda (to appear) point out, there are numerous reduplicants in Ndebele, like *dleyi-* or *dlayi-*, two possible reduplicants of *dl-el-a* 'eat-for/at,' that have no counterpart in the set of actual or even possible words in Ndebele. If OO correspondence theory is relaxed, as Downing proposes, so as to allow correspondence between morphological subconstituents of a word, then the theories become quite close; the interest in comparing OO correspondence to MDT essentially comes down to how the sets of potentially corresponding items are defined in the former approach.

In an independent development of OO correspondence, Steriade (1997; 1999) allows correspondence between any part of the reduplicant and any other morpholexical consitutent with listed or predictable status, even if it has a different meaning. Thus far, however, we have not seen evidence of the need for this added power in analyzing reduplication. The two copies in reduplication can differ phonologically and morphotactically, but they always have the same meaning.

2.5   Conclusion

This chapter has assembled support for two of the essential claims of MDT, repeated below:

(61)   **The Thesis of Morphological Targets**: reduplication doubles
morphological constituents (affix, root, stem, word), not phonological
constituents (mora, syllable, foot)

The Thesis of Semantic Identity: the constituents that reduplication
doubles are identical semantically, but not necessarily in any other way

Although phonological identity often follows, indirectly, from semantic identity, in that the usual means of ensuring the latter is to use the same morphemes in each copy, phonological identity is epiphenomenal, not an extrinsic or intrinsic requirement. The epiphenomenality of phonological identity, and the propensity of reduplicative constructions to introduce phonological differences between the two copies, are the subjects of Chapters 3 and 4.

3 Morphologically conditioned phonology in reduplication: the daughters

Phonology is often morphologically conditioned. It can be sensitive to part of speech, as in Acehnese, where /p/ dissimilates to /s/ before another labial in verbs, but not in nouns (Durie 1985:32, 79–81, 95–96); in Japanese (McCawley 1968; Poser 1984) or Kaulong (Ross 2002), where accent assignment works differently in noun and verb roots, or in any of innumerable other examples. Phonology is also commonly conditioned by morphological construction type. For example, some phonological effects occur only in compounding constructions. Rendaku voicing in Japanese applies at the internal juncture of compounds, but not at stem-affix junctures; moreover, it applies only within a particular subtype of compounding, namely compounds with head-modifier semantics and Yamato vocabulary (e.g. Itô & Mester 1986; 1995b; 1996a). Similarly, Malayalam exhibits junctural gemination in one but not the other of its two compounding constructions (Mohanan 1995). Other phonological effects are specific to certain affixation contexts. For example, vowel-initial suffixes in Turkish divide into two sets: those which trigger intervocalic velar deletion (e.g. the possessives: *bebek* 'baby,' *bebe-in* 'baby-2SGPOSS'), and those which do not (e.g. the aorist: *gerek* 'be necessary,' *gerek-ir* 'be necessary-AOR') (see, for example, Inkelas & Orgun 1995). Many phonological effects are associated with only a single affix in a language. For useful overviews of morphologically conditioned phonology, see, among others, Ford and Singh 1983; Dressler 1985; Spencer 1998; Booij 2000; Comrie 2000. It is very likely that many languages meet Ezard's (1997:35) characterization of the Austronesian language Tawala: "phonological processes are mostly applied to a subset of the data; rarely does a rule apply consistently," i.e. across all morphological contexts.

It is important to understand reduplicative phonology within this general context of morphologically conditioned phonology. Reduplicative constructions sometimes exhibit phonological effects that are different from the phonological effects found in some other constructions within the same language. This should not be surprising, given that reduplication is a morphological construction and that phonology is often morphologically sensitive. Nonetheless, reduplicative phonology is often discussed as a distinct phenomenon, with theories proposed for it that have no connection to nonreduplicative morphologically conditioned phonology.

The empirical question confronting scholars of reduplication is whether reduplicative phonology is qualitatively different, in any systematic way, from the phonology of nonreduplicative constructions, or whether all types of phonological patterns that can occur in conjunction with reduplication constructions can also occur with nonreduplicative constructions. The answer to this question ought to determine whether reduplicative phonology can be handled within the theory of morphologically conditioned phonology that is needed anyway, or whether there must be a special theory just to handle reduplicative phonology. With respect to this question, theories of reduplication separate into two classes: Native Identity and Coerced Identity theories. The difference lies in the extent to which special reduplicative phonology is tied to the dimension of base-reduplicant identity that makes reduplication unique, or whether reduplicative phonology falls out from purely general principles of morphologically conditioned phonology.

MDT is a Native Identity theory. It seeks to understand reduplicative phonology in particular within the larger context of morphologically conditioned phonology in general and does not posit any special phonological status for reduplicative constructions. Some early phonological copying theories, like Marantz's (1982) Copy and Association theory or Steriade's (1988) Full Copy theory in which reduplicants start out as total copies of their bases and are then modified by morphologically conditioned phonological rules, are also Native Identity theories in that they take identity as the starting point but do nothing special to maintain it. Coercive Identity theories, from Wilbur's (1973) Identity Principle to McCarthy and Prince's (1995a) Base-Reduplicant Correspondence Theory (BRCT), have taken the opposite tack, arguing that the phonological patterns that occur in reduplication are intrinsically tied to an identity requirement holding between reduplicant and base. Coercive Identity theories predict that at least some reduplicative phonology will be unparalleled outside of reduplication; Native Identity theories predict all reduplicative phonology to follow from the same principles generating morphologically conditioned phonology outside of reduplication.

Both this chapter and the next argue, on the basis of a broad survey of reduplicative phonology, for the Native Identity approach, pointing to the parallels between the phonology of reduplicative and nonreduplicative constructions to support the view that reduplicative phonology is not qualitatively different from nonreduplicative phonology and, specifically, that reduplicative phonology is not identity-driven. Rather, true insight into reduplicative phonology comes from looking at reduplication in its full morphological context.

These two chapters are organized around several predictions about reduplicative phonology. All follow from the basic architecture of MDT, specifically from the MDT claim that each node in a reduplication construction – first daughter, second daughter, mother – is associated with a cophonology, or subgrammar. This architecture is explicated in §3.1.

The first phonological prediction of MDT, sketched below, is that the phonological effects that one finds within individual daughters in reduplication constructions will be the same kinds of effects one finds applying outside of reduplication:

(1) **Generalized Phonology Prediction:**
The set of phonological effects found applying within reduplication is
equivalent to the set of morphologically conditioned phonological
effects found outside of reduplication. There is nothing unique about the
phonology of reduplication constructions.

Evidence for this prediction, a version of which was originally introduced by Steriade (1988), is presented in §3.2.

A second prediction of MDT is that that the phonological effects applying in the two daughters in a reduplication construction can be divergent.

(2) **Independent Daughter Prediction**:
The phonological effects associated with the two copies in reduplication
are independent.

Two different factors contribute to this prediction, which distinguishes MDT sharply from phonological copying theories in which one copy is dependent phonologically on the other. The first is that, as seen in Chapter 2, the daughters in reduplication have morphologically separate inputs which may differ phonologically; the second is that the cophonologies of the daughters in reduplication are independent of each other and may also differ. In both respects MDT differs profoundly from theories that privilege one copy ("Base") and use it to derive the other copy. The prediction of phonological independence of the two daughters is explored in §3.3.

The third distinctive prediction of MDT is that reduplication constructions as a whole, not just the daughters within them, may be associated with distinctive phonology.

(3)   **The Mother Node Prediction**:
       Reduplication constructions may be associated, as a whole, with
       morphologically conditioned phonological effects.

These special effects are, of course, subject to the Generalized Phonology
Prediction: there is nothing unique to reduplication about them. The effects of
this sort that we will see are also capable of being associated with nonreduplicative morphological constructions. Mother node effects are largely discussed in
Chapter 4.

MDT is a layered theory, in that it assumes that the output of the phonology applying to daughters is the input to the phonology applying to mother
nodes in morphological constructions. The particular layered structure proposed for reduplication accounts for a number of effects which require extra
statements in theories not assuming layering. These are discussed primarily in
Chapters 4–6.

3.1   Cophonologies

MDT uses cophonologies, or phonological grammars associated with particular
morphological constructions, to model morphologically conditioned phonology
in general. Cophonologies within a language have been motivated independently of morphologically conditioned phonology to handle variation (Anttila
1997; Itô & Mester 1997; Anttila & Cho 1998) and what Zuraw calls patterned lexical exceptions (Zuraw 2000, also Itô & Mester 1995a; b). The use
of cophonologies for the phonological patterns associated with different morphological constructions was pioneered in Orgun 1994; 1996; Inkelas, Orgun
and Zoll 1997 and has been developed in much subsequent work (Itô & Mester
1996b; Orgun 1997; Inkelas 1998; Inkelas & Orgun 1998; Orgun 1999; Yu
2000; 2003).

The cophonology approach is a natural evolution of ideas put forward in the
theory of Lexical Morphology and Phonology (LMP; see, for example Pesetsky
1979; Kiparsky 1982a; b; Kaisse & Shaw 1985; Mohanan 1986; Pulleyblank
1986; Inkelas 1990), which handles morphologically conditioned phonology by
sorting the morphological constructions of a language into sequentially ordered
groups, each associated with its own distinct phonological grammar. In LMP,
phonological rules themselves are, in principle, quite general; it is the grouping
together of rules and morphological constructions within morphological levels
that produces morphological conditioning of phonology. Much research has
shown LMP in its original form to be both too strong and too weak. It is too

strong in claiming that levels are strictly ordered relative to one another, a point argued in, for example, Mohanan 1986; Hargus 1988; Inkelas and Orgun 1995; 1998. It is too weak in the sense that it omits from consideration many phonological effects which are too morphologically specific to merit positing an entire level, and thus requires building very specific morphological information back into some phonological rules or constraints (Inkelas 1998). For example, stress shift is associated with Level 1 morphology in English (e.g. Kiparsky 1982b), yet only a subset of Level 1 suffixes actually induce stress shift. Level 1 suffixes not inducing stress shift have to be associated with an extrametricality rule (e.g. Hayes 1981) that is stipulated to apply to some but not all Level 1 suffixes. This very specific kind of stipulation falls outside the scope of what level ordering can do.

Cophonology theory shares with LMP the ambition of making phonological alternations themselves fully general. Every morphological construction – each compounding, affixation, zero-derivation, truncation construction, and so on – is associated with a cophonology, which may potentially differ from the cophonologies of other constructions. In cophonology theory phonological rules or constraints are never themselves indexed to particular morphological contexts; it is the entire bundle of rules or the specific ranking of constraints constituting the cophonology itself which is morphologically indexed. Cophonology theory differs from LMP in abandoning the failed claim that morphological conditioning boils down to dividing the lexicon into a few ordered components each with fully general phonology.

Building on Anttila 1997 and suggestions in Inkelas and Orgun 1998 and Stump 1998, we assume that the cophonologies of any given language are constrained by what we have called in other work (Inkelas & Zoll 2003) the "Master Ranking," a partial ranking of constraints that every cophonology in the language conforms to. The Master Ranking is in some ways similar to proposals such the Stratum Domain or Strong Domain hypotheses of LMP, which were attempts to constrain the degree to which phonological strata in the same language could differ. These last hypotheses, however, presuppose that strata are extrinsically ordered; the arguments against stratum ordering are voluminous (see, for example, Mohanan 1986; Hargus 1988; Hualde 1988; Inkelas & Orgun 1995; Inkelas 1998; Inkelas & Orgun 1998). Cophonologies are intrinsically unordered. Their relative ordering follows from the intrinsic or extrinsic ordering of the morphological constructions with which they are associated.

Below are schematic representations of compounding and affixation, illustrating the association of cophonologies with morphological mother nodes. As discussed in Chapter 1, the formalism adopted here is based on Orgun's (1996) Sign-Based Morphology, though the relevant generalizations are available to other morphological frameworks as well:

(4)   a. Compounding schema:

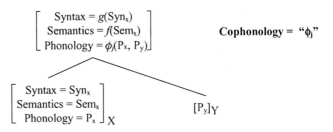

$$\begin{bmatrix} \text{Syntax} = g(\text{Syn}_x, \text{Syn}_y) \\ \text{Semantics} = f(\text{Sem}_x, \text{Sem}_y) \\ \text{Phonology} = \phi_i(\text{P}_x, \text{P}_y) \end{bmatrix} \quad \textbf{Cophonology} = \text{``}\phi_i\text{''}$$

$$\begin{bmatrix} \text{Syntax} = \text{Syn}_x \\ \text{Semantics} = \text{Sem}_x \\ \text{Phonology} = \text{P}_x \end{bmatrix}_X \quad \begin{bmatrix} \text{Syntax} = \text{Syn}_y \\ \text{Semantics} = \text{Sem}_y \\ \text{Phonology} = \text{P}_y \end{bmatrix}_Y$$

    b. Affixation schema:

$$\begin{bmatrix} \text{Syntax} = g(\text{Syn}_x) \\ \text{Semantics} = f(\text{Sem}_x) \\ \text{Phonology} = \phi_j(\text{P}_x, \text{P}_y) \end{bmatrix} \quad \textbf{Cophonology} = \text{``}\phi_j\text{''}$$

$$\begin{bmatrix} \text{Syntax} = \text{Syn}_x \\ \text{Semantics} = \text{Sem}_x \\ \text{Phonology} = \text{P}_x \end{bmatrix}_X \qquad [\text{P}_y]_Y$$

What is important for purposes of this chapter is simply the fact that distinct cophonologies can be associated with the mother node of each distinct morphological construction. It is when cophonologies differ across morphological constructions that we say that phonology is morphologically conditioned. We illustrate the use of cophonologies to model morphologically conditioned phonology with the example of Turkish velar deletion, below.

Stem-final velar deletion is a typical morphologically conditioned phonological alternation. Some suffixes trigger it and others do not. (On velar deletion, see, for example, Zimmer & Abbott 1978; Sezer 1981; Inkelas & Orgun 1995; Inkelas 2000.)

(5)   a. Dative suffix: triggers velar deletion

Nominative	Dative	Gloss
bebek	bebe-e	'baby'
inek	ine-e	'cow'

b. Aorist suffix: does not trigger velar deletion

Past	Aorist	Gloss
gerek-ti	gerek-ir	'be necessary'
bırak-tı	bırak-ır	'leave'

To describe this split among affixes it is necessary to posit at least two cophonologies for Turkish, shown below:

(6) a. Cophonology ϕ_1: *VKV » Max-C *delete velar consonants ("K") intervocalically*
b. Cophonology ϕ_2: Max-C » *VKV *preserve velars even intervocalically*

Affixation constructions triggering velar deletion, like the dative, are associated with Cophonology ϕ_1; affixation constructions not triggering velar deletion, like the aorist, are associated with Cophonology ϕ_2.

(7)
Dative suffix (triggers velar deletion) Example:

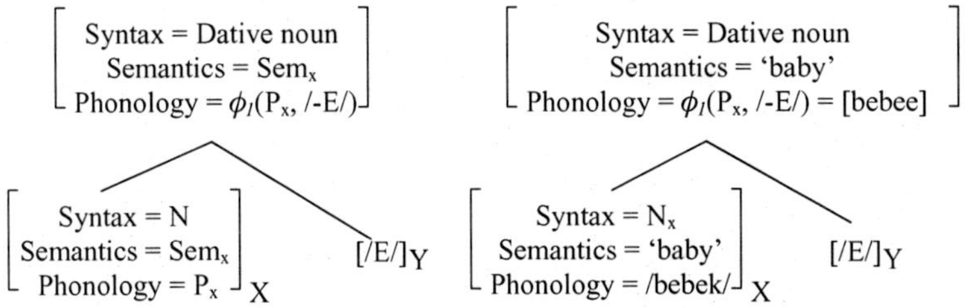

Aorist suffix (doesn't trigger velar deletion) Example:

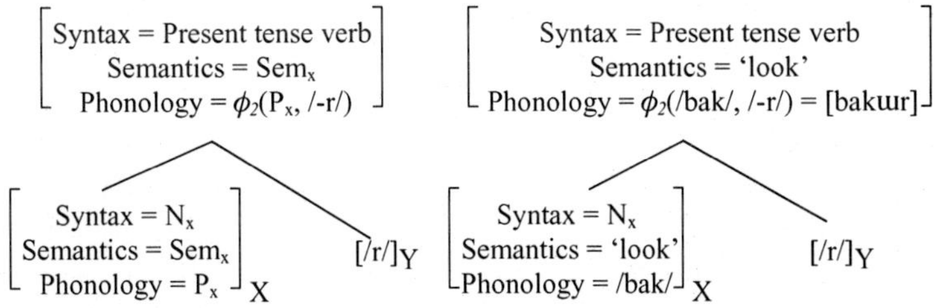

As observed in Chapter 1, constructions can treat affixation as realizational, as well, although we generally opt throughout this work to represent affixation as item-based, for reasons of graphical clarity.

Cophonologies are a theoretically economical method of describing morphologically conditioned phonology, in that cophonologies are needed independently to describe language-internal variation and, if desired, patterned exceptions or stratal effects in the lexicon. The use of cophonologies also permits phonological rules or constraints to be morphologically purely general; it is the distribution of cophonologies, and their differences from one another, that captures morphological conditioning of phonological patterns.

In comparing cophonology theory to alternatives, it is important to recognize not only its theoretical economy but also two important predictions that cophonology theory makes regarding the behavior of morphologically conditioned phonology. The first is scope. Each cophonology has scope over the daughters of the morphological construction with which it is associated, but not over any other material. The second prediction, which is related, is the inside-out nature of the phonology–morphology interface. It follows intrinsically from associating cophonologies with nodes in morphological structure that the output of applying phonology to the base of a morphological construction – e.g. to the base of affixation – will serve as input to the phonology applying to the derived construction – e.g. to the stem produced as a result of affixation. The output of mother cophonologies can never serve as input to daughter cophonologies; "outside-in" effects are not describable. The inside-out character of phonology–morphology interaction has long been recognized; theories without layered cophonologies have had to stipulate base priority to generate the effects (e.g. Kenstowicz 1996; Benua 1997 *inter alia*).[1]

3.1.1   *Cophonologies vs. indexed constraints*

Many researchers have developed approaches to the phonology–morphology interface which do not utilize cophonologies. It is important to assess these approaches for their ability to capture generalizations about the scope and inside-out nature of the interface. The most widespread alternative to cophonologies in use today is constraint indexation in Optimality Theory, which maintains one single constraint ranking for the language as a whole but splits constraints into sets whose members are indexed to specific morphemes or morphological constructions and are ranked independently (see, for example, Benua 1997; Alderete 1999; Itô & Mester 1999; Alderete 2001). Constraint indexation is capable of emulating many of the effects of cophonologies, though it does not intrinsically generate the scopal and inside-out predictions of cophonology theory.

Cophonologies and individual constraint indexation work similarly in simple cases, such as in the accentual differences between nonderived nouns and verbs in Tokyo Japanese. The presence and location of accent in nonderived nouns (8a) is unpredictable and must be lexically specified; for verb roots, by contrast, while the presence or absence of lexical accent itself is unpredictable, the location of accent (if any) is predictable: accent falls on the syllable containing the penultimate mora of the verb stem (8b) (Poser 1984:51–52, citing McCawley 1968). The data below are taken from Smith 1997:7–8, citing Haraguchi 1977 and Poser 1984:

(8) a. Nouns   b. Verbs

ínoti	'life'	kák-u	'write'
kokóro	'heart'	nayám-u	'worry'
atamá	'head'	kumadór-u	'graduate'

The cophonological approach to this contrast would posit a verb stem cophonology in which accent placement constraints (FɪxLoc) outrank accentual Faithfulness (FᴀɪᴛʜLoc) (9a), and a noun stem cophonology in which the ranking is the reverse (9b).[2]

(9) Noun stem cophonology: FᴀɪᴛʜLoc(Accent) » FɪxLoc(Accent)
     Verb stem cophonology: FɪxLoc(Accent) » FᴀɪᴛʜLoc(Accent)

The indexed constraint account, developed by Smith 1997, is conceptually similar; it splits accentual Faithfulness into two versions, with the noun-specific version ranked above, and the other version ranked below, FɪxLoc:

(10) FᴀɪᴛʜLoc$_{Noun}$(Accent) » FɪxLoc(Accent) » FᴀɪᴛʜLoc(Accent)

Any given pair of cophonologies can always be unpacked in this manner into a single ranking with multiple, indexed versions of the constraints whose ranking differs in the cophonologies. Thus if one attends to the phonology of only a single morphological constituent at a time, the cophonological and indexed constraint approaches will always be exactly equivalent.

It is in morphologically complex words, more than one of whose morphological subconstituents is associated with distinctive phonology, that the two approaches diverge. The indexed constraint approach does not automatically make either the scopal or the inside-out predictions of cophonology theory (although, as we noted earlier, it can stipulate the effects; see, for example, Benua 1997; Alderete 1999; 2001). The virtue of making these predictions in reduplication is discussed below, and more extensively in Chapter 4, under the rubric of "layering," and it is for this reason that we adopt cophonology theory in this work.

3.1.2 *Cophonologies in reduplication*

Three morphological constituents play a role in the MDT approach to reduplication: the two daughters and the mother. The daughters are the stem-forming constructions that independently generate the two semantically identical stems (as discussed in Chapter 2); the mother is the reduplication construction itself, which puts those two stems together and associates the result with a particular meaning. Each constituent in the construction is associated with a cophonology:[3]

(11)   Mother node:
        Cophonology Z

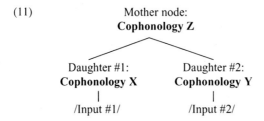

        Daughter #1:   Daughter #2:
        Cophonology X   **Cophonology Y**
              | |
          /Input #1/   /Input #2/

The three cophonologies may potentially differ from one another. Any of them may also differ from the cophonologies of other constructions in the language, resulting in the appearance of reduplication-specific phonological effects.

Consider, by way of illustration, intensive reduplication in Sanskrit, as discussed in Steriade 1988:108 (forms are prefinal, lacking the application of vowel coalescence rules):[4]

(12)   kan-i-krand-   'cry out'
        tai-tvais-   'stir'
        dau-dyaut-   'shine'
        sa:-svap-   'sleep'
        ga:-grabh-   'seize'
        va:-vyadh-   'pierce'

The two copies are differentiated in two phonological respects: the first copy is truncated down to a single syllable, and its initial consonant cluster (if any) is truncated to its least sonorant consonant ($kr \rightarrow k$, $sv \rightarrow s$, etc.).

In MDT these modifications are performed by the cophonology of the first daughter (Cophonology X). In Cophonology X, markedness constraints (e.g. *COMPLEX, which bans complex onsets) rank higher, relative to faithfulness, than they do in the cophonology of the second daughter (Cophonology Y) or the mother (Cophonology Z). The contrast in rankings is shown below.

(13)   Cophonology X: *Complex, Dep-V » Max-C
        Cophonologies Y, Z: *Dep-V, Max-C » Complex

Truncation is also accomplished in Cophonology X; a constraint limiting the output to a single heavy syllable ranks above Max-seg in Cophonology X, but is low-ranked in Cophonologies Y and Z:

(14)   Cophonology X: Output = $\sigma_{\mu\mu}$ » Max-seg
        Cophonology Y, Z: Max-seg » Output = $\sigma_{\mu\mu}$

A third aspect of Sanskrit intensive reduplication is the *i* vowel appearing between the two copies of the verb root. Steriade characterizes this vowel as a morphological requirement of the construction as a whole; its presence is not required by general syllable structure requirements of Sanskrit. Clusters arising across other kinds of morpheme boundaries are not, as a rule, broken up with *i* (for example, Steriade (1988) cites the reduplicated perfect form *va-vrk-tám*, based on the root 'cut up' where *-tám* is a suffix, on p. 126). In MDT the *i* vowel is inserted by the mother node cophonology of the intensive reduplication construction. Cophonology Z breaks up consonant clusters across its internal boundary, as shown below. Contiguity ensures that *i* does not break up clusters internal to either daughter:

(15)   Cophonology Z: CONTIGUITY » *CC » DEP
        Cophonologies X, Y: CONTIGUITY, DEP » *CC

It is important to note that nothing in this MDT account is reduplication-specific. The generality of all of the phonological statements predicts that the effects that happen, in a given construction in some language, to be reduplicant-specific can occur in a nonreduplicative construction in that or some other language.

We demonstrate in the remainder of this chapter and in Chapter 4 that the three cophonologies in (11) successfully generate the attested range of reduplicative phonological effects without the need for any phonological statements that are specific to reduplication, and that each of the predictions of MDT, sketched in the introduction, is correct.

3.2   Typical daughter modifications

Theories of Coerced Identity take the independence of base-reduplicant faithfulness (BR-FAITH) and input-output faithfulness (IO-FAITH) as the driving force behind reduplication-specific phonological effects (Wilbur 1973; McCarthy & Prince 1995a; Struijke 2000a). If this thesis is correct, then it should be the case that reduplicative phonology differs from the phonology of other morphological constructions not involving reduplication, since identity plays no role in the latter. By contrast, Native Identity theories, like MDT, treat all morphologically conditioned phonology in the same way and predict no difference between the kinds of effects found in reduplication and those found elsewhere. The Generalized Phonology Prediction of MDT says that reduplicative phonological effects are neither a subset nor a superset of the types of morphologically conditioned phonological effects outside reduplication. In this prediction, MDT shares with Steriade (1988) the view that the mechanisms (truncation, or segmental changes) "that frequently accompany reduplication are operations independent of and unrelated to the copying process central to reduplication" (p. 75).

In MDT, any phonological effect distinguishing the output form of the base or reduplicant from its input is accomplished either in the daughter cophonologies or in the mother cophonology. We focus in this section on the effects found in daughter cophonologies. These consist of assimilation, dissimilation, deletion, insertion, truncation, augmentation, lenition, fortition, and neutralization – in short, the set of phonological effects observed in languages generally. None is limited to reduplication. For example, syllable structure simplification – cluster simplification, length neutralization, coda deletion – is often cited as a hallmark of reduplicant phonology; onset cluster simplification occurs, for example, in reduplicants in Sanskrit intensive reduplication (e.g. *kan-i-krand-* 'cry out'; Steriade 1988:108) and Tagalog 'just finished' construction (e.g. *ka-ta-trabaho* 'just finished working'; McCarthy & Prince 1999b:252, citing Bowen 1969; see also, for example, Ramos & Caena 1990:38, Schachter & Otanes 1972:362). But onset cluster simplification is of course not specific to reduplicants; many languages allow onset clusters only in morphologically or phonologically prominent positions. In Lango (Nilotic), for instance, onset clusters (of which the second consonant is necessarily a glide) occur only root-initially (Noonan 1992:7); Babine (Athapaskan) permits complex onsets only word-initially (Hargus 1995). Burmese, discussed in Chapter 4, simplifies syllable onsets in compounds, also a nonreduplicative environment. Similar points can be made for rime simplification and the neutralization of segmental contrasts. Comparison of Alderete et al. 1999 and Steriade 1988, who survey the kinds of neutralizations or simplifications that occur in reduplicants, and Barnes 2002, who surveys the kinds of neutralizations or simplifications that can be positionally conditioned and are independent of reduplication, shows complete parallelism. We have found nothing reduplication-specific in this respect about the contents of Cophonologies X and Y.

This observation extends as well to the more arbitrary, morphophonological effects that are sometimes observed in reduplication, particularly truncation and input–output dissimilation. Neither is a natural phonological rule, setting them apart from the ordinary kinds of reductions of markedness discussed above, but like the markedness-reducing effects, neither is specific to reduplication, either.

Consider, for example, truncation, which in MDT is what results in partial reduplication: the stem-forming construction producing the relevant daughter is associated with a truncating cophonology. In the case of Diyari reduplication, for example, the relevant cophonology truncates its input down to a foot (McCarthy & Prince 1999b:263, citing Austin 1981 [see also Poser 1989]):

(16)   a. wiḻa-wiḻa   'woman'
        b. t̪ilpa-t̪ilparku 'bird sp.'

Truncation is handled in Optimality Theory by ranking the constraints that induce foot truncation (LEX≈PWD and PWD≈FOOT) above IO-FAITH.

(17)   [t̪ilpa]
            | ⇐ Cophonology: PWD≈FOOT » IO-FAITH
        /t̪ilparku/

Because there is nothing specific to reduplication in the contents of daughter cophonologies, MDT makes the prediction that a comparable truncation process might occur in a nonreduplicative context as well. This is of course correct; and pointing it out was a major contribution of McCarthy and Prince 1986 (published in edited form as McCarthy & Prince 1999b). As shown by McCarthy and Prince, Weeda 1992, and others, truncation comparable to what is found in reduplication can also serve as the sole morphological marker of constructions, e.g. the Central Alaskan Yupik hypocoristics in (18), from Weeda 1992 (based on work by Anthony Woodbury):[5]

(18)   iluʁaq   iluq   'male cross cousin of male' 163
        qəɬuqi:n (HBC)   qəɬuq   (name)   163
        cupəɬaq   cupəɬ   (name)   163
        aɲivʁan   aɲif   (name)   163
        kalixtuq   kalik   (name)   163
        qətunʁaq (HBC)   qətun   'son'   163

The Generalized Phonology Prediction holds true even of reduplicative dissimilation, an effect which has often been discussed in reduplication-specific terms (see, for example, Yip 1997; 1998; Kelepir 2000, among others). Dissimilation is quite common in cases of Melodic Overwriting (discussed in Chapter 2) constructions, as discussed, for example, in Emeneau 1955; Apte 1968; Abbi 1991, and others. In Abkhaz, for example, an echo-word construction meaning 'X etc.' doubles a word and replaces the onset of the second copy with /m/ (a) (Bruening 1997, based on a manuscript by Bert Vaux). If the word already begins with /m/, however, /č'/ is used instead (b):

(19)   a. čə́-k'   čə́k'-mə́k'   'horse'
           gaʒá-k'   gaʒák'-maʒák'   'fool'
           pəstəh°-k'   pəstəh°k'- məstəh°k'   'fog, mist'
        b. maát   maát č'aát   'money'
           maš°ə́r-k'   maš°ə́rk'-č'aš°ə́rk'   'miracle'
           maʒá-k'   maʒák' č'aʒák'   'secret'

Similar effects are found in cognate constructions throughout Asia (see Abbi 1991 for an overview), as well as in the emphatic adjective partial reduplication construction, discussed in Chapter 2, found throughout Turkic (e.g. Johanson & Csato 1998) and in Armenian (Vaux 1998).

Yip (1997; 1998) characterizes such cases in reduplication-specific terms. Using a BRCT-like constraint, REPEAT, to drive reduplicative identity, she invokes a higher-ranking constraint, *REPEAT, to drive (minimal) dissimilation between base and reduplicant.

Of course, however, dissimilation that takes place across base and reduplicant can generally be described equally well as dissimilation that takes place between input and output, for one of the daughters in reduplication. Instead of assuming that the reduplicant-initial *m*-prefix in Abkhaz is dissimilating (to *č'*-) with respect to the initial *m*- of the base, we could equally well assume that it is dissimilating with respect to the initial input consonant of the reduplicant:

(20)   Input–output dissimilation (MDT)   Base-reduplicant dissimilation (BRCT)

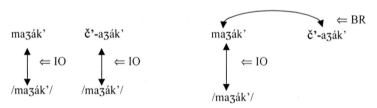

Input–output dissimilation is observed in nonreduplicative contexts where IO correspondence is the only descriptive possibility, as in the famous "toggle" cases of voicing or vowel length in Nilotic languages; see Kurisu 2001 for a recent overview of these and other cases. Input–output dissimilation can be triggered in overtly marked morphological contexts as well.[6] For example, input-output quantity dissimilation is triggered in stems by the location-forming suffix -*an* in Tagalog (Schachter & Otanes 1972:98), as illustrated below:

(21)   a. if base has penultimate long vowel, length shifts to preceding open
             syllable, else vanishes
             gu:lay   'vegetables'   gulay-an   'vegetable garden'
             ta:goʔ   'hide'   taguʔ-an   'hiding place'
             hala:man   'plant'   ha:laman-an   'garden'
             lanso:nes   'sp. of fruit' lansones-an   'place for growing lansones'
         b. if base has penultimate short vowel, it lengthens
             hiram   'borrow'   hi:ra:m-an   'place for borrowing'
             ʔaklat   'book'   ʔakla:t-an   'library'
             kumpisal   'confess'   kumpi(:)sa:l-an 'confessional'
             taraŋkah   'lock'   ta:raŋka:h-an 'gate'

Length dissimilation is only part of the story; when the stem-final vowel
lengthens, as in (21b), so does the stem-initial vowel, as well, optionally, as
other stem-medial vowels in open syllables. Schachter and Otanes report similar behavior for several other suffixes. According to Schachter and Otanes
1972, all syllables with long vowels are stressed; it is thus conceivable that
the alternations above are ultimately stress-related, but the pattern is clearly
dissimilatory, regardless of the precise prosodic parameter along which the
dissimilation occurs.

Given that input–output dissimilation is necessary in order to describe
nonreduplicative phonological effects, Occam's Razor suggests it is also the
right analysis of reduplicative dissimilation as well.

The conclusion reached here, namely that none of the phonological modifications typically found in reduplication is reduplication-specific, finds interesting
echoes not only in the Native Identity approach of Steriade (1988) but also
in the following statement of Alderete et al. (1999), who argue for a Coerced
Identity approach to reduplication:

(22)   Reduplicant/Inventory Relation III (Alderete et al. 1999)
         Any phonological restriction on the reduplicant of one language is a possible
         restriction on the whole of another language.

By this Alderete et al. mean that the constraints driving reduplicant-specific
phonotactics in one language are the same constraints that, ranked differently, drive general, nonreduplicative phonotactics in some other language(s).
However, the data surveyed in this work suggest that Alderete et al. are
too narrow in singling out reduplication. The statement in (22) would be
more accurate if 'the reduplicant' were replaced by "a morphological construction," recalling the original Generalized Phonology Prediction of MDT,
reworded below to refer more explicitly to Optimality Theory and constraint
ranking:

(23)   **Generalized Phonology Principle (Optimality Theory version):**
          A constraint ranking which in one language may be indexed to a particular
          set of morphological constructions may in some other language be indexed
          to a different set of constructions, possibly larger, possibly smaller.

It has often been noted that opaque or unnatural phonological alternations
are more likely to be restricted to a small set of morphological constructions
than to be fully general. One would not want to claim that any phonological
alternation which is found in reduplication in one language has the potential of
being a fully general process in another; rather, the claim put forth there is that
the alternations associated cross-linguistically with reduplication are neither a
proper subset nor a superset of the alternations associated with morphological
constructions of any kind, across languages.

3.3   Divergent modification

Textbooks describe two prototypical cases of reduplication: perfect reduplication, in which both copies surface in the shape they assume as independent
words, and reduplication in which one of the copies is modified phonologically in some way. BRCT is designed to capture these two kinds of cases.
Either the reduplicant matches the base exactly, satisfying BR identity, or it
deviates in some way, either by truncating or by improving its phonological
well-formedness (IO-FAITH » Markedness » BR-FAITH).

MDT predicts a third possibility: both copies can be modified, in potentially
independent ways (the Independent Daughter Prediction). The next sections
illustrate this prediction with cases in which both copies undergo distinct morphologically conditioned phonology. We term this situation "divergent modification." MDT is alone in predicting it to occur.

3.3.1   Hua

As seen in Chapter 2, Hua intensifying reduplication (Haiman 1980) involves
total reduplication in which each copy is subject to final vowel modification. In
the first copy, the final vowel is replaced with *u*; in the second copy, the final
vowel is replaced with *e*. The data are repeated in (24); recall that *hu* is a support
verb.

(24)   kveku kveke hu   'crumple'   kveki   'crumple'
          ebsgu ebsge hu   'twist and turn' ebsgi   'twist'
          ftgegu ftgege hu   'all coiled up'   ftgegi   'coil'
          ha-varu ha-vare hu   'grow up'   ha-vari   'grow tall'

In Chapter 2 this case was analyzed as an instance of double Melodic Over-writing. Reduplication calls for daughters which are semantically identical but consist of different lexical types; one is a u-stem, meaning it must be formed by an existing semantically vacuous construction which replaces the final vowel with *u*, and the other is an *e*-stem, formed by a comparable construction which effects e-replacement. Those who, like Alderete et al. (1999), draw a sharp distinction between Melodic Overwriting and phonological modification in the direction of increased phonological well-formedness might not consider Hua to represent divergent modification. We are not committed to the view that Melodic Overwriting and cophonological modification are always distinguish-able; certainly a realizational view of morphology would not necessarily want to distinguish the two. From a larger perspective, it does not matter what is causing the differentiation between base and reduplicant. What matters is that they are both different, not only from each other, but also from their inputs. Nonetheless, we present next several cases which fall more clearly into the category of divergent cophonological modification.

3.3.2   *Hausa tonal modification*
As described by Newman (2000:74ff.), numerous augmentative Hausa adjec-tives of the form X-*eːCèː* coexist with a synonymous reduplicated construction in which the same base, X, appears in both daughters with a suffix *-àː*. The first copy has all High tone; the second, all Low:[7]

(25)   gansameːmèː   ~   gansamaː-gànsàmàː   'tall and stout'   76
       shaɽtaɓeːɓèː   ~   shaɽtaɓaː-shàɽtàɓàː   'long and sharp'   76
       zungureːrèː   ~   zunguraː-zùngùràː   'long, tall'   76

The base of these constructions is in most cases bound, not appearing (even with a vowel suffix) as a free word; however, Newman notes a few forms like *gabzàː* 'heap up a lot of something,' presumably historically the base of *gabjeːjèː* 'bulky' and *gabzaː-gàbzàː* 'huge (people)' (p. 76).[8]

A similar construction is reported by Newman (1989b:251); Niepokuj (1997:56) and Downing (2000a) offer discussion and additional data. Neither copy is tonally faithful to the isolation form:

(26)   càkʷàliː   'slush'   cakʷal-càkʷàl   'slushy'
       jiniː   'blood'   jinaː-jìnàː   'bloody'
       ɽàbèːniyaː   'dangling'   ɽabeː-ɽàbèː   'pendulous (breasts)'

For an overview of tonal replacement patterns of this kind, see Downing 2004. In the present MDT analysis, the formation of the reduplicated H-L

adjectives in (26) calls for daughters of different types, in that the first requires
a cophonology assigning High tone, while the second requires a cophonology
assigning Low tone. Both daughters impose *-a:* stem-finally.

(27)   Daughter #1 cophonology: H tone imposed (and *-a*: suffixed)
        Daughter #2 cophonology: L tone imposed (and *-a*: suffixed)

3.3.3   *Tarok: divergent TETU*

In Tarok (Benue-Congo; Nigeria), nominal reduplication expresses third singular possession (Robinson 1976 [R]; Sibomana 1980 [S]; 1981; Longtau 1993;
Niepokuj 1997 [N]). In reduplicated forms, as illustrated by the reduplicated
polysyllabic nouns in (28), the tone of the second copy is neutralized to Mid:

(28)   a-fini   a-fini-fini   'his/her yarn'   N23
        a-górò   a-górò-goro   'his/her cola-nut' N23
        ì-gìsàr   ì-gìsàr-gisar   'his/her broom'   N23
        a-ríjìyá   a-ríjìyá-rijiya (alt: a-ríjìyá-jiya)   'his/her spring'   N23
        a-dànkálì   a-dànkálì-dankali (alt: a-dànkálì-kali) 'his/her potato'   N23

The interest of the Tarok facts lies in the divergent modification exhibited
by the two copies of a monosyllabic base. Neither copy is faithful to the input,
and each shows neutralization along a different dimension. As shown in (29),
reduplication of monosyllables manifests tonal reduction in the second copy,
and truncation and vowel neutralization in the first copy. In the first copy, the
final consonant deletes and all vowels raise to [+high]. In the second copy, tone
(which in Tarok can be High, Low, or Mid) is neutralized to Mid.

(29)   ì-ján   ì-jí-ja:n   'his twin'   R206
        a:-sán   a:-só-sa:n   'his rope'   R203
        ì-tòk   ì-tù-tok   'his chair'   S203
        ì-gʸel   ì-gi-gʸel   'his/her chin'   N115

The Morphological Doubling Theory reduplication construction for Tarok
monosyllables selects two semantically identical daughters, each subject to its
own (distinct) cophonology:[9]

(30)   [tù-tok]
                                        ╱   ╲
                                    [tù]   [tok]
X: Vowel raising and truncation ⇒ | | ⇐ Y: Reduction to Mid tone
                                   /tòk/   /tòk/

Cophonology X effects truncation and vowel raising by ranking the following
constraints above IO-FAITH: OUTPUT=CV, which mandates truncation to a

light syllable, and *V[-high], which neutralizes the height of the reduplicant vowel to the unmarked value, [+high]. Both effects are observed in *tù-tok* (31). Failure to truncate causes a fatal violation of the templatic constraint (31a, b), and failure to raise the vowel crucially violates the vowel markedness constraint (31c). The optimal outcome is a light syllable with a high vowel (31d).

(31)

Cophonology X	/tòk/	Output=CV	*V[-high]	IO-FAITH
a.	tòk	*!	*	
b.	tùk	*!		*
c.	tò		*!	*
☞ d.	tù			**

In the second daughter in the reduplication construction, the only alternation is neutralization of tone to Mid. Cophonology Y thus ranks the tonal markedness constraints above tonal faithfulness:

(32)

Cophonology Y	/tòk/	*High, *Low	IO-FAITH	*Mid
a.	tòk	*!		
☞ b.	tok		*	*

The problem for the Basic Model of BRCT presented by Tarok arises with tonal neutralization in the second copy, which, because it is not truncated, would be analyzed as the base. With respect to tone, the reduplicant is *more faithful* to the input than the base is. Accounting for this while maintaining that IO-FAITH is responsible for base faithfulness results in a ranking paradox.[10] We know independently that IO-FAITH must outrank the tonal markedness constraints (*High, *Low) since High, Low, and Mid all occur in nonreduplicated forms:

(33)

	tòk	IO-FAITH-Tone	*High, *Low
☞ a.	tòk		*
b.	tok	*!	

In standard BRCT (McCarthy & Prince 1995a), IO-FAITH is the same as IB-FAITH. Herein lies the divergent modification ranking paradox. The ranking required for nonreduplicated forms, namely IO-FAITH-Tone » tonal markedness constraints, incorrectly predicts preservation of the base tone in reduplication. Consider the candidates in (34). BR-FAITH-Tone is shown low-ranked here, but this is immaterial; the fact is that no ranking of the constraints in (34) will correctly identify (34a) as the winner. Candidate (34d) violates a proper subset of the constraints violated by candidate (34a), so candidate (34a) can never win.

(34)

	RED-tòk	IO-FAITH-Tone	*High, *Low	BR-FAITH-Tone
(☞) a.	tù-tok	*!	*	*
b.	tu-tok	*!		
c.	tù-tòk		**!	
💣 d.	tu-tòk		*	*

Because MDT generates reduplicant and base independently, it handles both mappings solely in terms of IO-FAITH and markedness constraints. The fact that constraints can be ranked independently in the two cophonologies means there is no ranking paradox.[11]

3.3.4   Parallel modification

If reduplicant and base can be associated with divergent cophonologies, neither of which is general in the language, it should also be possible to find cases in which both copies are associated with the same cophonology. We call this phenomenon "parallel modification." It is of interest because, although predicted to be possible by MDT, parallel imposition of many kinds of phonological modifications typical of reduplication (truncation, contrast reduction within the reduplicant) had previously been thought not to occur. The foundational logic of BRCT rules out parallel contrast reduction effects (McCarthy & Prince 1994a; 1995a); Generalized Template Theory (McCarthy & Prince 1994c; d; Urbanczyk 1996) was added to BRCT in order to rule out parallel truncation.

As demonstrated in this work, however, parallel modification does occur, supporting MDT in its prediction that the phenomenon is possible. Newman (2000) describes a Hausa construction forming adjectives from common nouns via "full reduplication of the underlying noun, preserving the original tone. This is accompanied by shortening of the final vowel of both parts" (Newman 2000:27):

(35)   gishiri: gishiri-gishiri   'salt/salty'
        bùhu: bùhu-bùhu   'sack/sacklike'
        gà:ri: gà:ri-gà:ri   'flour/powdery'
        mà:kubà: mà:kubà-mà:kubà   'mahogany tree/dark brownish color'

This is parallel modification. In a derivational approach, parallel modification would be handled by first making the modification in question, and then reduplicating the result:

(37)

Step 1	truncation mà:kubà: → mà:kubà
Step 2	reduplication mà:kubà → mà:kubà mà:kubà

In MDT, parallel modification occurs as a result of the fact that in the reduplication construction in question, both daughters impose the same cophonology. Recall that the daughters in reduplication are themselves constructions that take a morpheme or collection of morphemes as input and map them, via a specific cophonology, to an output which serves as one of the two inputs to the reduplication construction. If we assume, as in Chapter 2, that every morphological construction in the language is identified by some sort of index, which we will call type (following the type hierarchy literature), then to model a reduplication construction in which both daughters are the product of the same construction, we specify that the daughters agree not only semantically but also in type. Type features are nonsemantic diacritic features of the sort that are needed anyway to represent things like conjugation or declension class, or nonsemantic gender.

Each daughter of the Hausa construction illustrated in (35) is the product of the same stem-forming construction, shown below, which modifies noun stems by shortening the final vowel and produces stems of type #47:

(38)   Stem-forming construction: Example:

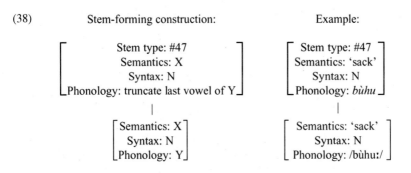

The reduplication construction responsible for generating the forms above simply calls for two type #47 stems, which it concatenates, identifying the output as an adjective, as below:

(39)   Denominal adjective reduplication (for data in (35))

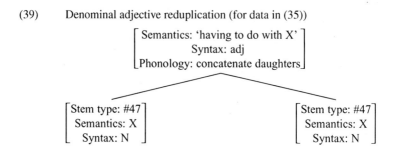

The MDT account of Hausa denominal adjectival reduplication retains the insight behind the derivational approach to these data sketched in (37). In the MDT account, one construction, i.e. the stem-forming construction (#47) which produces each of the daughters, truncates nouns, while another construction calls for two truncated nouns and groups them into a constituent labelled "adjective." Thus the output of truncation is the input to the cophonology of the mother node of the reduplication construction, which concatenates the two copies. The resulting schema, compiled into one representation, is shown below:

(40)

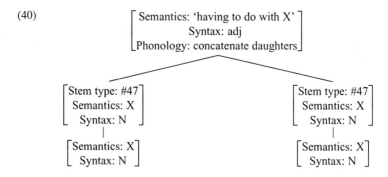

While nonderivational, this maps closely to the idea of "first truncate, then copy."

Parallel application of reduplication-specific phonological modification presents a challenge for standard BRCT. To illustrate this prediction, we again use Hausa adjective formation, which shortens final long vowels in both copies in reduplication (*màːkubàː* → *màːkubà-màːkubà*). In order for the final long vowel to shorten in the base, it has to be the case that the ban on final long

vowels (*V:]) outranks IO-FAITH, which preserves input vowel length. No
matter where BR-FAITH ranks, it will ensure that the reduplicant also has a
final short vowel:

(41)

		long-RED	BR-FAITH	*V:]	IO-FAITH
a.	long-short	*		*	
b.	long-long			**	
(☞) c.	short-short				*
d.	short-long	*		*	*

The problem is that Hausa does not shorten final long vowels generally (not
even in other reduplication patterns), and, therefore, the ranking *V:] » IO-
FAITH cannot be correct. The only way for BRCT to describe the Hausa
pattern would be to adopt cophonologies, such that for adjective formation,
*V:] » IO-Faith, but for other constructions, IO-Faith » *V:]. This move would
bring BRCT closer to MDT but would vitiate the central tenet of BRCT, which
is that it is the relative ranking of BR-Faith that distinguishes reduplicative
phonology.[12]

   Interestingly, BRCT is capable of generating a superficially similar parallel modification effect. McCarthy and Prince (1999a) credit René Kager and
Philip Hamilton for independently observing what has come to be known as
the "Kager–Hamilton problem": given base-reduplicant correspondence (as in
BRCT), it is logically possible for a truncated reduplicant to cause a base to
become truncated as well. This can happen in case BR-FAITH is ranked so
high that a reduplicant-specific constraint on prosodic size (RED = X) is indirectly imposed on the base as well. Thus, for example, the ranking RED =
σ_μ, BR-FAITH » IO-FAITH would produce a situation where bases and reduplicants are both truncated to light syllables. The belief that such phenomena
do not occur inspired the development of Generalized Template Theory (GTT;
McCarthy & Prince 1994c; Urbanczyk 1996), a serious modification to BRCT
which prohibits the use of direct prosodic constraints on reduplicant size. However, the existence of doubled truncated nicknames like *JoJo* or *CoCo* (from
Josephine or *Collette*) suggests, as observed by Downing (2000a), that in fact
there may be no empirical basis to the "Hamilton–Kager" problem; any time
truncation and reduplication are in a morphological feeding relationship, the
appearance of double truncation can be generated, with or without GTT, and
GTT is therefore unnecessary.[13]

Parallel affixal modification is fairly common in reduplication, as discussed in Chapter 2. For example, Hausa forms frequentatives, which Newman (2000) describes as "pseudoplural deverbal nouns" (p. 196), from verbs via modification of stem tone, truncation and suffixation. As is general throughout Hausa verbal morphology, the vocalic suffix, here -*e*, replaces the verb's inherent grade suffix (if any). As shown below, stem tone is also replaced with a L*H melody in both copies:

(42)   gyaːràː   'repair'   gyàːre-gyàːre   'corrections'   196
       tàmbayàː   'ask'   tàmbàye-tàmbàye   'repeated questioning'   196
       sàssaƙà   'carve'   sàssàƙe-sàssàƙe   'repeated carving'   196
       shaː   'drink'   shàːye-shàːye   'drinks, repeated drinking'   196

Newman notes (p. 196) that the form each copy takes in frequentative reduplication is identical to the stative form of the same verb, e.g. *sàssàƙe* 'carved.' However, Newman argues that the frequentative and stative constructions are not synchronically related, either functionally or semantically. What this shows is that Hausa has a stem-forming construction producing L*H verbs ending in -*e*:

(43)   Construction: Example:

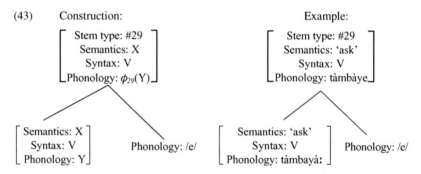

Stem #29 is a semantically neutral stem-forming construction (on stem types, see Aronoff 1994; Blevins 2003). It produces stems for use in other constructions. The frequentative construction calls for two semantically identical stems of type #29. The stative calls for one.

Note that the stem-forming construction itself involves melodic overwriting of two kinds: the replacement of the verb's final vowel by -*e*, and the replacement of the verb's tones by Low. The choice to model these two replacements differently, one as a semantically empty morph and the other in the cophonology of the construction, is arbitrary; both modifications, or neither, could have been attributed solely to the cophonology. This ambiguity of analysis derives from the more general issue of whether morphology is item-based or realizational, an issue on which we would like to remain as neutral as possible, and which does not affect our central claim.

3.3.5   *Double modification outside of reduplication*

Support for the MDT approach which uses independent daughter cophonologies to perform the modifications found in double daughter modification examples is that exactly the same mechanism is needed outside of reduplication. Two familiar examples are Japanese loanword clipping, which applies to each member of borrowed compounds (44a), and two processes of nickname formation in English, illustrated in (44b, c), which clip each of two juxtaposed words down to initial syllable-sized units.[14]

(44)

Double truncation outside of reduplication
a. Japanese clipped compound loanwords (Itô 1990:220)
waado purosessaa   → waa puro 'word processor'
paasonaru koNpyuutaa   → paso koN 'personal computer'
paNtii sutokkiNgu   → paN suto 'panty stockings'
sukeeto boodo   → suke boo 'skate board'

b. Stanford University compound clipping slang
Corner Pocket in the Tresidder Union → Co Po
Florence Moore Hall   → Flo Mo
Frozen Yogurt   → Fro Yo
Memorial Auditorium   → Mem Aud
Memorial Church   → Mem Chu
Residential Education   → Res Ed
Stanford University Employees   → SU Emps

c. English shorthand slang
slo-mo   'slow motion'
ficto-facto documentary based on very little fact
SoHo   neighborhood in New York south of Houston St.
hi-fi   'high fidelity'
sci-fi   'science fiction'
Bo-Jo   'Bob Jones university'
fin-syn   from 'financial syndication' = proposed FCC policy to ease up
            on control of the networks

Clearly, the ability of both members of a compound to be truncated shows that double truncation itself is not a property of reduplication alone. The construction posited for Hausa double reduplicative truncation, above, could easily be adapted to account for compound truncation in Japanese or English. It would be necessary to remove the semantic identity requirement from the daughters, and, of course, to alter as needed the semantic and syntactic description of the mother node.

3.4   Daughter independence vs. base-dependence

The evidence assembled thus far clearly shows that daughter cophonologies are independent of one another and that base and reduplicant have morphologically independent (though semantically equivalent) inputs. Insofar as MDT guarantees this independence, it predicts the absence of the phenomenon termed "base-dependence," in which the output form of one copy depends on the output form of the other. Such a situation cannot be directly modeled in MDT, since in MDT the outputs of the two daughters in reduplication are not in a correspondence relationship. The following sections survey the evidence for base-dependence and find it wanting.

3.4.1   *Reduplicant shape*

The strongest arguments for base-dependence have been made on the basis of reduplicant shape. The most commonly described scenario is that in which prefixing reduplicants exhibit CV vs. VC allomorphy, such that the CV allomorph is used when the base is C-initial and the VC allomorph is used when the base is V-initial. McCarthy and Prince (1999b) analyze several such cases in terms of base-dependence, subsequently formalized in the Optimality Theory frameworks (e.g. McCarthy & Prince 1993; 1995a). The idea is simple. In such languages, the reduplicant is constrained to be a light syllable. CV reduplicants meet that description, but VC reduplicants (prefixed to V-initial bases) do not, since the final C of a VC reduplicant is necessarily syllabified as the onset of the surface syllable containing it. The only reason, according to McCarthy and Prince, that the C in question finds its way into the reduplicant at all is that it can supply an onset to the following base. An example from McCarthy and Prince's (1986) analysis of Orokaiva (published in McCarthy & Prince 1999b), is presented below:

(45)   From McCarthy and Prince 1999b (example (16), p. 250)

If reduplicant shape were determined solely within Cophonology X, VC ~ CV allomorphy would be very difficult for MDT to handle.

However, our survey of the literature shows that the evidence for base-dependent reduplicant shape is very slim, if not nonexistent. The prediction of MDT that base-dependence should not occur appears to be correct.

3.4.1.1   Orokaiva, Roviana, Tawala

We begin our discussion with McCarthy and Prince's (1986) original analysis of Orokaiva (Binandere; Papua New Guinea), published (with emendation) in McCarthy and Prince 1999b. McCarthy and Prince's discussion of Orokaiva is based on Healey, Isoroembo and Chittleborough 1969 (HIC), from which McCarthy and Prince cite the following examples of pluractional reduplication (p. 249; see HIC, p. 35):[15]

(46)	Bare stem	Pluractional	Shape of reduplicant	Gloss
a.	waeke	wa-wa-eke	CV	'shut'
	hirike	hi-hi-rike	CV	'open'
	tiuke	ti-ti-uke	CV	'cut'
b.	uhuke	uh-uhuke	VC	'blow'

In their 1986 manuscript, McCarthy and Prince propose a base-dependent analysis in which the reduplicant is a syllable; it copies a final base consonant just in order to provide a hiatus-breaking onset consonant for the following base. If this were the correct analysis, it would be difficult to implement straightforwardly in MDT, since the reduplicant cophonology (X) does not have access to the base. In the published, revised version of the (1986) manuscript, however, McCarthy and Prince (1999a:251) reject the base-dependent analysis, proposing instead that Orokaiva repetitive reduplication is infixing, and that the reduplicant has a fixed CV shape, as shown below:

(47)	Bare stem	Pluractional	Shape of reduplicant	Gloss
a.	waeke	wa-wa-eke	CV	'shut'
	hirike	hi-hi-rike	CV	'open'
	tiuke	ti-ti-uke	CV	'cut'
b.	uhuke	u-hu-huke	CV	'blow'

Consideration of all of the data and discussion in Healey, Isoroembo, and Chittleborough 1969, strongly suggests that McCarthy and Prince's revised analysis is the correct one. Healey, Isoroembo, and Chittleborough (1969) cite thirteen reduplicated pluractional forms. Only two are vowel-initial: the *uhuhuke* form cited by McCarthy and Prince (1986), and another form, *indidike* 'eat' (Healey, Isoroembo & Chittleborough 1969:36), which is correctly handled by the infixation analysis, but not by the base-dependent prefixation analysis:

(48)   Bare stem   indi
        Prediction of base dependence analysis: VC reduplicant   *in-indi-ke
        Prediction of infixation to first CV: CV reduplicant   in-di-dike

Since the infixation account works neatly for all the data, and since CV infixing reduplication is common not only in the world's languages in general but in Oceanic languages in particular, we may safely conclude with McCarthy and Prince (1999b) that Orokaiva does not present evidence for base dependence.[16]

We have not found other robust examples of the kind of CV ~ VC reduplicative allomorphy, conditioned by whether the following base begins with a C or a V, that would signal base dependence.[17] There are certainly cases, like Roviana (Corston-Oliver 2000), where phonological alternations applying at the mother node level give rise to phonologically conditioned CV ~ VC allomorphy. However, Roviana is not a case of base-dependence; all of the surface reduplicative allomorphs can be derived from the same basic (C)VC reduplicant structure. In Roviana, the general method of forming imperfectives is to reduplicate the first two syllables of the verb root. As shown below, when the first two syllables are both CV, the second V is often deleted from the reduplicant (49a, b). If V-deletion creates a geminate, simplification occurs (b):

(49)   Imperfective   V-deletion,
        Verb root   reduplication degemination
        ──
        peka   'dance'   peka-peka   pek-peka   470
        raro   'cook'   rara-raro   rar-raro → ra-raro   470

In the case of a vowel-initial verb, the reduplicant would be VCV. The final vowel of the reduplicant fuses with the initial vowel of the base, giving the appearance of VC reduplication.

(50)   Imperfective   V-deletion,
        Verb root   reduplication degemination
        ──
        ene   ene-ene   en-ene   'walk' 470

The result is superficial CV ~ VC reduplicant allomorphy. However, because the C-final reduplicative allomorphs can be derived from a V deletion rule at the mother node, there is no need to attribute *en-ene* to base-dependent reduplication.

A similar analysis is probably correct for another apparent case of base-dependence in Tawala, an Austronesian language of Papua New Guinea (Milne Bay Area; Ezard 1980; 1997). Progressive aspect is marked by verb root reduplication. Roots that begin with a CVV sequence reduplicate as CV, as shown in (51a) (Ezard 1980:147, Ezard 1997:43).[18] Vowel-initial roots systematically reduplicate as VC (51b), as shown by these data from Ezard 1980:147:

(51) a. gae   ge-gae   'to go up'
         tou   tu-tou   'to weep'
         beiha   bi-beiha   'to search'
         houni   hu-houni   'to put it'
      b. apu   ap-apu   'to bake'
         atuna   at-atuna   'to rain'
         otowi   ot-otowi   'to make an appointment'

Before concluding that Tawala exhibits base-dependent CV ~ VC reduplicative allomorphy, however, it is important to take note of what happens with CVCV-initial bases (see Ezard 1997:41–42); the data below are taken from Ezard 1980:147:

(52)   hopu   hopu-hopu   'to go down'
       geleta   gele-geleta   'to arrive'
       hune-ya   hune-huneya   'to praise (tr.)'
       bahanae   baha-bahanae   'to speak (lit. talk-go)'
       hanahaya   hana-hanahaya   'to bite'

The data in (52) suggest that the target output shape for the reduplicant is not CV but CVCV, which affects the interpretation of the data in (51). The data with apparent VC reduplicants may very well instead be instantiating VCV reduplication and experiencing a V-V $\rightarrow$ V simplification like that of Roviana. Indeed, there is independent evidence for vowel elision in Tawala. Ezard (1997) describes a regular process by which the initial vowel of the derivational prefix *om-* is elided following a vowel-final prefix, thus, for example, /hi-om-hoe/ $\rightarrow$ *himhoe* 'they left' (p. 36). Ezard also describes a process by which morphemes containing a lexical vowel sequence undergo the loss of the first vowel when another morpheme follows in the same word or phrase: *i-mae* '3sG-stay = he stayed,' vs. *i-me duma* '3sG-stay very = he stayed a long time' (p. 37).

If we accept vowel elision in (52), then the data in (51b) and (52) fall together. In each case the output of the reduplication is two moras. What requires explanation is not the VC allomorph in (52) but the CV allomorph in (51a). Although we cannot be sure, Ezard's observation about VV reduction in non-final morphemes may well be relevant here. If indeed VV $\rightarrow$ V simplification is taking place at Cophonology Z (or even at the word level or phrasally), the output of the reduplicant may in these cases be bimoraic (CVV) as well.

3.4.1.2   Other possible cases

There are more claimed cases of base-dependent reduplicative shape than we can analyze here. Mokilese progressive verbs, for example, exhibit CVC reduplication for consonant-intial stems (e.g. *pɔdok* 'plant' → *pɔd-pɔdok*) and VCC reduplication for V-initial stems (e.g. *andip* 'spit' → *and-andip*, *alu* 'walk' → *all-alu*) (Harrison 1973; 1976, analyzed in Levin 1985a; Blevins 1996; see also discussion in McCarthy & Prince 1999b, McCarthy & Prince 1995a:308). Reduplicant-final gemination, as in *all-alu*, could easily be accomplished at Cophonology Z and need not be stipulated as a property of the reduplicant. Double consonant copying, as in *and-andip*, is more of a concern, since in MDT the *d* would have to be preserved in Cophonology X. Without pretending to resolve this issue here, we do note that all of the VC_iC_j reduplication examples provided by Harrison involve homorganic consonant clusters, as the *nd* in *andip*. It is possible that the homorganicity of these clusters inhibits simplification in Cophonology X. Ulu Muar Malay, analyzed by Kroeger 1990 and Wee 1994, is a case in which the reduplicant (the first copy) consists of material from the left and right edge of the input; whether the right edge material surfaces depends on the nature of the initial consonant in the second copy. However, it is possible to assume that Cophonology X always includes the final consonant in its output, and that Cophonology Z simplifies impossible clusters, just as we assume it simplifies vowel sequences in Tawala and Roviana.

McCarthy and Prince 1999b cite several examples of VC* reduplication as candidates for a base-dependence analysis, e.g. Oykangand prefixing reduplication (e.g. *eder* → *ed-eder* 'rain') and Mangarayi pluralizing infixing reduplication (e.g. gabuji → g-ab-abuji 'old person'). Because the reduplicants in these languages have a fixed shape, base dependence is not strictly necessary in their analysis; the reduplicant can be derived in a context-free manner, as MDT requires. McCarthy and Prince argue, however, that only a base-dependence analysis can explain the VC* shape of the reduplicant: it ends in a consonant because it always precedes a vowel with which that consonant can syllabify. (McCarthy & Prince dispute Sommer's [1981] claim that the canonical syllable in Oykangand is VC*.) Their argument, subsequently formalized in the Optimality Theory framework, is typological; they point to cross-linguistic generalizations about the shape and position of reduplicants, particularly infixed ones. McCarthy and Prince (1999b) state, for example, that fixed VC prefixing reduplication is unattested (except, apparently, in the case of strictly V-initial languages like Oykangand; p. 251), and that no language will exhibit CV reduplication which is infixed after the first consonant (the mirror image of Mangarayi) (McCarthy & Prince 1994b). However, more recent work by Yu (2003) and McCarthy (2002a) has cast doubt on statements of this kind. Yu (2003) cites two languages, for example, which infix a consonant after the first consonant of the stem (the Austronesian language Leti, discussed in Blevins 1999, Yu 2003:89, and references cited therein; and the Pingding dialect of Mandarin Chinese [Yu 2003:91 and references therein]). In the absence of compelling individual cases requiring base-dependence, and in the absence of strong typological universals connecting reduplicant shape to segmental context, we conclude that MDT is correct in generating the daughters of reduplication independently of one another.

3.5 Conclusion

In this chapter we have documented a number of cases in which both daughters in reduplication are modified, and we have provided analyses making use of the principle in MDT that requires only semantic identity between the two daughters in reduplication and allows the daughters to diverge phonologically and morphotactically.

By accounting for reduplicative phonology using the same method – cophonologies – which we use to account for nonreduplicative phonology, we correctly predict that all of the types of phonological effects that occur in reduplication occur outside of reduplication as well. Morphological Doubling Theory is economical, in not using any reduplication-specific phonological rules or constraints; it also makes the right predictions about the phonology of reduplication. Theories that focus solely on reduplication fail to capture the fundamental parallels between reduplicative and nonreduplicative phonology.

4   Morphologically conditioned phonology in reduplication: the mother node

Chapter 3 demonstrated the need for independent daughter cophonologies in the reduplication construction that is the centerpiece of Morphological Doubling Theory (MDT). This chapter shows that, in addition, a cophonology associated with the mother node, i.e. indexed to the construction as a whole, is required in order to handle junctural alternations conditioned by the juxtaposition of the two daughters in a reduplication construction. To illustrate briefly what we call junctural effects, consider the case of vowel reduction/syncope in Lushootseed (Hess 1977; Hess & Hilbert 1978; Bates 1986; Hess 1993; Bates, Hess & Hilbert 1994; Hess 1995; Urbanczyk 1996). In the Lushootseed diminutive reduplication construction, an unstressed /a/ either reduces to [ə] (1a) or, when the resulting consonant cluster is legitimate, deletes altogether (1b) (Urbanczyk 1996). Since the diminutive prefix is usually stressed, in most cases the base vowel reduces. However, when the base vowel is stressed, the vowel of the reduplicant alternates. This is a classic junctural effect: the environment for the alternation is provided by the concatenation of the two pieces of the construction, and the process is agnostic with respect to the affiliation of the unstressed vowel it strikes.[1]

(1)				
a.	s-túləkʷ	s-tú-tələkʷ	'river'/'creek'	167
b.	wális	wá-w'lis	'type of frog'/'Little Frog (wife of p'ic'ikʷ)'	167
c.	q'aXa-cut	q'ə-ʔq'áXa-cut	'uncover, bring to light'/'show self a little'	169

The application of reduction in Lushootseed is taken up in more detail in §4.4 (see particularly §4.4.4).

Other languages exhibit junctural alternations that apply in some morphological constructions but fail to apply in reduplication. One such example involves stress assignment in Indonesian (Cohn 1989). As shown in (2a), in compounds, where there are potentially two primary stresses, the stress of the first word is subordinated. The behavior of compounds contrasts with that of reduplication, however, in which primary stress persists in both copies (2b). The underapplication of junctural effects of this sort is taken up in §4.3. Data are taken from Cohn 1989:185–88:

(2)   a. tùkaŋ cát   'artisan-print = printer'   *túkaŋ cát
        b. búku búku 'books'   *bùku búku

Our surveys have found that the range of junctural alternations occurring in reduplication is as broad as the range of junctural alternations generally, including epenthesis, lenition, metathesis, coda sonorization, assimilation, dissimilation, and syncope. Carrying on with the argument developed in Chapter 3, this chapter demonstrates that reduplication-specific phonology requires the same approach as other morphologically specific phonology, and provides evidence for the mother node cophonology provided in the MDT reduplication construction. We first illustrate our general approach to junctural alternations, arguing that the existence of reduplication-specific junctural effects that target the base require any descriptively adequate theory of reduplication to include layered phonologies, i.e. cophonologies or constraints indexed to constructions as well as to terminals. Cases discussed include so-called underapplication; we demonstrate that MDT, rather than a theory built around base-reduplicant correspondence, such as BRCT (Base-Reduplicant Correspondence Theory; McCarthy & Prince 1995a), is the right way to account for them. The final piece of this argument considers, and then rejects, a potential alternative to layered phonologies, namely Existential Faithfulness (∃-FAITH) (Struijke 1998; 2000a; b), on the grounds that it is both insufficient and unnecessary.

4.1   General approach to junctural phonology

To illustrate our general approach to junctural effects, consider the behavior of stems affixed with dominant suffixes in Japanese (Poser 1984), recently discussed from an Optimality Theory perspective by Alderete (1999; 2001).[2] In Japanese, morphemes may be accented or unaccented. When a dominant accented suffix attaches to a stem, it deletes the stem accent (if there is one), and the word is realized with the suffixal accent (3a). The loss of stem accent triggered by dominant affixes contrasts with the behavior of stems concatenated with a recessive suffix (3b), in which case the stem accent, if present, prevails (Alderete 2001:202):

(3)   a. Accented stem + Dominant accented suffix: stem accent deletes
          /adá + ppó$_{Dom}$ + i/ ada-ppó-i 'coquettish'
        b. Accented stem + Recessive accented suffix: stem accent prevails
          /yóm + tára$_{Rec}$/   yón-dara 'if he reads'

This case dramatically illustrates an important feature of construction-specific junctural phonology: the alternation conditioned by the presence of the affix (in this case accent deletion) is a property of the whole affixed stem, not just of the triggering affix itself.[3] Such effects can only be modeled by a theory that allows constraints or cophonologies to be indexed to particular *constructions*, rather than to hold only over terminals. Following the approach developed by Inkelas (1998) for similar data, we propose that dominant and recessive affixes are associated with different cophonologies. As shown schematically in (4), in the cophonology associated with dominant affixes, *ACCENT outranks stem faithfulness, which results in deletion of stem accent. In the cophonology associated with recessive affixes, the ranking of these constraints is reversed, thus preserving the lexical accent of the stem.

(4)   Dominant suffix schema   Recessive suffix schema
    FAITH_SUFFIX » *ACCENT » FAITH_STEM   FAITH_STEM » *ACCENT » FAITH_SUFFIX

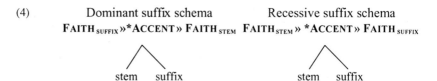

        stem   suffix   stem   suffix

The need to reference constructions in stating subphonological patterns transcends the extensive debate about the use of cophonologies vs. indexed constraints.[4] Any adequate account of subphonological junctural patterns must refer to constructions. Poser (1984), who indexes tone deletion to dominant affixes, specifies that deletion has scope over the base of affixation; Alderete (1999; 2001) indexes his accent deletion constraint not to the dominant affix itself but to the affixed stem. As Inkelas (1998) argues, cophonologies do a better job of correctly predicting what all approaches recognize: the scope of deletion is the affixed stem – the mother node, in constructional terms.

4.2   Reduplication-specific alternations

We return to reduplication-specific junctural effects by examining the case of Dakota coronal dissimilation. Dakota morphology uses reduplication to mark the plurality of inanimate subjects as well as the iterative, distributive, and intensive forms of verbs (Patterson 1990:90). Reduplication in Dakota is described as a process that occurs to the right of the root, copying the final syllable (Shaw 1985; see also Boas & Deloria 1941 and, more recently, Steyaert 1976; Marantz

1982; Sietsema 1988; Patterson 1990).[5] The data in (5) illustrate the pattern for vowel final roots; the reduplicant is boldfaced (Shaw 1985:184):

(5) ixá   ixá-**xa**   'to smile' / 'to grin' (reduplicated)
     skokpá o-skókpa-**kpa**   'to be scooped out' / 'puddle'

Consonant-final roots always have a final epenthetic stem-forming /a/. In reduplication, however, this vowel is not copied (Shaw 1985:184):[6]

(6) /ček/   ček-a   ček-ček-a   'stagger'
     /čap/   čáp-a   čap-čáp-a   'trot'
     /t'is/ t'iz-a t'is-t'iz-a 'draw tight'
     /khuš/ khúž-a khuš-khúž-a 'lazy'

If the first coronal in a cluster of coronals is {t, č, n, d}, it becomes dorsal, but this happens only if the cluster straddles the juncture between reduplicant and base (Shaw 1985:184):

(7) /žat/   žag-žát-a   'curved'
     /theč/ thek-théč-a   'be new'
     /čheč/ čhek-čhéč-a   'to look like'
     /nin/   nig-nín-a   'very'

Dissimilation does not occur word-internally or in lexical compounds (Shaw 1985:184):

(8) sdod + čhí-ya   'know.I + you-cause'   'I know you'
     phed + nákpa-kpa 'fire + crackle (reduplicated)' 'sparks'

The relevant constraints governing this alternation are shown in (9):

(9) IO-IDENT(Place) penalizes a change of place features between input
                      and output
     *COR-COR   assesses a violation for a cluster of two coronals

In reduplication, *COR-COR must outrank IO-IDENT in order to force coronal dissimilation. Outside of reduplication, by contrast, the opposite ranking must hold.[7] With only a single hierarchy and one IO-IDENT constraint, the result is an apparent ranking paradox:

(10) a. Ranking for coronal dissimilation in reduplication:
         *COR-COR » IO-IDENT(Place)
      b. Ranking for no coronal dissimilation outside reduplication:
         IO-IDENT(Place) » *COR-COR

MDT, which permits different cophonologies within a language, encounters no paradox; it associates the different rankings in (10) with different constructions (11). In each case, the relevant cophonology must be a property of the construction as a whole, since the triggering environment for dissimilation is junctural. In MDT terms, this translates into mother node cophonologies. The necessity for such cophonologies provides strong support for the layered structure of the MDT model of reduplication.

(11)   Reduplication   Compounding
     [Dissimilation cophonology]   [Non-dissimilation cophonology]

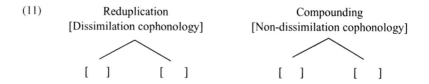

    [ ]   [ ]   [ ]   [ ]

The standard BRCT indexing solution to potential ranking paradoxes that arise in reduplication – faithfulness specific to the reduplicant – cannot work here, because it is a consonant of the base rather than the reduplicant that dissimilates. The problem is identical to the Divergent Modification Ranking Paradox from Chapter 3. First, since coronal dissimilation does not occur in unreduplicated words, it must be the case that IO-IDENT(Place) outranks *COR-COR in Dakota. The tableau in (12) shows how this ranking blocks dissimilation in unreduplicated forms. High-ranking IO-IDENT(Place) penalizes dissimilation of the coronal to velar (12b), rendering the more marked sequence of two coronals intact in the optimal form (12a).

(12)

	/phet – nákpakpa/	IO-IDENT(Place)	*COR-COR
a. ☞	phed – nákpakpa		*
b.	pheg – nákpakpa	*!	

The problem Dakota raises, however, is that reduplication-specific coronal dissimilation targets a consonant in the base. Because in BRCT, IO-Faithfulness constraints are responsible for bases in and out of reduplication, the ranking of IO-IDENT(Place) over *COR-COR should prevent the alternation from targeting any base, even in reduplication. This is shown in the following tableau: IR-IDENT(Place) is necessary to guarantee faithfulness of the reduplicant to the input (13c), but it cannot subvert the protection of the base by the high-ranking IO-IDENT(Place).

(13)

	/sut-R E D-a/	IO-I D E N T(Place) IR-I D E N T(Place)	*C O R-C O R
☞ a.	sut-súut-a		*
(☞) b.	suk-súut-a	*!	
c.	suk-súuk-a	*!	

It is clear that the solution for Dakota lies in having a cophonology specific to the reduplication construction, as we propose above.[8]

4.3   Reduplication-specific non-alternation

Further support for layered phonologies comes from junctural alternations that fail to apply. Indonesian stress assignment is a familiar example of junctural underapplication in reduplication. In the variety of Indonesian analyzed in Cohn 1989, words carry a single primary stress, which is usually penultimate. This culminativity is enforced in compounds by the demotion of the main stress of the first member of a compound to secondary stress (14) (Cohn 1989:188).

(14) tùkaŋ cát   'artisan + print = printer'
      anèka rágam   'various + way = varied'
      polùsi udára   'pollution + air = air pollution'
      ìkut   sərtá   'go along + part of = included'
      lùar   nəgərí 'outside + country = abroad'

Stress subordination fails to apply in unaffixed reduplication, however, where two primary stresses persist (Cohn 1989:185):

(15) hák-hák   'rights'
      búku-búku   'books'
      kərá-kərá   'monkeys'
      kəcíl-kəcíl   'small-DIST'
      waníta-waníta   'women'
      minúman-minúman   'drinks' (n.)
      màšarákat-màšarákat   'societies'
      kəkuráŋan-kəkuráŋan   'lacks' (n.)
      kəmàšarakátan-kəmàšarakátan   'societies (abstract)'

The MDT analysis of Indonesian associates different cophonologies with the compounding and reduplication constructions. They differ crucially in the ranking of CULMINATIVITY, which permits only one primary stress in the output, and IDENT$_{IO}$-stress, which preserves primary stress:

(16)   Compounding cophonology: CULMINATIVITY » IDENT$_{IO}$-stress
        Reduplication cophonology: IDENT$_{IO}$-Stress » CULMINATIVITY

As this demonstration illustrates, MDT treats underapplication as nonapplication; it is analyzed with garden-variety input–output faithfulness constraints. In BRCT, underapplication is analyzed as purposeful, blocking an alternation that would, if it occurred, destroy the identity of reduplicant and base. Consider the sketch of Cohn and McCarthy's (1998) BRCT analysis of Indonesian in (17), which appears as a small part of their comprehensive account of the complex stress patterns in the language and parallels the independently arrived at Coerced Identity account proposed in Kenstowicz 1995. Cohn and McCarthy argue that CULMINATIVITY[9] is outranked by constraints enforcing metrical identity between the base and the reduplicant, which we abbreviate here as BR-METRICALFAITH.[10] Crucially, the constraint is violated when corresponding vowels disagree in degree of stress. Therefore, the reduplicated form with two primary stresses (17a) is optimal, since the stress subordination in (17b) introduces a fatal difference between the two copies:[11]

(17)

	[RED-buku]	BR-METRICALFAITH	CULMINATIVITY
☞ a.	búku-búku		*
b.	bùku-búku	*!	

4.3.1   BR-Faith is insufficient

A Native Identity theory such as MDT, where identity in reduplication is a by-product of MS feature duplication but is not actively maintained by the phonology, does not attribute underapplication to constraints on base-reduplicant identity. With regard to underapplication, the MDT approach makes at least two predictions that distinguish it from BRCT. First, MDT predicts that underapplication is possible under any kind of morphological conditioning, regardless of identity. Second, MDT predicts that there will be underapplication effects that occur in reduplication that are not identity enhancing. Both of these predictions are correct, with the result that the Coerced Identity approach to underapplication in BRCT is insufficient as it stands. To make BRCT descriptively adequate requires including the kind of indexed cophonologies/constraints that are at the heart of MDT. In doing so, BR-FAITH constraints become redundant.

4.3.2   Underapplication all over
Recall the Generalized Phonology Prediction from Chapter 3:

(18)   **Generalized Phonology Prediction:**
         The set of phonological effects found applying within reduplication is
         equivalent to the set of morphologically conditioned phonological effects
         found outside of reduplication. There is nothing unique about the phonology
         of reduplication constructions.

With respect to underapplication, the Generalized Phonology Prediction
leads us to expect that underapplication is a potential property of all morphologically conditioned phonology, not just of reduplication. This prediction
is certainly true. For example, alternations that occur in derived environments
often underapply in nonderived environments (see, for example, Kiparsky 1993,
as well as Inkelas 2000; Anttila in press for recent overviews). Moreover, in
many languages the phonological alternations of one stratum fail to apply in a
different stratum, as has been well documented, for example, in English, Malayalam, Kashaya, Sekani, and Turkish among others (see, for example, Orgun
1996; Inkelas 1998; Anttila 2002 for recent overviews). It is also common to
find underapplication in words of a particular morphosyntactic category. Smith
(1997; 1998) documents cases in which alternations applying in verbs in some
languages underapply in nouns. In other cases an apparently arbitrary class of
morphemes fails to trigger an alternation found in other constructions. Consider,
for example, a morphologically conditioned syncope process in Hopi, described
by Jeanne (1982). For roots subject to syncope, their final vowel deletes when
a suffix is added (19a). In all other roots, syncope underapplies (19b).

(19)

	Non-future	Future		
a. *Syncope applies:*	soma	som-ni	'tie'	246
	yiŋʸa	yiŋ-ni	'enter (pl)'	246
	mooki	mok-ni	'die'	246
	hiiko	hikʷ-ni	'drink'	246
b. *Syncope underapplies:*	maqa	maqa-ni	'give'	248
	pana	pana-ni	'put in'	248
	qatɨ	qatɨ-ni	'sit'	248
	ʔöki	ʔöki-ni	'arrive (pl)'	248

Along the same lines, we find a morphologically conditioned syncope alternation in Piro (Arawakan) (Matteson 1965; Kenstowicz & Kisseberth 1979).
According to Matteson (1965:36), in Piro, "Arbitrary vowel loss occurs preceding certain suffixes and incorporated postpositives." The data in (20), based on

the stems *neta* 'I see' and *yopnuha* 'he wards off there,' serve as illustration. For any given stem, some suffixes arbitrarily trigger deletion of the final vowel (20a), while others do not (20b):

(20)   a. *Syncope applies:*

LOCATIVE	net-ya	yopnuh-ha
3SG.OBJ	net-lu	yopnuh-lu

   b. *Syncope does not apply:*

ANTICIPATORY	neta-nu	yopnuha-nu
YET	neta-wa-lu	yopnuha-wa-lu

The cophonologies at the heart of MDT are general enough to encompass the full range of underapplication effects found cross-linguistically. These cases clearly require indexation of cophonologies or constraints to syntactic categories (noun/verb), arbitrary affixation constructions (e.g. in Piro), and so on. BRCT's identity-based account of underapplication, on the other hand, is insufficient. With the recognition that underapplication (non-application) is not a special feature of reduplicative phonology, and that indexed constraints/cophonologies are necessary, BR-FAITH constraints are rendered superfluous in the analysis of underapplication.

4.3.3   *Non-identity-enhancing underapplication in reduplication*

Because the MDT account of underapplication does not rely on phonological identity, it predicts that there will be cases where underapplication occurs in reduplication even when it is not identity enhancing. This is in contrast with the expectation in BRCT, where base-reduplicant identity is at the heart of reduplication-specific effect. Again, the prediction of MDT is the correct one. Chamorro (Topping 1973), for example, exhibits underapplication of a stress shift, independent of any plausible identity considerations. Consider the data in (21), taken from Topping 1973. Default stress in Chamorro is penultimate. When a suffix attaches to a root, it shifts the stress over to the right to maintain penultimate stress:

(21)   a.

karéta	'car'	108
karetá-hu	'my car'	108
karetá-ta	'our (incl.) car'	108
kareta-n-mámi	'our (excl.) car'	108
kareta-n-ñíha	'their car'	108

   b.

hásso	'think'	42
h-in-ásso	'thought'	42
h-in-assó-mu	'your (sg.) thought'	42
h-in-asso-n-mámi	'our (excl.) thought'	42

While the penultimate stress pattern is preserved under suffixation (21a) and infixation (21b), it is disrupted by both of the CV reduplication patterns in Chamorro. Final CV reduplication, which serves to intensify adjectives, negatives, and directional adverbs (Topping 1973:183), repeats the final CV of the stem. As shown in (22), this reduplication pattern results in antepenultimate stress.

(22)

ñálang	'hungry'	ñá**lala**ng	'very hungry'
métgot	'strong'	mét**gogo**t	'very strong'
buníta	'pretty'	bu**níta**ta	'very pretty'
guátu	'there, in that direction'	guá**tutu**	'furthest'
mági	'here, in this direction'	má**gigi**	'nearest'
		ni há**yiyi**	'no one else'
		ni guá**huhu**	'not even me'
		hi taimá**nunu**	'no matter how'

Klein (1997) presents a Coerced Identity account of the underapplication of default stress in the intensive reduplication construction. He argues that stress shift is inhibited in reduplication because it would ruin the otherwise perfect identity between the reduplicant and the base:

(23)

		/RED-buníta/	BR-IDENT(STRESS)	PENULT
a.	*normal application*	bunitá-ta	*!	
☞ b.	*underapplication*	buníta-ta		*

A more comprehensive look at the language reveals, however, that Coerced Identity cannot be at the root of underapplication in Chamorro. A second reduplicative construction, which copies the first CV of the stressed syllable, also fails to shift stress, despite the fact that there would be no consequences for identity. Stressed CV reduplication serves a variety of functions, including nominalization (24a) and the marking of continuative aspect (24b). In the resulting forms stress surfaces on the antepenultimate, rather than the penultimate, syllable. Data are taken from Topping 1973:

(24)

a.	hátsa	'lift'	**háha**tsa	'one that was lifting'	102
b.	saga	'stay'	**sása**ga	'staying'	192, 259
	s-um-ága	'lived'	s-um-**ása**ga	'living'	191–192
c.	átan	'look at'	**á'a**tan	'looking at'	171
d.	táitai	'read'	**táta**itai	'reading'	259
e.	hugándo	'play'	hu**gága**ndo	'playing'	259

In this case, assuming a high-ranked Non-Finality constraint, either the reduplicant or the base must carry the stress. Klein's account incorrectly predicts that for this construction, stress shift should apply normally, since normal application of stress shift (25a) does not increase the severity of the BR-IDENT(STRESS) violation:

(25)

		/RED- sága /	BR-IDENT(STRESS)	PENULT
☛* a.	*normal application*	sa-sá-ga	*	
b.	*underapplication*	sá-sa-ga	*	*!

Coerced Identity cannot be the right analysis of underapplication in Chamorro. The pattern bears out the prediction of MDT that underapplication in reduplication is not tied to identity enhancement. In this case, as we will also argue below for Indonesian and Klamath, apparent underapplication is simply non-application: the cophonology in question does not enforce the pattern in question.[12]

4.3.4   *Layering and underapplication*
Klein's analysis of Chamorro highlights the danger of theorizing on the basis of a reduplicative construction without taking into account the broader picture of the morphology of a language. In that case, while one reduplication construction appears to be consistent with the Coerced Identity view of underapplication, it is clear that Coerced Identity cannot motivate underapplication in the whole set of constructions (including other reduplication constructions) taken together.

To make the point that underapplication is not in general motivated by identity requirements, we return to Indonesian reduplicative underapplication, another case which has been analyzed from the Coerced Identity perspective, as discussed above. We show, by looking at reduplication in the context of affixation generally, that the apparent identity affect is ephemeral; instead, Indonesian shows a cophonological difference between application and non-application of stress reduction which happens to give the appearance of identity preservation in some cases.

Indonesian stress forms the basis of an intriguing argument for the Coerced Identity account of underapplication, presented by Kenstowicz (1995) and Cohn and McCarthy (1998). The argument hinges on the stress patterning of reduplicated forms.

The default location of main stress in Indonesian is penultimate. Penultimate main stress is reassigned under suffixation; stresses further to the left are subordinated (Cohn 1989:176):

(26) a. bicára   'speak'
          məm-bicará-kan   'speak about (something)'
          məm-bicàra-kán-ña   'speak about it'
      b. acára   'plan'
          məŋ-acará-kan   'plan (something)'
          məŋ-acàra-kán-ña   'plan it'

Reduplication does not conform perfectly to the generalization that the rightmost stress is primary and others are secondary. A focus of Cohn (1989) is the fact that the copies in reduplication bear equal stress, as shown on the left in (27). Intriguingly, however, stress subordination does apply when a reduplicated stem is suffixed; as shown on the right in (27), such forms pattern exactly like the suffixed stems in (26) with regard to stress shift and subordination (Cohn 1989:185):

(27) búku-búku   'books'   [bùku-bukú]ña   'the books'
      waníta-waníta   'women'   kə[wanìta-waníta]an   'womanly'
      màšarákat-màšarákat   'societies' [màšaràkat-màšarakát]ña   'the societies'
      minúman-minúman   'drinks' n. [minùman-minumán]ña   'the drinks'

Stress shift and subordination under affixation decrease identity between the two copies. Kenstowicz (1995) and Cohn and McCarthy (1998) independently argue that this is a kind of TETU effect; once identity is disrupted for other reasons, unmarkedness emerges.[13] As modeled in (28), the unmarkedness effect in this case is stress reduction; the disruption in identity is caused by stress shift upon suffixation. As seen, the addition of a suffix to a reduplicated form forces the main stress on the second copy to shift rightward (by high-ranking PENULT). This shift induces non-identity between the two copies, since it results in differently stressed syllables in each. Given that perfect identity is impossible, the effects of CULMINATIVITY emerge, triggering stress subordination in the first copy in typical TETU fashion:[14]

(28)

	[RED-buku-ña]	"PENULT"	BR-METRICALFAITH	CULMINATIVITY
a.	búku-búku-ña	*!		
b.	búku-bukú-ña		*	*!
☞ c.	bùku-bukú-ña		*	

Note that in Cohn and McCarthy's analysis it is crucial that BR-METRICAL FAITH is assessed categorically. Although the optimal candidate, (28c) obscures metrical faithfulness in two ways (location and degree of stress), it can win only if this leads to a single violation of the BR-FAITH constraint. Otherwise, it would be bested by the candidate in (28b), whose base and reduplicant are more faithful to each other but which violates CULMINATIVITY.

The characterization of normal application of stress subordination as a TETU effect contrasts with the treatment of this phenomenon in a Native Identity theory such as MDT, where BR-FAITH constraints play no role. In the Native Identity view, it is an accidental (although functionally understandable) fact about the reduplication construction that its cophonology happens not to trigger stress subordination. Adding a suffix to a reduplicated form introduces a new layer of structure and a new cophonology, one that includes regular stress subordination:

(29)   Native Identity view:

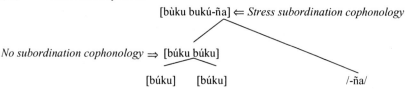

The BRCT view is appealing in its apparent explanation of a pattern that in MDT is essentially arbitrary. However, further facts show that stress subordination in affixed reduplicated words is in fact a consequence not of TETU, but of cophonological layering, as predicted by MDT. Consider first the data in (30), drawn from Cohn (1989:185). Bases with only a single stressable vowel, which include both monosyllabic bases and disyllabic bases where one of the vowels is a schwa, exhibit the same pattern of stress subordination as do the polysyllabic forms seen in (27). The downgrading of primary to secondary stress does not apply in reduplicated forms – except where the reduplicated word is followed by a suffix. What distinguishes the data in (30) from those in (27) is that stress never shifts. Because the words have only one stressable vowel, stress is final; under suffixation, it stays put, due to the penultimate stress generalization. No stress shift occurs – but stress subordination takes place regardless:

(30)
pás	'try'			di [pàs-pás]kan	'tried on, repeatedly'
kərá	'monkey'	kərá-kərá	'monkeys'	[kərà-kərá]an	'toy monkey'
kəcíl	'small'	kəcíl-kəcíl	'small (dist.)'	məŋ[əcìl-ŋəcíl]kan	'to belittle s.t.'

Cohn and McCarthy (1998) recognize stress subordination in these forms as a potential problem for their analysis of underapplication. In the Coerced Identity scenario, stress subordination should occur in reduplication only as a TETU effect when other factors make perfect identity impossible. However, there is no obvious cancellation of metrical identity in these short words: stress does not shift. The prediction would thus appear to be that stress subordination should not occur either; BR-identity in stress degree should be preserved:

(31)

	[RED-pas-kan]	BR-METRICALFAITH	CULMINATIVITY
a.	pàs-pás-kan	*!	
☞* b.	pás-pás-kan		*

Cohn and McCarthy solve this problem by proposing that although stress does not shift, metrical structure changes under suffixation by virtue of enlarging the second metrical foot to two syllables. Footing differences are argued to trigger likewise a violation of BR-METRICALFAITH; the decision among candidates is thus again passed down to CULMINATIVITY, with the result that only the second stress retains its primary status:

(32)

	[RED-pas-kan]	BR-METRICALFAITH	CULMINATIVITY
☞ a.	(pàs)-(pás-kan)	*	
b.	(pás)-(pás-kan)	*	*!

As noted earlier, this analysis relies heavily on the unorthodox assumption that BR-METRICALFAITH is evaluated categorically. This mode of violation constitutes a significant departure from standard assessment of faithfulness constraints in Optimality Theory (Prince & Smolensky 1993) and Correspondence Theory (e.g. McCarthy & Prince 1995c; d). In general, it is crucial for a faithfulness constraint to be violated for every infraction. Consider, for example, a language where high-ranking *COMPLEX penalizes complex codas and simplifies them by deleting all but the postvocalic consonant (e.g. *hand* → *han*). As shown by the tableau in (33), the pattern would be impossible to generate if faithfulness is evaluated categorically, since IO-MAX-C could not serve to minimize deletion. A NOCODA constraint, ranked anywhere, would always favor the candidate with maximal deletion, i.e. (c).

(33)

	/hand/	*COMPLEX	IO-MAX-C	NOCODA
a.	hand	*!		
b.	han		*	*!
☞ c.	ha		*	

In the Indonesian stress case, this problem is exacerbated further by the fact that, in a fully developed analysis, the single metrical BR-METRICALFAITH constraint would have to be broken down into a family of metrical faithfulness constraints, as is standard in any analysis of stress (see, for example, Kager 1999 for an overview). In that case, we would not expect to see the TETU effect at all. Since suffixed output candidates violate foot identity regardless of whether or not stress subordination occurs, the candidate that at least preserves the same degree of stress would always be optimal:

(34)

	[RED-pas-kan]	BR-IDENT (STRESS DEGREE)	BR-IDENT (FOOT MEMBERSHIP)
a.	(pàs)-(pás-kan)	*!	*
☞ b.	(pás)-(pás-kan)		*

Even if it were possible to work out the technical details of Cohn and McCarthy's Indonesian analysis, the deeper issue is whether or not the intuition Cohn and McCarthy, and Kenstowicz, pursue for Indonesian is the right one, cross-linguistically. The intuition behind their analysis is that if a language has a phonological alternation that fails to apply in reduplication, the inhibition is due to BR identity; only when perfect identity is impossible for independent reasons is the alternation predicted to apply, in the manner of TETU.

Our investigations, detailed below, fail to support this intuition. Lack of application of a phonological alternation in reduplication is due to its absence from the cophonology associated with that reduplication construction; application of the alternation when the construction is embedded in further morphology is due to the presence of the alternation in the cophonology associated with the higher morphological constructions. Interestingly, this is the analysis originally given to Indonesian by Cohn (1989); we have found its counterpart to be the correct analysis in numerous other cases as well.

4.3.5   Klamath

We illustrate our argument against the equation of phonological underapplication with maintenance of base-reduplicant identity with Klamath intensive reduplication, a well-known case for which that equation has been made (McCarthy & Prince 1995a).[15] The relevant phonological alternation in Klamath is vowel reduction/syncope. Both prefixes and root reduplication trigger vowel reduction in the second syllable of the derived stem (Barker 1963; 1964).[16] If the second syllable is closed, its vowel reduces to schwa (35a, b). If the second syllable would be open, the vowel deletes (35c, d) altogether. Henceforth, page numbers for data taken from Barker (1963) are prefixed with "B63"; those for data taken from Barker (1964) are prefixed with "B64."[17]

(35)

	Plain stem	Prefixed stem	
a.	domna	so-d[ə]mna	B63:121
	'hears, obeys, understands'	'hear each other'	
b.	čonwa	hos-č[ə]nwa	B63:166
	'vomits'	'cause to vomit'	
c.	qabaːta	has-q[Ø]baːta	B63:310
	'sets something heavy up	'causes s.o. to put a heavy or	
	against'	pronged object up against'	
d.	wp̓eq̓a	ʔi-p[Ø]q'a	B63:308
	'hits in the face with a long	'puts plural objects on the face'	
	instrument'		

Barker (1964) considers Intensive reduplication to be prefixal (though, since reduplication is total, no evidence identifies either copy as the reduplicant as opposed to the base).[18] As shown in (36), the Intensive does not trigger vowel reduction.

(36)

	Plain stem		Intensive	
a.	/beq̓-l̀i/	'be bay colored, dawn'	beq-beq-l̀i	B63:61
b.	/Liw'-a/	'shiver (from fatigue, hunger)'	Liw-Liw'-a	B63:229

McCarthy and Prince (1995a), who adopt Barker's prefixing analysis of Intensive reduplication, argue that the failure of vowel reduction to apply in the Intensive is a BR-identity effect. Their analysis relies not only on BR correspondence but also on backcopying, a possibility unique to BRCT, in which the surface form of the reduplicant can influence, via BR correspondence, the surface form of the base. McCarthy and Prince's (1995a) backcopying analysis is illustrated by the tableau in (37). The constraint called REDUCE stands for the set of constraints that motivate vowel reduction and deletion; it is outranked by IO-FAITH-σ_1, which protects the vowel in the initial syllable from reduction/deletion, with the result that only the second syllable is normally affected (as in (35)). In the Intensive form shown in (37), normal second syllable reduction, which would affect only the base (37a), is blocked because it would render the base and the reduplicant non-identical. Reducing both copies, which would also maintain identity, fatally violates the high-ranking IO-FAITH-σ_1 (37b) that protects the initial syllable from reduction. The optimal solution is to reduce neither (37c):

(37)

	/INT-Wič-lì/	IO-FAITH-σ_1	BR-FAITH	REDUCE
a.	W[ə]č-W[ə]č-lì	*!		
b.	Wič-W[ə]č-lì		*!	*
☞ c.	Wič-Wič-lì			**

If this is the right analysis, then the failure of reduction in Intensive reduplication requires some version of BR faithfulness, and would be incompatible with MDT. However, the backcopying analysis has two major drawbacks. First, it does not take into account the fact that vowel reduction also fails to apply in certain nonreduplicative morphological contexts; second, it does not take into account the fact that reduction does apply in some reduplicative contexts. The BR identity analysis presupposes an implicational connection between reduplication and lack of vowel reduction which simply does not exist, a point made by Zoll (2002), on which this discussion draws; Park (2000) reaches similar conclusions as well. To support this view, we present some background on Klamath morphology.

The verb in Klamath consists of a number of prefix classes, a root, and a variety of suffixes (Barker 1964; Delancey 1991; 1999):

(38)

Distributive	Causative, Reflexive- reciprocal	Causative, Transitive	Classifiers	Intensive	**Root**	Suffixes

Vowel reduction is morphologically conditioned, applying only in certain zones of the verb. As shown below, vowel reduction/deletion of the second syllable in the morphological domain is *not* triggered by suffixes (39a, b), nor does it apply root-internally (39c) (White 1973; Thomas 1974). Roots are underlined:

(39) a. se-tpek-bli-bg-a se-tp[ə]k-bli-pg-a *se-tp[ə]k-bl[ə]-pg-a B64:155
          'reaches back of oneself'
      b. boːs-dgi-diːl-a → boːs-tgi-diːl-a *boːs-tg[Ø]-diːl-a B64:141
          'turns black underneath'

Bare roots and root-suffix sequences are contexts where BR identity is not at stake; thus some other mechanism is needed to prevent vowel reduction in these domains, while allowing it in prefixed stems like those in (35). MDT assumes, as for all morphologically conditioned phonology, a cophonological difference. Stems, consisting of root plus suffixes, are associated with a cophonology that does not enforce vowel reduction (IO-FAITH » REDUCE). By contrast, prefixes like those in (35) are associated with a cophonology that does enforce vowel deletion in noninitial syllables (IO-FAITH-Initial » REDUCE » IO-FAITH).

The same cophonological differences found outside of reduplication also obtain among reduplication constructions. Vowel reduction fails to apply in the Intensive reduplication construction (36), as we have seen; however, it does apply in another reduplication construction: the Distributive (40).

(40) qlin   'chokes . . .' qli-ql[ə]n   'choke (Distributive)'   B63:321
      domna   'hears,   so-d[ə]mna   'hear each other (Distributive)' B63:121
                obeys . . .'
      čonwa   'vomits'   hos-č[ə]nwa   'cause to vomit' (Distributive)   B63:166
      pag-a   'barks'   pa-p[Ø]g-a   'bark (Distributive)'   B63:296

McCarthy and Prince (1995a) distinguish Distributive reduplication from Intensive reduplication by splitting BR-FAITH into two constraints, one specific to the Distributive reduplicant and one specific to the Intensive reduplicant. REDUCE ranks below BR-FAITH-Intensive and above BR-FAITH-Distributive. This is essentially equivalent to the cophonology approach that MDT takes, without invoking BR-FAITH at all: Distributive stems are associated in MDT with the cophonology REDUCE » IO-FAITH, while Intensive stems are associated with the cophonology IO-FAITH » REDUCE. Because construction-specific constraint reranking – cophonology differentiation – is needed anyway in Klamath, IO-FAITH is sufficient to account for the observed variation. BR-FAITH in general, and backcopying in particular, are superfluous.

A concern even greater than superfluity for the backcopying analysis is an incorrect prediction that it generates. Recall that on the backcopying analysis of simple reduplicated stems, Reduction/Deletion is blocked in the reduplicant because it is word-initial; BR identity is responsible for its blockage in the BASE (37). The backcopying analysis therefore clearly predicts that when RED is *not* word-initial, and thus not protected by positional faithfulness, reduction *will* occur in both RED and BASE (McCarthy & Prince 1995a:349). However, as illustrated by the forms in (41), when an Intensive is preceded by a prefix that normally triggers second syllable vowel reduction, only the syllable immediately following the prefix reduces.

(41)
a. /Wič/   'be stiff'
    Wič-Wič-ỉi   'stiff'   B63: 458
    Wi-W[ə]č-Wičỉi   'stiff (Dist)'   * Wi-W[ə]č-W[ə]č-ỉi   B64:121

b. /Leq̓/   'whisper'
    Leq-Leq̓-a   'whispers'   B63:228
    Le-L[ə]q-Leq̓-a   'whisper (Dist)'   *Le-L[ə]q-L[ə]q̓-a
    se-L[ə]q-Leq̓-a   'whispers to oneself, *se-L[ə]q-L[ə]q̓-a
                       to each other'

c. /Wit'/   'flop'
    Wit-Wiỉ-a   'flops'   B63:458
    Wi-W[ə]t-Wit-kang-a 'flop around (Dist)' *Wi-W[ə]t-W[ə]t-kang-a
    sni-W[ə]t-Wit-kang-a 'make s.t. flop around' *sni-W[ə]t-W[ə]t-kang-a

The prediction that reduction will be backcopied to the base, yielding the starred forms in (41), is illustrated below. Only REDUCE violations for the second syllable are shown:

(42)

	se-RED-Leq̓-a	IO-F,AITH-Initial	BR-FAITH	REDUCE	IO-FAITH
a.	se-Leq̓-Leq̓-a			*!	
(☞) b.	se-L[ə]q̓-Leq̓-a		*!		
♠ c.	se-L[ə]q̓-L[ə]q̓-a				*

McCarthy and Prince (1995a) cite a different form which they interpret as showing that prefixed Intensive forms do show reduction in both base and reduplicant: /sw'V-RED-ciq̓-a/ → swi-c[ə]q-c[Ø]q̓a 'shake the head' (1995a:349), which has reduction in the reduplicant and deletion in the base. This form is assumed to be representative of prefixed reduplicated forms in Klamath generally. (McCarthy & Prince observe that the form is problematic in that the reduplicant and base reduce differently: schwa in the reduplicant, and deletion in the base.)

An exhaustive search of Barker (1964) reveals, however, that this form is not representative and that double reduction of prefixed intensive stems is not the norm. Crucially, there are no examples in which an unprefixed intensive stem, without reduction, coexists with a prefixed counterpart showing reduction in both reduplicant and base. As the examples below illustrate, either the unprefixed form shows a regular Reduction/Deletion pattern targeting the second syllable (43a), or there is no unprefixed form given (43b, d). The predicted alternation between a doubly reduced prefixed form and an unreduced plain form is unattested.

(43)

	Root	Reduplicated	Prefixed reduplicated	
a.	/čiq̓/	čiq-cq̓a	sẇi-č[ə]q-č[Ø]q̓-a	B63:76
		'shakes'	'shakes the head (like a horse)'	
b.	/k̓ač̓/		tga-k̓[ə]č-k[Ø]č̓-ač̓	B63:197
	'from earth to sky'		'stands from earth to sky (said of a character in a myth)'	
c.	/peL'/		sẇe-p[ə]L-p[Ø]l̀-a	B63:300
	'shake all over'		'shakes all over, shakes oneself (as a dog)'	
d.	/qt̓aq̓/		sa-qt̓[ə]q-qt[Ø]q̓-a	B63:324
	'clap the hands'		'claps the hands together'	

Under any account, forms like *č[ə]q-č[Ø]q'-a*, which exhibit double reduction even when unprefixed, are lexical exceptions and must be listed as such. Given this, the patterning of the rest of the data reflects normal application of vowel reduction.

In summary, the failure of the Intensive to trigger reduction is not directly attributable to BR identity. Instead, it must be attributed to the association of the Intensive construction with a non-reducing cophonology. The side-by-side structures in (44) of an Intensive verb and a prefixed Intensive verb show how the differential application of reduction in the two cases follows directly from the association of the appropriate cophonologies with the constructions involved. Each arrow represents the effect of the cophonology associated with the mother node just above:

(44)   Unprefixed Intensive   Prefixed Intensive

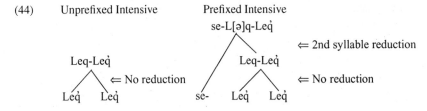

Zoll (2002) argues that the association of Intensive reduplication with a non-reducing cophonology is not arbitrary but follows from the fact that the Intensive construction is stem-internal, thus subsumed under the generalization that reduction does not apply stem-internally. This analysis accords with the insights of Barker (1964) and White (1973), who treat Intensive reduplication essentially as root-root compounding.

By contrast, the Distributive, a late morphological process, patterns with stem-external prefixes in triggering vowel reduction. The association of clusters of morphological constructions, or zones in the word, with similar cophonologies is the kind of pattern that stratal ordering was originally developed to handle; it can be captured in cophonology theory through meta constructions; see, for example, Inkelas and Orgun 1998; Stump 1998; Anttila 2002 for discussion.

In summary, the failure of vowel reduction in Intensive reduplication in Klamath is a case of normal non-application of Reduction/Deletion stem-internally, not backcopying underapplication. The proposed cophonology analysis is capable not only of distinguishing constructions triggering reduction from those which do not, but also of correctly predicting the outcome in forms containing both kinds of constructions. In the latter respect it is more descriptively adequate than the backcopying analysis argued for in McCarthy and Prince 1995a. Our reanalysis thus eliminates Klamath as support for BR correspondence, while also making the more general point that morphological investigation is essential to the understanding of the non-application of a phonological alternation.[19]

4.4   ∃-Faith

The MDT view that reduplicative phonology is simply a subcase of morphologically conditioned phonology, modeled in exactly the same way, contrasts sharply with the BRCT view, stated most strongly by Spaelti (1997):

> all deviations from complete identity between the two parts of the reduplication are due to [TETU]. In contrast to this any unexpected identity between the reduplicant and the base [is] the result of what I will call IDENTITY INDUCED FAILURE OF ALTERNATION (IIFA). These two concepts constitute the entirety of the theory of reduplication.   (p. 43)

The difficulty with this view, as we have seen, is that it does not extend to the broader range of morphologically conditioned phonology found across languages, nor does it fully account for the phonology of reduplication itself.

One proposal within the BRCT framework that has made some inroads into the latter problem is existential faithfulness (∃-FAITH), a proposal by Struijke (1998; 2000a; 2000b), building on earlier work by Raimy and Idsardi 1997;

Spaelti 1997; Fitzgerald 2000 (see also Rose 1999) which addresses the issue of ranking paradoxes arising when alternations which are not fully general in the language target the base of reduplication. One such paradox arises in Dakota (§4.2), where coronal dissimilation applies across the internal juncture only in reduplication; Tarok, in Chapter 3, represents another ranking paradox in which reduplication-specific neutralization applies to the base. Klamath, in which vowel reduction applies to the base in some cases of reduplication but not generally in the language, is yet another such example. In each case, the paradox is the same. For the alternation in question to apply to the base of reduplication, it must be the case that the relevant markedness constraint (set) outranks IO-FAITH. That predicts, however, that the alternation will also occur outside reduplication, which is not true.

Perhaps the best-known example in the literature of a reduplication-induced ranking paradox comes from diminutive reduplication in Lushootseed, discussed earlier in this chapter, and one of the languages highlighted in the work of Struijke (2000a; b). Lushootseed exhibits a process of unstressed vowel syncope/reduction. Earlier work on Lushootsheed (Hess 1977; Hess & Hilbert 1978; Broselow 1983; Bates 1986; Hess 1993; 1995) observes that reduction frequently occurs between voiceless obstruents; Urbanczyk (1996) demonstrates that the alternation targets unstressed vowels, primarily the low vowel /a/. An overview of the morphological conditioning of syncope, oversimplified in a crucial way to be clarified shortly, is as follows. In unreduplicated words, reduction is optional, leading to free variation (a), while in reduplicated words, reduction is obligatory (b). Which vowel reduces – reduplicant or base – depends on the location of stress, as discussed in Urbanczyk 1996 and references therein. Whether an unstressed /a/ syncopates or reduces is predictable from segmental environment; we subsume both processes under the term "reduction." The data below are taken from Urbanczyk 1996:

(45)

a.	caq'(a)	'spear, jab'	cá-cq'	'act of spearing big game on water' 167
	šaXʷ-il	'grass, hay'	sá-ʔsXʷ-il	'(short) grass, lawn' 167
	wális	'type of frog'	wá-w'lis	'Little Frog (wife of *p'ic'ikʷ*)' 167
	laq-il	'late'	lá-ʔlq-il	'be a little late' 167
	q'aXa-cut	'uncover'	q'ə-ʔq'áXa-cut	'show self a little' 169
b.	sčúsad ~ sčúsəd			'(established) star' 166
	híqab ~ híqəb			'too, excessively' 166
	qacágw=ac ~ qəcágw=ac ~ qcágw=ac			'ironwood, ocean spray, spiraea' 166
	Xáλ'=al=ap ~ Xəλ'=ál=ap			'steer a canoe with a paddle held over the stern (like a rudder)'

The ranking paradox lies in the fact that the constraint rankings driving the pattern in bases of reduplication are clearly different from those driving the pattern in unreduplicated bases. In particular, the ranking that entails obligatory reduction in diminutive reduplication, REDUCE » IO-FAITH, incorrectly predicts obligatory reduction outside of reduplication as well.[20]

The cophonology approach would resolve this paradox by positing two cophonologies, one associated with unreduplicated stems, and one associated with the reduplication construction.

(46)   Reducing cophonology: REDUCE » IO-FAITH
        Optionally reducing cophonology: IO-FAITH ~ REDUCE

Existential faithfulness, or ∃-FAITH, addresses the paradox without appealing to cophonologies by introducing a modified type of IO faithfulness which calls for every segment and feature of the input to have some correspondent in the output. The only difference between ∃-FAITH and IO-FAITH, which it is intended to replace, is that, in reduplication, ∃-FAITH is satisfied by the appearance of input material in either the reduplicant or the base. The following definitions of ∃-MAX and ∃-IDENT, members of the ∃-FAITH family, are taken from Struijke 2000a:

(47)   a. ∃-MAX$_{IO}$ (p. 21)
           Let seg ∈ input: then there is some seg' ∈ output, such that seg ℜ seg'
           Every segment in the input has some correspondent in the output
        a. ∃-IDENT$_{IO}$ (p. 24)
           Let seg ∈ input be in the domain of ℜ, and seg is [αF]: then there is
           some seg' ∈ output, such that seg ℜ seg' and seg' is [αF].
           *Some output segment corresponding to an input segment preserves
           the feature specification [aF] of that input segment.*

∃-FAITH gives BRCT some purchase on the reduplication-specific junctural effects discussed in previous sections by potentially substituting for constraint indexation to the reduplication construction. ∃-FAITH limits certain types of alternations to just the context where one correspondent of an input segment is preserved. Struijke's analysis of Lushootseed appeals to ∃-FAITH to distinguish reduplication from nonreduplicative contexts. The insight is intuitive: reduction is, in principle, optional in both constructions. In nonreduplicated constructions, reduction is in a tug of war with ∃-FAITH, which is violated whenever reduction is satisfied. In reduplicative constructions, however, ∃-FAITH is satisfied even when reduction applies in the base, because the input vowel is still preserved intact in the reduplicant.

(48)

		/sčúsad/	Ǝ-FAITH	REDUCE
☞ a.	no reduction	sčúsad		*
b.	reduction	sčúsəd	*!	
		/RED-cáq'/		
c.	no reduction	cá-caq'		*!
☞ d.	reduction	cá-cq'		

If Ǝ-FAITH can not only resolve the ranking paradox which MDT resolves using different cophonologies but also predict which construction – reduplication or nonreduplication – will be associated with which pattern, Ǝ-FAITH would be an appealing alternative to cophonologies.

To evaluate the potential of Ǝ-FAITH to obviate cophonologies, we turn now to an in-depth exploration of the intuitions underlying Ǝ-FAITH and the predictions it makes. We ultimately conclude that Ǝ-FAITH is neither necessary nor sufficient in accounting for reduplicative phonology, nor can it extend, as cophonologies do, to nonreduplicative morphologically conditioned phonology.

4.4.1   Predictions of Ǝ-*FAITH*

Ǝ-FAITH potentially offers a way of understanding reduplicative phonology without recourse to cophonologies. The claim is that reduplicative phonology differs from nonreduplicative phonology for a functional reason: the existence of two correspondents for each output permits neutralization to occur once in reduplication even in languages that do not permit the corresponding neutralization process outside of reduplication.

This is not, however, the right generalization. As we will see, reduplicative phonology does not differ from nonreduplicative phonology in precisely this way. Ǝ-FAITH is therefore not sufficient to account for the differences between reduplicative and nonreduplicative constructions in the same language. Moreover, even within reduplicative constructions in the same language we find variation for which Ǝ-FAITH cannot account. The mechanisms required to describe this variation render Ǝ-FAITH unnecessary. Ǝ-FAITH is therefore neither necessary nor sufficient to account for reduplication-specific phonology. The intuition it embodies is not correct in any general way.

In this section we explore four aspects of ∃-FAITH that lead to the conclusion we have just stated.

(49)   a. ∃-FAITH undergenerates, predicting no overapplication of
            reduplication-specific phonology
         b. ∃-FAITH undergenerates, being unable to derive construction-
            specific insertion in reduplication
         c. ∃-FAITH is superfluous in handling reduplication-internal
            differences in the same language
         d. ∃-FAITH does not capture parallels between reduplicative and
            non-reduplicative construction-specific phonology

4.4.2   Overapplication of reduplication-specific phonology

∃-FAITH predicts that if a neutralization occurs in either the reduplicant or the base which does not occur generally in the language, it should affect only segments in one copy and, in particular, it should affect only those segments which have intact correspondents in the other copy. The reason is that if the neutralization does not occur generally, ∃-FAITH must outrank the relevant Markedness constraint; from that ranking it follows that the neutralization can affect only one of the two output correspondents of the input structure in question.

This prediction is, however, incorrect. It is possible to find double application of neutralization in reduplication. We saw cases in Chapter 2 of double Melodic Overwriting in which neither reduplicant nor base preserved an input segment that, outside of reduplication, is always preserved. Of course, Melodic Overwriting presents extra complications, and it could be that ∃-FAITH is simply outranked in that case by the need for the Melodic Overwriting affix(es) to surface. However, the case of Hausa reduplicative adjective formation is a real counterexample to the predictions of ∃-FAITH.

In Hausa, "[a]djectives are formed from common nouns by full reduplication of the underlying noun, preserving the original tone. This is accompanied by shortening of the final vowel of both parts" (Newman 2000:27):[21]

(50)   gishiri: gishiri-gishiri   'salt/salty'
         bùhu: bùhu-bùhu   'sack/sacklike'
         gà:ri: gà:ri-gà:ri   'flour/powdery'
         mà:kubà: mà:kubà-mà:kubà   'mahogany/dark brownish color'

The process of vowel shortening that occurs in both copies in reduplication does not occur in the unreduplicated forms, nor is word-final vowel shortening a general process in the language. The fact that vowel length contrasts are generally preserved word-finally in Hausa means that ∃-FAITH must outrank the ban on long vowels: ∃-FAITH » *FINAL-V:

(51)

	/ bùhuː/	ꓱ-FAITH	*FINAL-Vː
☞	bùhuː		
	bùhu	*!	

Following the logic of ꓱ-FAITH, it is possible, in a language with the general ranking ꓱ-FAITH » *FINAL-Vː, to get final vowel shortening in reduplication – but only once (52b), and only if BR-FAITH is ranked very low:

(52)

		/RED-bùhuː/	ꓱ-FAITH	*FINAL-Vː	BR-FAITH
possible	a.	bùhuː-bùhuː		**	
possible	b.	bùhuː-bùhu (or bùhu-bùhuː)		*	*
impossible	c.	bùhu-bùhu	*!		

Given the ranking ꓱ-FAITH » *FINAL Vː, there is no ranking of BR-FAITH that can achieve overapplication of final vowel shortening (52c). The only outcome ꓱ-FAITH does not predict possible is the actual outcome in Hausa.

A theory with ꓱ-FAITH could, of course, describe this Hausa construction if we abandon the general ranking of the language and rerank ꓱ-FAITH below *Final-Vː for this particular construction:

(53) Hausa generally: ꓱ-FAITH » *FINAL Vː
      Hausa adjective reduplication: *FINAL-Vː » ꓱ-FAITH

But this move undermines the primary motivation behind ꓱ-FAITH, which was to resolve ranking paradoxes without resorting to reranking. Once reranking is introduced as a possibility, there is no longer any need for ꓱ-FAITH; we can simply use cophonologies, as MDT does, which utilize markedness constraints and standard IO-FAITH to generate the right outcomes. The cophonological approach to Hausa is shown below:

(54) Hausa generally: IO-FAITH » *FINAL Vː
      Cophonologies X and Y in adjective reduplication: *FINAL-Vː » IO-FAITH

Once we acknowledge the need to rerank Faithfulness (whether IO-FAITH or ꓱ-FAITH) and markedness constraints across reduplicative and nonreduplicative constructions, ꓱ-FAITH becomes unnecessary as a tool for distinguishing reduplicative and nonreduplicative phonology.

4.4.3   *Construction-specific insertion*

Another prediction resulting from reliance on ∃-FAITH as the instrument of reduplication-specific phonology is that reduplication-specific phonology will be limited to alternations that alter material within the reduplicant or the base, and will not include insertion of material between the reduplicant and base. This prediction follows from the standard assumption that epenthetic material, especially at morpheme junctures, does not belong to either morpheme (see, for example, Prince & Smolensky 1993: 20–21 for a recent statement in Optimality Theory).

This prediction is overly restrictive, as illustrated in (55) by data from Fox. As described in Jones 1919; Dahlstrom 1997 (see also Burkhardt 2002) and discussed more extensively in Chapter 5, vowel hiatus at the base-reduplicant juncture is resolved via *h*-epenthesis. Data are taken from Dahlstrom 1997:

(55)   amwe-h-amwe:wa   'he eats him'   219
        ayo-h-ayo:ya:ni   'I use it; conjunct'   219
        iwa-h-iwa   'he says'   219

While the process of epenthesis at VV junctures is completely general, the quality of the epenthetic segment is construction specific. Vowel hiatus across prefix-stem junctures is broken up by an epenthetic *t* (56a), rather than *h*. (In yet a third morphological context, discussed in Dahlstrom 1997, *n* is used instead.) A form with both epenthetic *t* and epenthetic *h* is shown in (56b); the reduplicated stem is bracketed:

(56)   a. ke-t-en-a:wa   'you say to him'   220
        ne-t-amw-a:wa   'I eat him'   220
        ke-t-a:čimo   'you tell a story'   220
        ne-t-ek^wa   'he says to me'   221
        b. ne-t-[ena-h-ina:pi]   'I look [there]'   216

Following Optimality Theory approaches to markedness (e.g. Smolensky 1993; Kiparsky 1994; DeLacy 2002), we assume that the quality of epenthetic segments is determined by the relative ranking of faithfulness and markedness constraints. On this standard view, Fox therefore requires (at least) two different junctural cophonologies, one for affix-stem constructions and the other for reduplication. We use segment-specific IO-DEP here; other analyses are also imaginable:

(57)   Affix-Stem construction: IO-DEP(h) » IO-DEP(t)
        Reduplication construction: IO-DEP(t) » IO-DEP(h)

Since epenthesis in Fox involves insertion *between* reduplicant and base, rather than modification internal to either constituent, the difference between the two types of constructions cannot be reduced to a consequence of BR-FAITH constraints alone; the epenthetic segment is outside the scope of BR-FAITH. More to the point, junctural epenthesis also cannot be reduced to Ǝ-FAITH. This is because the intent of Ǝ-FAITH is to make sure that everything present under-lyingly appears somewhere on the surface. It will not be violated by the presence of anything extra on the surface (unless it violates Ǝ-CONTIGUITY, by insertion within a morpheme). Recognizing this, Struijke uses M-SEG (McCarthy 1993) in place of DEP, in the context of a different discussion, to regulate epenthesis in reduplication:

(58)   M-SEG 'Every segment belongs to a morpheme.'

The substitution of M-SEG for DEP in Fox is straightforward, but to achieve the necessary construction-specificity of the epenthetic segment, an M-SEG analysis still requires constraint reranking across different morphological con-structions. We therefore reach the same conclusion arrived at above: Ǝ-FAITH cannot take the place of constraint reranking, or cophonologies, in accounting for reduplication-specific phonology. Again, given the existence of cophonolo-gies, Ǝ-FAITH is superfluous.

4.4.4   *Reduplication-internal variation*

Another crucial lacuna in Ǝ-FAITH theory is its inability to capture varia-tion across reduplicative constructions in the same language. We will illustrate this point using data from Lushootseed. Recall, from our earlier discussion of Lushootseed, the caveat that the picture of Lushootsheed reduction presented in (45) was oversimplified in a crucial way.[22] The information missing from that picture is the following. As discussed in Urbanczyk 1996 and the literature cited therein, Diminutive reduplication is not uniformly subject to reduction. Rather, some stems reduce invariably when they reduplicate, including those shown in (45a), while others invariably fail to reduce when they reduplicate (Urbanczyk 1996:184ff.). The data below are taken from Urbanczyk 1996:186; unreduced unstressed /a/ vowels in reduplicated stems are in boldface:

(59)   Plain stem   Diminutive stem

Plain stem	Diminutive stem	
Xaƛ'-il	Xá-Xaƛ-il	'argue'/'squabble'
ƛac'=ap-əb	ƛ'á-ƛac'=ap-əd	'belt'/'ant, small (lit. little cinched up one)'
talə	tá?-talə	'dollar'/'small amount of money'
čagʷ-is	čá-čagʷ-is	'become irritated'/?

According to Urbanczyk, stems which fail to reduce in reduplication represent a minority pattern; nonetheless, they must be accounted for. Urbancyzk proposes a constraint reranking account (p. 184), which is equivalent to using cophonologies. The behavior of non-reducing stems requires the ranking IO-FAITH » REDUCE.

(60)   Reducing cophonology: REDUCE » IO-FAITH
        Non-reducing cophonology: IO-FAITH » REDUCE

The problem for Ǝ-FAITH is that if Ǝ-FAITH is substituted for IO-FAITH, the distinction between these two patterns collapses. Ǝ-FAITH predicts reduction in reduplication regardless of where it is ranked with respect to REDUCE.

(61)

	/RED-Xaλ'-il/	Ǝ-FAITH (V)	REDUCE
(☞) a.	Xá -Xaλ'-il		*!
💣 b.	Xá -Xλ'-il		

By its very nature Ǝ-FAITH is incapable of being reranked in such a way as to account for the difference between reducing and non-reducing variants of the diminutive reduplication construction. The Ǝ-FAITH analysis must rerank BR-FAITH instead, as shown below:

(62)   Non-reducing cophonology: Ǝ-FAITH » BR-FAITH » REDUCE
        Reducing cophonology: Ǝ-FAITH, REDUCE » BR-FAITH

A tableau showing the correct result for a non-reducing stem is given below (compare to the failed tableau, above):

(63)

	/RED-Xaλ'-il/	Ǝ-FAITH (V)	BR-FAITH	REDUCE
☞ a.	Xá -Xaλ'-il			*
b.	Xá -Xλ'-il		*!	

The only way to save the Ǝ-FAITH approach from descriptive inadequacy is to permit reranking of BR-FAITH and REDUCE across different reduplication constructions, as shown below.

(64)   Reducing reduplicative construction: Ǝ-FAITH, REDUCE » BR FAITH
        Non-reducing reduplication construction: Ǝ-FAITH, BR FAITH » REDUCE

But as soon as this is done, Ǝ-FAITH immediately becomes superfluous. Once we accept reranking of BR-FAITH with respect to Markedness constraints across different constructions, we have essentially emulated the MDT cophonology analysis, which requires neither Ǝ-FAITH nor BR-FAITH. As shown below, IO-FAITH and Markedness, ranked suitably in the two relevant cophonologies, are all that is needed:

(65)   Reducing cophonology: REDUCE » IO-FAITH
        Non-reducing cophonology: IO-FAITH » REDUCE

Ǝ-FAITH thus plays no role, in the end, in explaining the applicability of reduction in reduplication in Lushootseed. While the intuition it is intended to capture – that reduplication will exhibit more neutralization than is permitted outside reduplication, because of the increased opportunity it has to preserve input contrasts – is not falsified by the data, it is true only for a circumscribed portion of the data. A fully general approach to reduplicative phonology requires consideration of that data in a broader context.

Lushootseed is by no means unique; many other Salish languages exhibit variation in the application of syncope/reduction inside and outside of reduplication (on Bella Coola, for example, see Newman 1971; Broselow 1983; Nater 1984; 1990; Carlson 1997; Raimy & Idsardi 1997). Farther afield, we find variation of a different type in Hausa, where codas neutralize differently not only inside and outside of reduplication but also within the set of reduplication constructions the language possesses. Hausa imposes fairly strict constraints on codas throughout the language. Coronals are allowed the most leeway, exhibiting the following variety of behaviors (data and generalizations from Newman 2000):

(66)   Outside reduplication: plosives rhotacize; fricatives do not
                                  alternate (a)
        Most reduplication: all coronals rhotacize, including fricatives (b)
        Pluractional reduplication: all coronals geminate (c)

a.	ɓa:tà:		'to damage'	233
	ɓàr̃na:		'damage (n.)'	
cf.	kasko:		'earthen bowl'	233
	fizga:		'grab, snatch'	233
b.	/gwado:/ gwàr̃-gwado:		'proportion, moderation'	235
	/maza/ mar̃-maza		'very quickly'	235
	/kwà:sa:/ kwar̃-kwà:sa:		'driver ant'	235
c.	/fita/ fif-fita	(~ fir̃-fita)	'go out'	425
	/gasà:/ gag-gàsa:	(~ gar̃-gàsa:)	'roast'	425

It is clear that reduplicative phonology is not monolithic in nature.

4.4.5   *Parallels between reduplicative and nonreduplicative phonology*

The final argument against relying on ∃-FAITH to understand the differences between reduplicative and nonreduplicative phonology is the body of evidence in which the morphologically conditioned phonological effects that set some reduplication constructions apart from other constructions in the language find parallels in nonreduplicative constructions in the same language as well. Not only is reduplicative phonology not internally monolithic; it is also not distinct, in aggregate, from nonreduplicative phonology.

Like a blunt knife, ∃-FAITH divides constructions into reduplicative vs. nonreduplicative ones with respect to their predicted phonological behavior. However, we have seen from Lushootseed and Hausa that reduplication constructions in the same language are not identical in their phonology. What we will show now is that the same kinds of differences found among reduplicative constructions are found among nonreduplicative constructions as well, motivating a view like that in (c):

(67)

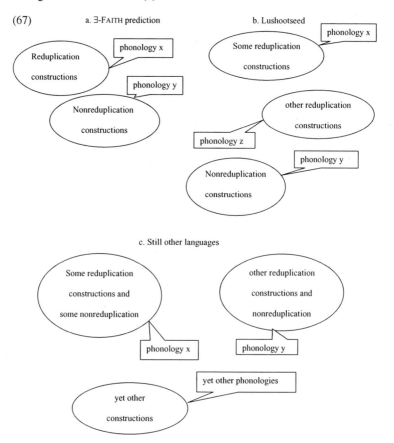

The facts we discuss are of a familiar type; the novelty in our discussion lies only in pointing out their implications for ∃-FAITH.

4.4.5.1 Reduplication and other derived environments

In Tohono O'odham (Uto-Aztecan), the primary differentiation in phonological behavior lines up with the distinction between morphologically derived and morphologically underived words. Stress assignment in Tohono O'odham places main stress on the initial syllable, followed by alternating secondary stress. The interesting twist in Tohono O'odham is that *nonderived* words prohibit final stress (69a), but *derived* ones permit it (69b) (Hill & Zepeda 1992; Fitzgerald 1999; 2000; Yu 2000 (Y); Fitzgerald 2001 (F); on Tohono O'odham phonology generally, see also Zepeda 1983; 1984; Hill & Zepeda 1998):

(68)   a. Nonderived words: *no stress on final syllable*
kí:	'house'	Y118
pí:ba	'pipe'	Y118
ʔásugal	'sugar'	Y118
síminǰul	'cemetery'	Y118

      b. Derived words: *stress permitted on final syllable*
cíkpan-dàm	'worker'	Y119
má:ginà-kam	'one with a car'	Y119
pímiàndo-màd	'adding pepper'	Y119

As shown in (69), reduplicated words pattern with derived words in allowing secondary stress to fall on the final syllable:

(69)
pí-pibà	'pipes'	Y119
pá-padò	'ducks'	F942
sí-sminǰùl (cf. síminǰul 'cemetery')	'cemeteries'	F945
tá-tablò	'shawls'	F945

This is a species of derived environment effect.[23] For our purposes, what makes it interesting is that it shows one common classification of words into subphonologies: derived vs. underived, where the derived words include both reduplicated and unreduplicated words. Yu (2000) demonstrates that the only approach to this derived environment effect that can succeed is one that includes distinct cophonologies for derived and underived words, as shown in (70). Simplifying Yu's analysis somewhat, the difference between the two cophonologies amounts to the relative ranking between PARSE-σ, which favors metrification of all syllables, and constraints that penalize final stress, represented here as NON-FINALITY (Prince & Smolensky 1993):

(70)   a. Underived: NON-FINALITY » PARSE-σ
        b. Derived: PARSE-σ » NON-FINALITY

Tohono O'odham manifestly requires indexation of cophonologies (or constraints) to broad construction types. ∃-FAITH is irrelevant, since reduplication patterns with nonreduplicative derivation. Fitzgerald (2001) proposes to derive the different stress patterns using a monostratal ranking, arguing that what drives final stress is a morpheme-to-stress constraint. In the case of suffixed words, this principle acts transparently to attract stress to the suffix. As Yu shows, however, this analysis is problematic for various reasons, the simplest being the fact that imperfective truncation attracts stress to the final syllable despite providing no overt morpheme on which the stress can surface:

(71)   Imperfective Perfective
---

a. síkon   síko   'hoe object (imperf/perf)'   Y130
b. wáčuwì-čud   wáčuwìc   'make someone bathe (imperf/perf)'   Y130
   bathe-CAUS
c. wákon-amɨd   wákon-àm   'go and wash (imperf/perf)'   Y130
   wash-to go

Yu's cophonology account works straightforwardly for these data. Imperfective truncation is a morphological construction whose output is morphologically derived; it therefore undergoes final stress assignment, a property of all cophonologies associated with morphologically derived environments.[24]

4.4.5.2   Reduplication and compounding

In Roviana (New Georgia; Northwest Solomonic subgroup of Oceanic), reduplication and compounding pattern together to the exclusion of other morphological constructions in three phonological respects (Corston-Oliver 2002:470): stress, vowel deletion, and consonant cluster reduction.[25] As shown in (72a), stress falls on the first syllable of both constituents in reduplication and in compounding. In suffixed words, by contrast, there is just one stress allowed per morphologically complex word (with the exception of the stressed transitive suffix -*i* [p. 469]).[26] As shown in (72b), both CVCV reduplication and compounding also optionally delete the second V in the first constituent; this apparently does not occur in other morphological constructions. Finally, as shown in (72c), clusters resulting from vowel deletion are simplified in the same way in reduplication (RED) and compounding (CPD): nasals assimilate in place to a following voiceless stop, geminates degeminate, and oral consonants optionally delete:

(72)

a.	RED	'ha^mbo-'ha^mbotu-ana[27]	'sit-sit-NML = chair'	469
	CPD	'βetu-'lotu	'house-pray = church'	469
b.	RED	ha^mbo-ha^mbotu-ana ~	'chair'	470
		ham-ha^mbotu-ana		
		peka-peka ~ pek-peka	'dance-dance = dancing'	470
	CPD	βetu-lotu ~ βet-lotu	'church'	470
c.	RED	heɣe-heɣere ~ heɣ-heɣere ~ he-heɣere	'laugh-laugh'	470
		ra-raro (< rar-raro < raro-raro)	'cook'	470
		pino-pino ~ pim-pino (< pin-pino)	'star'	470
	CPD	<no examples given>		

Even though vowel and consonant reduction are neutralization effects that could, in reduplication, be attributed to ∃-FAITH, an ∃-FAITH account would do nothing to capture the parallelism between reduplication and compounding with respect to these effects.

Parallelism, in particular languages, between compounding and reduplication constructions has often been noticed; a common response has been to propose that reduplication and compounding both operate on prosodic words. While this may well be the right approach to Roviana reduplication, it still does not eliminate the need for cophonologies. Vowel deletion is not a general phenomenon at the end of prosodic words in Roviana; thus, it is still necessary to specify, cophonologically, its occurrence in reduplication and compounding.

A similar constellation of reduplication and compounding is manifested in Burmese. As is typical of languages in the Tibeto-Burman family, Burmese imposes strict constraints on syllable structure. Complex onsets are allowed only in the "main," or "full" syllable of the word; a preceding "minor" syllable is permitted only a simplex onset. Green (2002) analyzes "full" syllables as feet and treats complex onsets as being licensed only foot-initially. Synchronic alternations show that this distributional generalization is actively enforced. As analyzed in VanBik 2003, Burmese has a process of compounding marked phonologically by voicing of the initial obstruent of the second member (e.g. *pè* 'peanut' + *pouʔ* 'rot/putrid' = *pè-bouʔ* 'fermented soybean'). Compounds are subject to reduction, whereby the rime of the first member reduces to [ə], and its onset simplifies and, if the second member begins with a voiced obstruent, voices:[28]

(73)
	a.	pà	+ moú	→	pə-moú
		'cheek'	'mound'		'prominence of cheek'
	b.	nwà	+ má	→	nə-má
		'cow'	'female'		'female cow'

c. θwà   + te?   → ðǝ-de?
   'tooth'   'rise'   'canine tooth'
d. pyà   + tu   → bǝ-du
   'bee'   'hammer' 'hornet'

Even though the onset reduction in reduplication might normally call out for an ∃-FAITH account, the clear parallelism between compounding and reduplication shows that ∃-FAITH is irrelevant in this reduction process.

4.4.5.3 Random grouping of things with same cophonology

Hausa is known for its distinction between affixes which preserve base tone and those which replace base tone with a fixed melody. Newman (1986; 2000) terms these "non-tone-integrating" and "tone-integrating," respectively. Whether or not a given affix is tone-integrating (the majority pattern) is, at least synchronically, an essentially arbitrary fact about that affix.

As illustrated below, reduplication constructions are no different from affixation constructions in subdividing, arbitrarily, into those that are tone-integrating and those that are not. The number of reduplication and affixation constructions in Hausa is very large; we have selected only four here, for illustration. The interested reader is encouraged to consult Newman (2000), from whose work this data is drawn, as well as Downing (2004) for a recent survey of such effects.

(74)   a. Tone-integrating, nonreduplicative: plural -*ai*; L*H (p. 434)
           ɗa:lìbi: (HLH) → ɗà:lìb-ai (LL-H) 'student(s)'
           àlmùbazzàr̃i: (LLHLH) → àlmùbàzzàr̃-ai (LLLL-H) 'spendthrift(s)'
           màka:nikè: (LHHL) → màkà:nìk-ai (LLL-H) 'mechanic(s)'
        b. Non-tone-integrating; nonreduplicative: -*wa:* verbal noun former; (L)H
           (p. 705)
           kar̃ànta: (HLH) → kar̃àntâ:-wa: (HLH͡-LH) 'read(ing)'
           tso:ratar̃ (HHH) → tso:ratâr̃-wa: (HHH͡-LH) 'frighten(ing)'
        c. Tone integrating; reduplicative: Hypocoristic formation; L*HH output
           tone (p. 348)
           Àlhajì (LHL) → Àlhàji:-ji (LLH-H)
           La:dì (HL) → Là:di:-di (LH-H)
           Mùɗɗe (LH) → Mùɗɗe:-ɗe (LH-H)
        d. Non-tone-integrating; reduplicative: pluractional CVG- (p. 425–26)[29]
           dà:gurà: (LHL) → dàd-dà:gurà: (L-LHL) 'gnaw at (pluractional)'
           girma (HH) → gig-girma (H-HH) 'grow up (pluractional)'
           mutù (HL) → mur̃-mutù (H-HL) 'die (pluractional)'

The relevance of these data to the theoretical treatment of morphologically conditioned phonology is discussed by Inkelas (1998), who applies the terms "dominant" and "recessive" to tone-integrating and non-tone-integrating constructions. Inkelas argues on grounds of scope and layering that each morphological construction must be associated with a cophonology which either deletes or preserves input tone.

The distinctive tonal phonology of certain Hausa reduplication constructions has nothing to do with special reduplicative faithfulness. First, tone-integrating reduplication completely wipes out input stem tone; ∃-FAITH is playing no role. Second, tone-integrating affixation shows the same behavior. The differences between reduplication and nonreduplication constructions are identical to the differences obtaining within reduplication, on the one hand, and within nonreduplication constructions, on the other.

4.4.6   Wrapup

Our discussion of ∃-FAITH has revealed that even in a theory with ∃-FAITH constraints, it is still necessary to appeal to cophonologies to capture the full range of reduplicative phonology. Once cophonologies are invoked, ∃-FAITH becomes superfluous. ∃-FAITH is neither necessary nor sufficient in the analysis of reduplicative phonology.

The main problem with ∃-FAITH lies with its twin presuppositions that reduplicative phonology is different from nonreduplicative phonology and that the difference emanates from base-reduplicant identity. Both presuppositions, however, derive from an overly narrow focus on reduplication. By situating reduplication in the larger context of morphologically conditioned phonology, we have found that the same cophonological approach needed outside reduplication is necessary, and sufficient, to account for reduplicative phonology as well.

Part of the appeal of ∃-FAITH lies in its evocation of a commonly held view that contrast preservation is a desideratum of grammar. Reduplication, offering two chances to preserve each input contrast, might therefore be expected to behave differently from other constructions. Syntagmatically, certainly, we have seen that ∃-FAITH is not substantiated. The paradigmatic function of contrast preservation is harder to evaluate, and may have some truth. It is possible that functional pressures to recover input information have created a situation in which reduction is more likely, statistically, within reduplication; we do not know, and it would take a massive diachronic and synchronic study to be able to test this hypothesis. In any case, if one looks only at the types of reductions that are possible, one finds that reduplicants have no special status.

4.5   Conclusion

Reduplication constructions, as wholes, are often associated with phonological effects not observed generally in the language. We have argued at length that this phenomenon is exactly parallel to the phenomenon of morphologically conditioned phonology outside of reduplication. Theories that approach reduplication out of morphological context and focus exclusively on effects that appear related to the phonological identity between bases and reduplicant miss the larger picture and unnecessarily burden the theory with reduplication-specific analytical tools.

5 *Morphologically driven opacity in reduplication*

One of the objectives driving theories of reduplication is accounting for opacity effects, to which reduplication is perceived to be exceptionally prone. Opacity is the situation in which an alternation which, elsewhere in the language, is normally conditioned in some particular environment either exceptionally fails to apply in the expected environment or exceptionally applies in another environment where it is not supposed to (Kiparsky 1973a). In reduplication, the former phenomenon is termed "underapplication"; the latter, "overapplication."

Dakota (Shaw 1980:344–45) provides an example of the kind of opacity with which reduplication is rife. In Dakota, velars palatalize after /i/; spirants voice intervocalically. In the example of CVC reduplication, below, velar palatalization "overapplies" in the sense that it is conditioned transparently in the first copy of the root but not in the second:

(1)   wičʰá-ki-čax-čax-ʔiyèya   'he made it for them quickly'   (/kax/)
       napé kí-čos-čoz-a   'he waved his hand to him'   (/kos/)

Because of languages in which reduplication appears to be the only morphological context exhibiting a given pattern of overapplication or underapplication, opacity has emerged as a hallmark of reduplication. In a number of theories (Clements 1985, Mester 1986, McCarthy & Prince 1995a), reduplicative opacity is given special treatment that distinguishes it from other kinds of opacity. Recent work on reduplication (McCarthy & Prince 1995a, building on Wilbur 1973) has attributed reduplicative opacity effects to principles of base-reduplicant identity. These approaches presuppose that opacity effects increase identity between base and reduplicant.

This chapter, building on the results of Chapters 3 and 4, presents a different view. In MDT reduplicative opacity follows from the morphology of reduplication constructions, which often conspires to obscure the conditions on the application of phonological processes. The same approach that is taken in MDT to opacity in nonreduplicative constructions carries over to reduplication as well, without the need for reduplication-specific proposals like BR correspondence.

The perception that opacity is particularly prevalent in reduplication derives from the fact that there are multiple sources for opacity in any given reduplicated word. A principal factor is the morphological layering intrinsic to the MDT reduplication construction, which gives rise to the cyclic, or stratal, interactional effects to which Kiparsky (2000) attributes opacity in general.

In MDT, the output of the daughter cophonologies serves as input to the mother cophonology. There are thus three cophonologies involved, and any of them may produce opacity. For example, truncation within one of the daughters may render opaque another phonological alternation that the daughter undergoes. This type of daughter-based opacity occurs in Javanese, as discussed in §5.1. Alternatively, infixation of one daughter into the other at the mother node level may obscure phonological alternations conditioned within one of the daughters. Mother-based opacity of this kind is discussed in §5.2.1 and in the case studies in Chapter 6.

As we will show in a number of case studies presented in this chapter – Javanese, in §5.1, Eastern Kadazan and Chamorro, in §5.2, and Fox, in §5.5, among others – the cophonologies associated with reduplication in MDT are sufficient to account for opacity effects in reduplication. Reduplication-specific opacity-inducing mechanisms like Wilbur's Identity Constraint, or McCarthy and Prince's (1995a) BR correspondence relations, which have been invoked in phonological copying theories, turn out to be unnecessary once the role of morphology in reduplication is properly exploited. BR identity is not enhanced by all cases of reduplicative opacity; BR identity is therefore not a sufficient explanation for these effects. Further, identity-based theories of opacity make incorrect predictions about what kinds of reduplicative opacity are possible, as argued in §5.4.

Our claim that cophonologies and layering drive the opacity effects that have attracted attention in reduplication connects with the strong claim of Kiparsky 2000, according to whom all opacity effects, not just those in reduplication, arise through stratal ordering: a process on stratum n obliterates the environment which transparently conditions a process applying on stratum n-i. While we do not agree with Kiparsky that all phonological opacity has a stratal (layering) source, we do agree that much of the opacity found in reduplication is of this kind.

5.1   Daughter-based opacity: overapplication and underapplication in Javanese

Javanese is rife with instances of phonological opacity in reduplication, some of which have featured prominently in the theoretical literature (e.g. McCarthy &

Prince 1995a). Opacity in Javanese is daughter-internal, arising when truncation deletes input phonological structure that is crucial to determining the applicability of an alternation whose effects are opaquely present – or in some cases opaquely absent – on the material that survives truncation. Our understanding of Javanese is based on the following sources: Horne 1961 (H); Sumukti 1971 (S); Dudas 1976 (D); see also Uhlenbeck 1953; 1954. Many parallel effects occur in Johore Malay (Onn 1976).

5.1.1   /a/-raising: underapplication by truncation

Javanese has a total reduplication construction applying to adjectives and verbs; the construction is characterized by Dudas (1976) as indicating "various sorts of plurality – either of objects or actions – although there are certain cases where it is used in conjunction with a specific affix with a slightly different semantic import" (p. 202). According to Horne (1961), "Doubled adjectives . . . have a plural meaning: either they modify more than one noun, or they modify a plural noun . . . Some (not all) active verbs may be doubled . . . In general, the meaning conveyed by a doubled verb is a less purposeful action than for the single verb; perhaps it is performed without serious aim, or lazily. Or, it may be done over an extended period of time, or repeatedly" (pp. 221–22). The examples below are taken from Horne 1961:222–23. Because transcription systems for Javanese vowels vary across sources, we have converted all transcriptions of vowels to IPA here:[1]

(2) kirɔ   'think'   kirɔ-kirɔ   'about, approximately'
     takɔn   'ask'   takɔn-takɔn   'keep asking'
     wɔtjɔ   'read'   di-wɔtjɔ-wɔtjɔ   passive of 'read without concentration'
     turu   'sleep'   turu-turu   'fall asleep'

The reason Javanese has attracted interest in the reduplication literature is illustrated by the /a/ ~ /ɔ/ alternation in (3): /a/ surfaces before suffixes, as shown in (3b), but raises to /ɔ/ word-finally (3a) and in both copies in bare stem reduplication (3c). What has attracted attention are the data in (3d): when a stem is both reduplicated and suffixed, both of its copies end in /a/, despite the fact that the first is unsuffixed. Because /ɔ/ is expected when no suffix follows, /a/-raising can be said to be underapplying in the first copy of the verb roots in (d):[2]

(3) a. medjɔ   'table'   H70, D206
     b. medja-ku   'my table'   H70
        medja-mu   'your table'   H70
        medja-ne   'his/her table'   H70
     c. medjɔ-medjɔ   'tables'   D206, H70

d. medja-medja-ku   'my tables'   H70
   medja-medja-mu   'your tables'   H70
   medja-medja-ne   'his/her tables'   H70, D206

In a BR-identity approach (McCarthy & Prince 1995a), the opacity in (3d) could be attributed to the requirement that the final vowels in reduplicant and base must be identical, whether constrained in the second copy to be /ɔ/ (when final) or /a/ (when suffixed).

Our perspective on these data is entirely different. Supported by evidence from a number of suffixed reduplicated stems, we argue that /a/ raising is transparently conditioned within each daughter of reduplication. In (3c), the daughters are both bare stems; in (3d), they are both suffixed stems. The conditions inhibiting raising are rendered opaque in the first daughter of (3d) by truncation, which deletes the suffixal material entirely.

The two analyses are compared below:

(4)   Opacity by BR identity   Opacity by truncation

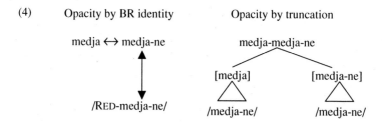

Although the data in (3) are neutral between the two analyses in (4), abundant evidence within Javanese supports the opacity-by-truncation analysis.

5.1.2   Suffix-triggered ablaut: overapplication by truncation
Initial support for holding truncation responsible for opacity effects in Javanese reduplication comes from the co-occurrence of reduplication with causative and locative suffixes. Javanese has three causative suffixes: the simple Causative /-(q)akɛ/, the Causative Imperative /-(q)nɔ/, and the Causative Subjunctive /-(q)nɛ/. There is a similar array of locative suffixes: the simple Locative /-(n)i/, the Locative Imperative /-(n)ɔnɔ/, and the Locative Subjunctive /-(n)ane/. The parenthesized consonants surface when the preceding root is vowel-final; recall that "q" represents [ʔ]. Although our sources (Horne 1961; Sumukti 1971; Dudas 1976) do not do this, it seems reasonable to treat /-(q)-/ and /-(n)-/ as general causative and locative stem formers, respectively; these consonantal suffixes, or their zero allomorphs, create bound stems to which one of the three available extensions must attach.

These consonantal causative and locative stem-forming suffixes trigger particular specific effects on the preceding stem vowel (Horne 1961:176, 208), which we will refer to by the cover term "Ablaut." Causative /-(q)-/ lowers /ɔ/ to /a/, /u/ and /o/ to /ɔ/, and /i/ and /e/ to /ɛ/; the Locative /-(n)-/ triggers these same effects as well as tensing /ɪ/ and /ʊ/ to /i/ and /u/. Illustrative examples are provided below. (Note that all of the verbs are cited in their full form and bear either the *ng-* active prefix or the *di-* passive prefix. On the *ng-* prefix in reduplication, see §5.1.4.)

(5)

Plain stem	Gloss of root	Causative	Locative	Alternation	
bisɔ	'can, be able'	di-bisa-q-ake	di-bisa-n-i	ɔ → a	H209, 178
laku	'walk'	nge-lakɔ-q-ake	nge-lakɔ-n-i	u → ɔ	H212, 179
(a)nggo	'use, wear'	ng-anggɔ-q-ake	ng-anggɔ-n-i	o → ɔ	H213, 180
bali	'return'	m-balɛ-q-ake	m-balɛ-n-i	i → ɛ	H209, 177
gawe	'make'	di-gawɛ-q-ake	ng-gawɛ-n-i	e → ɛ	H208, 178
apeq	'good, nice'	ng-apeq-ake	ng-apiq-i	eC → iC	H209, 177

When causative and locative stems are reduplicated, identical stem vowels occur in the two copies, parallel to the phenomenon manifested in the suffixed reduplicated stems in §5.1.1. In the case of causative and locative suffixation there is positive evidence pointing to the source of this effect. As shown in (6), the consonantal causative and locative stem formers surface on both copies when the root in question is vowel-final (see, for example, Sumukti 1971:97, Horne 1961:223, Dudas 1976:31). Double underlining identifies those vowels and consonants in the reduplicant for whose quality (or existence) the suffix is responsible:

(6)

	Root	Suffixed stem		Reduplicated suffixed stem	
a.	ambu 'odor'	ng-ambɔ-q-akɛ	(CAUS)	ngambɔq-ngambɔqake	D31
		ng-ambɔ-n-i	(LOC)	ngambɔn-ngambɔni	D31
b.	bali 'return'	m-balɛ-q-ake	(CAUS)	mbalɛq-mbalɛqake	D31
		m-balɛ-n-i	(LOC)	mbalɛn-mbalɛni	D31
c.	djərɔ 'deep'	n-djərɔ-q-ake	(CAUS)	ndjərɔq-ndjərɔ-qake	D31
		n-djərɔ-n-i	(LOC)	ndjərɔn-ndjərɔ-ni	D31
d.	uni 'sound'	ng-unɛ-q-ake	(CAUS)	unɛq-unɛ-q(a)ke	H216, S97
				'to berate'	
e.	tibɔ 'to fall'	tiba-q-(a)ke	(CAUS)	tibaq-tiba-q(a)ke	S97
				'repeatedly drop'	

Why do only the causative and locative stem-forming consonants, rather than the entire causative and locative suffix complexes, surface on the first copy? One possibility is morphological: perhaps only the causative and locative stem formers are present in the input to reduplication, with the extensions being added to the entire reduplicated stem. The other hypothesis, which we adopt here, is phonological: the reduplicant, i.e. the output of Cophonology X, is subject to a restriction that its syllable count cannot exceed that of the input root. We formalize this by positing a constituent, the Proot (Prt), which contains all of the syllables of the morphological root (Rt), plus any surrounding consonants which can syllabify into the Proot without increasing its syllable count (see (8) for formalization). Cophonology X truncates its input down to the Proot, which consists of the material in the morphological root plus any incorporated affixal consonants. In the schema below, representing the derivation of 'berate' in (6d), each daughter takes as input the Causative stem *ʃuneqʃake*, based on the input /uni-q-ake/. Cophonology X truncates its input down to the Proot, {uneq}; Cophonology Y is faithful.

(7) Causative stem formation: {uneq}ake   *Ablaut triggered by -q-*

/uni$_{Rt}$-q-ake/

Reduplication of causative stem: {unɛq}{unɛq}ake

                                          {unɛq}   {unɛq}ake
Cophon. X: truncation to Proot ⇒ | | ⇐ Cophon. Y: Identity
                                        {uneq}ake   {uneq}ake

Ablaut, triggered by the Causative stem former /-(q)-/, applies on the causative stem cycle; its effects are thus present in the *input* to the first daughter of reduplication. Because truncation removes most of the triggering suffix material, the ablaut is nearly opaque on the surface.[3]

Constituents like the Proot, based on but not identical to a morphological constituent, have a long history in phonological analysis; see, for example, Booij 1984; Nespor & Vogel 1986; Sproat 1986; Inkelas 1990; Booij & Lieber 1993, among many others. The role of P-constituents in reduplication has been explored by Cole (1994) and Downing (1998c; 1998d) (see also Pykllänen 1999), who document a number of onset overcopying cases in which a segment from an adjacent morpheme is incorporated (or "conscripted," to use Cole's term) into a following Proot, often to satisfy onset or minimality requirements on the root. Our analysis of Javanese is firmly rooted within this tradition of mismatches between morphological and prosodic constituents.

The Root-Proot (RP) correspondence constraints involved in truncating the output to a Proot which is based on the input morphological Root but which incorporates an adjacent non-Root consonant are given below:

(8) RP-Max-seg: All root segments should have correspondents in the Proot
RP-Max-syl: All root syllables should have correspondents in the Proot
RP-Dep-syl: All Proot syllables should have correspondents in the root
RP-Dep-seg: All Proot segments should have correspondents in the root
IP-Max-seg: All input segments should have correspondents in the Proot

In Javanese, RP-Max constraints are always satisfied; the Proot always includes the Mroot. Of interest is the potential for the Proot to contain affix material as well. The ranking illustrated in (9), RP-DEP-syl » IP-MAX-seg » RP-DEP-seg, results in inclusion of non-root input segments in the Proot when doing so does not add syllables to the Proot which lack correspondents in the root:

(9)

	uni-q-ake	RP-DEP-SYL	IP-MAX-SEG	RP-DEP-SEG
a.	{unɛ}qake		qake!	
b.	{unɛqake}	qa!, ke		qake
☞ c.	{unɛq}ake		ake	q
d.	{u}nɛqake		niqake	

Semantic evidence is consistent with this analysis of reduplicated causative and locative roots. The meaning of verb reduplication is inflectional, conveying randomness or casualness. Causative and locative affixation are clearly derivational. Thus even without any phonological evidence we would automatically expect the causative or locative to be present in the input to reduplication, as the MDT analysis claims, rather than the opposite.

Further evidence that suffixes whose effects are felt in both copies are in fact present in both inputs to reduplication, if not necessarily in both outputs, comes from the nominalizing suffix -/(a)n/, which surfaces as /-an/ following consonant-final stems and as /-n/ following vowel-final stems.[4] Like the causative and locative suffixes, the nominalizer triggers its own pattern of stem vowel ablaut:

(10)   a. tules   'write'   tulis-an   'handwriting, script'   H126
           raop   'wash face' raup-an   'water in which face   H126
                                             has been washed'
           tutop   'close'   tutup-an   'a closed house with   H126
                                             nobody at home'
        b. tuku   'buy'   tukɔ-n   'money for buying   H126
                                             something/things bought'
           wɔtjɔ   'read'   watja-n   'reading matter'   H126
           tampi   'receive'   tampɛ-n   'amount of money   H136
                                             received'

When vowel-final stems, i.e. those taking the /-n/ allomorph of the nominalizer, are reduplicated, the suffixal /-n/ surfaces, as expected under the MDT analysis, in both copies; not surprisingly, the ablaut patterns triggered by /-n/ appear in both copies as well:[5]

(11)   /uni/   'sound'   unɛ-n+unɛ-n   'noise, saying' S98
        /aŋgo/   'to wear'   aŋgɔ-n+aŋgɔ-n   'jewelry'   S98
        /ombe/   'to drink'   ombɛ-n+ombɛ-n   'beverage'   S98

When, however, the root is consonant-final, /-an/ surfaces only following the second copy. As predicted in the MDT account, the ablaut effects associated with the nominalizer are nonetheless found on both copies:

(12)   apeq   'good, nice'   apiq+apiq-an   'something nice'   H127
        ɛntoq   'receive, get'   ɛntuq+ɛntuq-an   'use, benefit'   H127
        ḍon   'descend; get off' ḍun+ḍun-an   'things which have been H127
                                                       taken off or unloaded'

The analysis already developed for reduplicated causative and locative roots extends straightforwardly to the nominalizer. Cophonology X truncates the suffixed, nominalized stem input down to its Proot, which consists of the input morphological root plus any adjacent material that can syllabify into the Proot without increasing its syllable count. This analysis correctly predicts that only the /n/ allomorph of the nominalizer will survive truncation; vowel ablaut effects, however, will surface in the output of Cophonology X regardless of whether suffixal material does. Example (13) shows nominalizer stem formation for vowel-final and consonant-final roots, and (14) illustrates the fate of Nominalized stems in reduplication:

(13)   {unɛn}   {apiq}an
          ∧   ∧   *Cophonology ablauts final stem vowel*
        /uni$_{Rt}$ -an/   /apeq$_{Rt}$ -an/

(14)

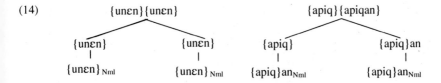

The MDT analysis in which reduplication operates on nominalized stems is consistent with cross-linguistic expectations about the relative ordering of morphological constructions in the same word; as a derivational process, nominalization is expected to occur inside of an inflectional process like Javanese reduplication.[6]

5.1.3   *Opacity in suffixation and reduplication: wrapup*

Our discussion of opacity in suffixed Javanese reduplicated stems began, in §5.1.1, with forms like *medjɔ-medjɔ* 'tables' and *medja-medja-ku* 'my tables'; we proposed there that the opaque distribution of /a/ and /ɔ/ in the output of reduplication is due to truncation. The daughters of the construction whose output is *medjɔ-medjɔ* are both [medjɔ]; the daughters of *medja-medja-ku* are both, on the MDT account, [medja-ku]. /a/-raising applies (or fails to apply) transparently in the daughters in both cases; its failure to apply in the first stem copy in *medja-medja-ku* is obscured by the fact that the suffix *-ku* is not part of the Proot and therefore does not survive truncation in the output of the first copy, as shown below:

(15)

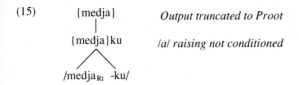

                      Output truncated to Proot

                      /a/ raising not conditioned

The question arises at this point as to why the *k* of *-ku* cannot syllabify into the Proot, yielding **medjak-medjaku*, in the same manner as the *-q* Causative stem former (as in (6)) or the *-n* allomorph of the Nominalizer (as in (11)). We hypothesize that a principle of Morpheme Integrity, along the lines of that proposed for Kinande by Mutaka and Hyman 1990, prevents the partial parsing of Javanese affixes into the Proot. Either the whole suffix (if consonantal) incorporates into the Proot, or none of it does. What distinguishes the Causative *-q* and Nominalizer *-n* suffix allomorphs is that they are monoconsonantal, able to syllabify in their entirety into a preceding vowel-final Proot.

5.1.4   Active prefix

The account developed thus far, which attributes opacity in suffixed reduplicated stems to truncation of the first stem copy to its Proot, provides insight into an interaction between prefixation and reduplication in Javanese that has been cited in the literature as support for BR Identity. The prefix in question is the Active prefix, one of two prefixes (the other being Passive *-di*) found on most transitive verbs (see, for example, Dudas 1976:14).

As shown in (16), the Active prefix, typical of nasal-final prefixes throughout Austronesian, fuses phonologically with the following root under certain phonological conditions, on which see Dudas 1976:14–15 and Horne 1961:103. If the root is vowel-initial, the Active prefix surfaces as [ŋ] (*ng*) or in some cases [m] (Horne 1961:103). The Active prefix surfaces as prenasalization on a following voiced obstruent (16b); it fuses completely with a following voiceless obstruent or sonorant, resulting in a fully nasal consonant (16c).[7]

(16)	a.	adjar	'learn'	ngadjar	D15
		uleh	'go home'	m-uleh	H103
	b.	bajar	'pay, salary'	m-bajar	D15
		golɛq	'get, seek'	ng-golɛq	D15
	c.	kɛləm	'become submerged'	ngɛləm	D15
		tulɪs	'write'	nulɪs	D15
		sijʊng	'canine tooth'	njijʊng	D15
		wɔtjɔ	'read'	mɔtjɔ	D15

The behavior of the Active prefix in reduplication has attracted attention in the literature (e.g. McCarthy & Prince 1995a) because of its propensity to occur on both copies. According to Dudas, when the verb root begins with the type of consonant with which the Active prefix does not fuse segmentally, the prefix can appear either on both copies or only on the first (17a, b). However, when the verb root begins with the kind of consonant with which the Active prefix does fuse, the prefix must be doubled (17c):

(17)	a.	ɪdaq	'to step'	ŋɪdaq-ɪdaq	'keep stepping'		S89
	b.	balɪq	'turn'	mbalɪq-mbalɪq-ake ~ mbalɪq-balɪq-ake			D30
	c.	tulɪs	'write'	nules-nules	'write aimlessly, without	H222
					accomplishing much'	
				nulɪs-nulɪs-ake	(*nulɪs-tulɪs-ake)		D30

Horne, who does not mention the possibility of phonological variation of the kind Dudas describes, presents the facts somewhat differently, stating that reduplication can either precede or follow Active prefixation (1976: 222–23). Horne offers forms like the following to illustrate the two options: First prefix, then reduplicate: *tules* 'write' → *nules* → *nules-nules*, or first reduplicate and then prefix: *isen* 'shy' → *isen-isen* → *ng-isen-isen*. The five examples Horne cites (1976:223) of this latter type begin with vowels or /l/, falling into the class of root types for which Dudas says Active prefix doubling is optional.

Unless a clear semantic difference can be found between the two construction types Horne describes (and see Uhlenbeck 1954 for suggestive discussion), we assume Dudas is correct in treating the difference as essentially phonological; however, the issue clearly requires further investigation by those better versed than we are in Javanese morphology. It should also be borne in mind that, according to Onn (1976), verb reduplication in Johore Malay patterns almost identically with Dudas's characterization of Javanese.

Assuming, with Dudas, that the distribution of the Active prefix is phonologically determined, the issue becomes one of under what conditions the nasal prefix can be recruited into the Proot. Both Downing (1998c; 1998d) and Cole (1994) have proposed to handle effects similar to these in other languages by conscripting a preceding consonant into a following Pword.[8] A prefix which has fused phonologically with the stem-initial consonant must be conscripted: /ng-tulis/ → *[nulis]*. Prefixes which retain their segmental integrity appear, on Dudas's description, to have the option of incorporating or not (e.g. *m-balɪq* → *m[balɪq]* ~ *[mbalɪq]*).

5.1.5   /h/-deletion: overapplication

/h/-deletion is the third alternation type (in addition to vowel changes and Active prefix nasal fusion) contributing to reduplicative opacity in Javanese; like Active prefix nasal fusion, it has been invoked as support for BR correspondence (McCarthy & Prince 1995a:285–87). However, BR correspondence is not needed in the analysis of /h/-deletion, whose behavior follows straightforwardly from the MDT analysis we have already developed.

Intervocalic /h/- deletion is triggered by certain, though not all, vowel-initial suffixes; (18) illustrates its application before Locative, Demonstrative, and Hortatory suffixes:

(18)   a. Locative   Stem

ng-adɔ-i	adɔh	'far'	D164
ng-akɛ-i	akɛh	'much, many'	D164
m-ili-i	pilɪh	'choose'	D164
nj-ala-i	salah	'mistaken'	D164

b. Demonstrative

ane-e	aneh	'strange'	D133
kɔkɔ-e (> kɔkɔwe)	kokoh	'rice mixed into soup'	D133

c. Hortatory

sarɛ-ɔ	sarɛh	'be patient!'	S92

/h/-deletion is suffix-specific; as illustrated below, for example, vowel-initial allomorphs of causative suffixes do *not* trigger /h/-deletion:[9]

(19)

	Causative	Stem		
	ng-adɔh-ake	adɔh	'far'	D164
	ng-akɛh-ake	akɛh	'much, many'	D164
	m-ilɪh-ake	pilɪh	'choose'	D164
	nj-alah-ake	salah	'mistaken'	D164

Because /h/-deletion is suffix-specific, it must be accomplished by the cophonology associated with the triggering suffixes. (We will assume that the relevant suffixes all trigger an /h/-deleting cophonology.) The following example illustrates Demonstrative stem formation:

(20)   {bəda}e   *Cophonology deletes intervocalic /h/*
                  ∧
         bədah$_{RI}$-e/

What has drawn attention in the literature is the following: In reduplicated suffixed /h/-final roots, /h/-deletion opaquely overapplies in the first copy when a vowel-initial suffix follows the second copy (and causes deletion there):

(21)

	Reduplication	Suffix + reduplication		
a.	bədah-bədah	bəda-bəda-e	cf. bədah 'broken'	D208
b.	ḍajɔh-ḍajɔh	ḍajɔ-ḍajɔ-e	cf. ḍajɔh[10] 'guest'	D209
c.	tɔngah-tɔngah 'middle'	tɔnga-tɔnga-e 'the middle'		H71
d.	kukʊh-kukʊh	kuku-kuku-w-e	cf. kukʊh 'solid'	D209
e.		njala-njala-i	cf. salah 'make a mistake'	D154–155
f.		oma-oma-an 'to play house'	cf. omah 'house'	S92
g.		saq-adɔ-adɔ-e 'as far as possible'	cf. adɔh 'far'	S92
h.		pili-pili-y-an	cf. pilɪh 'choose'	D154

The MDT analysis developed for Javanese reduplication handles these cases straightforwardly. The suffix triggering /h/-deletion is present in the input to both copies in reduplication; the first copy undergoes truncation to its Proot, preserving the effects of /h/-deletion but obscuring its suffixal trigger. This is illustrated below for the reduplicated demonstrative form of 'broken' (21a). The inputs to reduplication are both *[bəḍa]e*, itself the output of the Demonstrative stem-forming construction whose input is /bəḍah-e/:

(22)

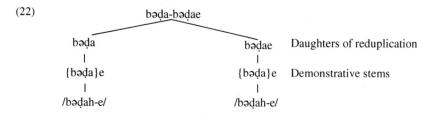

	bəḍa-bəḍae	
bəḍa	bəḍae	Daughters of reduplication
{bəḍa}e	{bəḍa}e	Demonstrative stems
/bəḍah-e/	/bəḍah-e/	

As with /a/-raising and nasal prefix fusion, /h/-deletion is opaque in the first copy because the environment which conditions its application within the suffixed stem is obscured by morphological truncation in reduplication.

5.1.6   Laxing: underapplication

Thus far in our discussion of Javanese we have seen several examples of overapplication and one example of underapplication (/a/-raising). A significant plank of support for the MDT analysis of opacity is that it predicts whether a given alternation which is transparent in the daughters of the reduplication construction will, as a result of reduplicative truncation, appear to exhibit overapplication vs. underapplication. If truncation obscures a trigger for the alternation (as in /h/-deletion), the result will appear to be overapplication; if truncation removes the environment inhibiting the alternation (as in /a/-raising), the result will appear to be underapplication. By contrast, in BRCT whether a given alternation overapplies or underapplies is an arbitrary effect of constraint ranking, not predictable from the nature of the alternation itself. We illustrate this point with our final case study from Javanese, a pattern of alternations in suffixed stems that affects both vowels and consonants.

As shown in (23), High Vowel Laxing laxes high tense vowels in stem-final closed syllables (Dudas 1976:55ff.).

(23)

UR	Plain	Demonstrative	Gloss
/apiq/	apɪq	apiq-e	'good (-demonstrative)'
/kluwung/	kluwʊng	kluwung-e	'rainbow (-demonstrative)'
/djupuq/	djupʊq	n-djupuq-ɔ	'go get (-hortatory)'
/tulis/	tulɪs	nulis-ɔ	'write (-hortatory)'
/wiwit/	wiwɪt	wiwit-an	'beginning (-substantive)'

Consonants alternate as well. As described by Dudas (1976:118–19), certain stem-final consonants alternate between "heavy" (voiced) and "light" (voiceless): they are voiceless word-finally or before a C-initial suffix, but voiced before V-initial suffixes, e.g. the Demonstrative, illustrated below:

(24)   Plain   Demonstrative

gaɪp	gaib-e	'secret'	D118
səbap	səbab-e	'because'	D118
bləbət	bləbəd-e	'protective cover'	D118
djogɛt	djogɛd-e	'the classical Javanese dance'	D118

Dudas terms this pattern Consonant Neutralization; we will refer to it instead as Devoicing. Both High Vowel Laxing and Consonant Devoicing underapply in reduplicated suffixed stems. Example (25) illustrates the failure of High Vowel Laxing to apply to the first daughter of a reduplicated suffixed (Demonstrative) stem; by contrast, it applies transparently in both daughters of a reduplicated unsuffixed stem:

(25)
a.	ḍuḍʊq	'place'	ḍuḍuq-ḍuḍuq-e	ḍuḍʊq-ḍuḍʊq	D207
b.	abʊr	'flight'	abur-abur-e	abʊr-abʊr	D207
c.	apɪq	'good, nice'	apiq-apiq-e	apɪq-apɪq	D207
d.	gilɪk	'cylindrical'	gilig-gilig-e	gilɪk-gilɪk	D207
e.	murɪt	'student'	murid-murid-e	murɪt-murɪt	D207

Similar behavior is exhibited by the stem-final consonants (25d, e); they transparently devoice in both copies of bare reduplicated stems but opaquely retain their underlying voicing in the first copy of a suffixed reduplicated stem.

Both of these underapplication effects follow directly from the MDT analysis developed thus far. Laxing and Consonant Devoicing apply transparently on the stem cycle; their conditioning environments are obscured by suffix truncation in the first copy of reduplicated suffixed stems. The Demonstrative stem-forming construction generating (25e) is shown below:

(26)   {murid}-e
          ∧
       /murit$_{Rt}$-e/

Neither Laxing nor Consonant Devoicing are conditioned in this stem; both transparently fail to apply. The appearance of underapplication in reduplication is a result of two factors: (a) the truncation, in Cophonology X, of the suffix which, on the stem cycle, renders the stem-final syllable open, permitting the vowel to remain tense and the consonant to remain voiced, and (b) the fact that Laxing and Devoicing do not reapply in Cophonology Z.

(27)

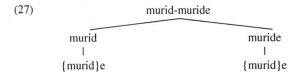

MDT does not predict that Laxing and Consonant Devoicing have to be opaque in the output of reduplicated suffixed stems. It would be possible, for example, within MDT for Laxing and Consonant Devoicing to apply again in Cophonology X, producing an output in which both copies – the first, truncated copy, and the second, intact copy – exhibit transparent phonology: *murɪt-murid-e*. The fact that they do not apply cyclically is an arbitrary fact about Javanese. What MDT does clearly predict, however, is that the opacity within each daughter is an effect of daughter-internal phonology; this is a prediction in which MDT differs sharply from BRCT or other Coerced Identity theories. In a BRCT account of Laxing, underapplication in *murid-muride* would follow from the fact that Laxing would disrupt BR identity if it applied in the first copy (where it is conditioned); therefore it is coerced to apply in neither. The problem is that identity would be maintained equally well if Laxing overapplied, yielding *murɪd-murɪde* with transparent application in the first copy by opaque application in the second copy. In BRCT what determines whether underapplication or overapplication of Laxing will be the outcome is relative markedness. If the constraint against a tense vowel in a closed syllable (*Tense/Closed) outranks the ban on a lax vowel in an open syllable (*Lax/Open), Laxing will overapply; if the ranking is reversed, Laxing will underapply. In MDT, by contrast, there is no means of deriving Laxing overapplication. Laxing is conditioned neither in the input nor in the output of the second copy in forms like *murid-muride*. If Laxing were a word-level alternation, rather than a stem-level alternation, MDT could describe the situation in which Laxing applied in the first copy but not in the second (the hypothetical *murɪt-muride*), but it could never generate *murɪt-murɪde*.

In summary, in every case of opacity we have surveyed in Javanese, the alternation is transparent in its domain of application (the stem); the opacity is generated when the stem in question is embedded in a reduplication construction which truncates that part of the stem orginally determining the applicability of the alternation. MDT not only describes this opacity effortlessly; it also correctly predicts whether the opacity will take the form of underapplication or overapplication.

5.1.7   Summary

In surveying opaque reduplicative phonology in Javanese, we have concluded that BR identity does not play a role. If anything, reduplication obscures identity, by virtue of the concomitant truncation. It is not the case in Javanese that reduplicative phonology creates or preserves identity that would not otherwise have existed.

In finding that reduplication operates on morphologically complex stems, we concur with the original insight of Dudas (1976), who concludes (p. 209) that reduplication is ordered after the phonological alternations in question.

A strong prediction that our analysis makes is that alternations internal to the daughters of reduplication may be rendered opaque by reduplication, but that word-level phonology, which applies to the output of reduplication, cannot be. This prediction appears to be correct. Glide Insertion (Dudas 1976:135–36) applies between two non-identical vowels when the first is tense and the second is lower or fronter than the first. In the examples below, Glide Insertion breaks up vowel hiatus resulting from *h*-deletion. Notice that it applies transparently, not opaquely: only the second copy in reduplication, not the first, is followed by an inserted glide:

(28)

	Stem		Reduplicated stem	Suffixed reduplicated stem		
a.	gadjɪh		gadjɪh-gadhɪh[11]	gadji-gadji-y-e	'salary'	D209
b.	kukʊh		kukʊh-kukʊh	kuku-kuku-w-e	'solid'	D209
c.	pilɪh	'choose'		pili-pili-y-an		D154

If Glide Insertion is a word-level rule, MDT has an explanation for why it applies only after the second copy, and not the first. The input to Glide Insertion in, say, (28b) is the output of reduplication, i.e. *kuku-kukue*. There is only one context for Glide Insertion, and it applies only once: *kukukukuwe*.

Our claim that the kind of opacity found in reduplication is simply the result of processes at a higher cophonology masking the triggers of processes in lower cophonologies resonates with the view of Kiparsky (1997:2):

> Insofar as templatic morphology functions as an operation on phonological representations (copying, truncation, etc.), it *must* show "overapplication" of phonological processes: processes triggered at the relevant level by the phonological context in the base will appear in the copied or truncated version, provided that the constraints on the reduplicant itself permit it (whether or not they are "opaque" there).

5.2 Mother-based opacity: infixation

In this section we look at two cases of opacity driven by interactions between the mother and the daughter. Both involve infixation.

5.2.1 Chamorro

In Chamorro, opacity results from the interaction between stem-level stress assignment and subsequent infixing reduplication (Topping 1973). Recall from our discussion of Chamorro in Chapter 4 that stress is normally penultimate, shifting rightward under suffixation:

(29)	karéta	'car'	108
	karetá-hu	'my car'	108
	karetá-ta	'our (incl.) car'	108
	kareta-n-mámi	'our (excl.) car'	108
	kareta-n-ñíha	'their car'	108

This penultimate stress pattern is perturbed by both CV reduplication patterns in Chamorro. Stressed CV reduplication, which copies the first CV of the stressed syllable, is illustrated in (30a). Final CV reduplication repeats the stem-final CV (30b).[12] Both patterns result in antepenultimate stress, rendering the predictable assignment of penultimate stress opaque.

(30)	a.	sága	'stay'	sásaga	'staying'	259
		hugándo	'play'	hug**ág**ando	'playing'	259
		hátsa	'lifted'	**háha**tsa	'one that was lifting'	102
	b.	métgot	'strong'	mét**gogo**t	'very strong'	183
		buníta	'pretty'	buní**tata**	'very pretty'	183
		dánkolo	'big'	dánko**lolo**	'very big'	183

The MDT analysis of Chamorro parallels that developed for Javanese. Penultimate stress assignment applies transparently in the stems which are input to reduplication, as shown below:

(31) Stem cycle: hugándo
             | $\Leftarrow$ Stem cophonology: PENULT-STRESS » *STRUC-STRESS
      /hugando/

Reduplication calls for two copies of each stem, the first of which is truncated by Cophonology X to (in the case of stressed CV reduplication) the initial CV portion of its stressed syllable. The second copy in reduplication, associated with Cophonology Y, preserves the stem intact. Cophonology Z infixes the output of Cophonology X into the output of Cophonology Y:

(32)   hugá-ga-ndo

Cophonology $X \Rightarrow$ ga   hugándo $\Leftarrow$ Cophonology Y
                              | |
                    hugándo $_{Stem[F]}$ hugándo $_{Stem[F]}$

The location of stress in the output of Cophonology Z is opaque in not following the regular penultimate stress rule. This type of opacity is so familiar that it
is hard to recognize, the distinction between affixes that occur within vs. outside
of the domain of stress assignment being so commonplace. Yet the obscuring
effect that subsequent affixation (here, infixation) can have on the conditioning
environment of a phonological alternation (here, stress assignment) plays an
important role in more complex examples of reduplicative opacity which we
analyze below.[13]

5.2.2   Eastern Kadazan

Opacity caused by infixation occurs in the reduplication system of Eastern
Kadazan, a Bornean language of Malaysia described by Hurlbut (1988) as
having "two or three times as many affixes . . . as, for example, in Tagalog"
(p. 1). The following example shows words containing both root reduplication
and affixes. To avoid prejudging the issue of where in the morphological layering
reduplication occurs, we list, on the left, the underlying representation of all
of the morphemes contained in the word (sans reduplication), with roots in
boldface, and on the right, the reduplicated words, with the duplicated sequence
in boldface. Infixes are set off by commas in the left-hand column but linearized
in the right-hand column. Data are based on Hurlbut 1988:[14]

(33)

'DIM-go/be_like'	/soN-**kaa**/	sang**kaka**a	77
'REC-move-I'	/ko-**puu**-ku/	ko**pupuu**ku	34
'ASS.COL-ignore-someone-RF'	/pog-**baya**-an/	pog**baba**yaan	60
'AF-DU.REC-AUG-obey'	/m-pi-ku-**bojo**/	miku**bobo**jo	107
'DES-lie_down'	/si-**kili**/	si**kiki**li	110
'COMP-N.INTEN-UN.DIST-spouse'	/N-o-piN-**savo**/	nopin**sasa**vo	92
'AF-CONT-lift'	/m-iN-**kakat**/	ming**kaka**kat	105
'AF-MID-POSS-go_around'	/m-pog-ki-**liput**/	mogi**lili**put	87
'EXAS-arrive/reach'	/to-**rikot**/	to**riri**kot	72
'COMP, MUL.REC-be_side_by_side'	/-in-, poi-**ganding**/	pinoi**gaga**nding	109
'AF, come'	/-um-, **ravung**/	**ruru**mavung	102
'catch_an_illness-UF-YOU'	/**ruvang**-o-ko/	**ruru**vangoko	112

'COMP, AF-DUR-to_sun' /-in-, m-mogin-**sidang**/ minogin**si**sidang 105
'COMPR-pock_mark'   /so-**gorontok**/   so**go**gorontok   49, 106

The reason for reserving judgment as to the hierarchical position of reduplication in the word is the behavior of vowel-initial roots (34). These show
doubling of the initial V of the root as well as the preceding, prefix-final C:

(34)

'AF-DU.REC-N.SER-paddle_a_boat' /m-pi-siN-**alud**/ mising**anga**lud   107
'COMP-N.INTEN-CONT-eat'   /no-ko-iN-**aran**/ nokoing**anga**ran   80
'AF-DISS-sleep'   /m-posiN-**odop**/   mosing**ongo**dop   60
'DIM-hold_in_hand'   /soN-**onggom**/   song**ongo**nggom   77

The MDT account of the data in (33) and (34) is that Eastern Kadazan
reduplication is infixing. As in Javanese, the Proot plays a crucial role. In Eastern
Kadazan, reduplication, a late morphological process, truncates the first copy
of the word down to the initial CV of the Proot and infixes the result directly
preceding the Proot in the second copy. The Proot, as in Javanese, consists of
those syllables projected from the morphological root. In the case of consonant-
initial roots, as in (33), the morphological root and the Proot are identical, and
reduplication reproduces the initial syllable. In the case of vowel-initial roots,
as in (34), the Proot can include a consonant from a preceding prefix if the
morphological root is vowel-initial; in such a case, reduplication reproduces
the syllable composed of that consonant and the root-initial vowel.

(35)   a. Consonant-initial root m-pi-ku-{**bojo**}   → mpiku-**bo-bojo**
        b. Vowel-initial root: m-posi{N-**odop**}   → mposi-**ngo-ngodop**

There is independent evidence in Eastern Kadazan that reduplication is infixing. Example (36) shows that when a vowel-initial root is not preceded by a
prefix, reduplication targets the initial CV portion of the root, skipping the initial
vowel:

(36)   'run_away-RF-I'   /**i**du-an-ku/   i+**du**+duanku   VCV   103
        'wait-RF-N.COMP.M'   /**in**dad-an-po/ in+**da**+dadanpo VCCVC 103, 116

The Proot requires an initial onset, as modeled by the constraint ranking
PROOT-ONSET » ALIGN-L(MROOT, PROOT); this requirement can either
cause material from outside the Mroot to be pulled into the Proot, as in (34) or
(35b), or, as in (36), it can cause the initial vowel in the Mroot to be excluded
from the Proot. Proot formation for a prefixless vowel-initial root is modeled
below:

(37)

	indad-an-po	P<small>ROOT</small>-<small>ONSET</small>	A<small>LIGN</small>(M<small>ROOT</small>,P<small>ROOT</small>)
☞ a.	in{dad}anpo		i
b.	{indad}anpo	*!	

Cophonology X truncates the stem to the initial CV of the Proot, and Cophonology Z positions the output of Cophonology X immediately preceding the Proot in the output of Cophonology Y.

(38)

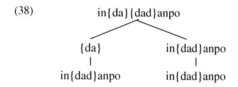

Further support for the infixation analysis is evidence that, completely independent of onset overcopying issues, the input to reduplication can be a morphologically complex stem. This assumption is crucial to the claim that reduplication is a late process. The data in (39) show that the Proot can contain the completive infix *-in-* (a) as well as what appear to be denominal verb stems (b, c):

(39)   a. -in- + vaal   /v-in-aal/   vi+vinaal   'It was made up'   101
           C<small>OMP</small>-make
        b. in-sada   /m-pog-iN-   mo+gi+ginsadano 'He catches fish   63
           V<small>BL</small>-fish   sada-no/   regularly'
        c. to-ruol[15]   /m-posiN-to- mosin+to+toruol 'She is pretending   60
           ?-?   ruol/   to have an illness'

The infix *-in-* is one of the outermost affixes (Hurlbut 1988:23); its reduplicability confirms that reduplication is a late morphological process, looking potentially deep into the word for the Proot.

   In sum, what appears initially to be onset overcopying is actually internal reduplication of a prosodic constituent (Proot), a phenomenon for which there is strong precedent in the form of internal reduplication of stressed syllables (as in Chamorro; see Yu 2003 for a recent survey). We have provided independent evidence for the two crucial parts of the analysis: reduplication is infixing, and reduplication operates on morphologically complex constituents.

   The semantics of Eastern Kadazan reduplication are also consistent with an analysis in which reduplication is a relatively late process. According to Hurlbut (1988:100), reduplication is basically semantically iterative, though its meaning can vary according to what other affixes are present in the word. Together with the *m*-prefix, reduplication marks progressive iterative aspect; together with completive aspect, reduplication gives the sense that the action of the verb was undertaken without purpose (or, apparently, in bad faith). The fact that the semantics of reduplication depends on the other affixes in the word is consistent with its being a late morphological process.

Further support for this conclusion comes from two examples illustrating whole-word reduplication (Hurlbut 1988). With what appears to be a purely iterative meaning, reduplication targets all three syllables of the complex stems *mingguli* in (40a) and *pointaamon* in (40b):

(40) a. tiap sodop **mingguli-mingguli** ka ino (102)
        'Every night that animal returned again and again'
      b. **pointaamon-pointaamon** dii iri tapon (51)
        'And as he was fishing he kept throwing in the fishing-line'
      c. /m-piN-guli/   AF-UN.DIST-return/repeat
        /po-iN-taam-on/ DERIVEDSTATE-CONT-throw_up-UF

Clearly, the observed variation is more plausible if reduplication is a late morphological process. If reduplication were the innermost morphological construction, the expectation would be variation between partial and total reduplication of the Proot, not the whole word; there would be no structural basis with respect to which partial Proot reduplication and total Word reduplication would form a natural morphological class.

Eastern Kadazan is just one of several languages in which infixation produces an apparent overcopying effect. Two other languages for which such effects have been of great interest to the theoretical literature are Chumash and Tagalog. They are discussed in Chapter 6.

5.2.3   Infixation in MDT

Infixation in MDT must be accomplished by Cophonology Z, which is responsible for collating the phonological outputs of its daughters. Infixation has been the subject of much recent work. The kind of infixation seen in Chamorro and Eastern Kadazan falls into the category of "positive prosodic circumscription" (McCarthy & Prince 1990; Lombardi & McCarthy 1991; McCarthy & Prince 1995b), alignment to a prosodic constituent (McCarthy & Prince 1994b), or Phonological Subcategorization (Yu 2003). In Chamorro, the reduplicant, which is truncated to the stressed syllable of its input, is positioned adjacent to the stressed syllable of its sister; in Eastern Kadazan, the reduplicant, itself a truncated Proot, is positioned adjacent to the Proot of its sister.

It is interesting that in both of these cases the reduplicant surfaces adjacent to the portion of the base that it phonologically resembles. As far as we know this is true generally of infixed reduplicants; see, for example, Tagalog and Chumash (Chapter 6), and the over fifty cases of internal reduplication documented in Yu 2003 (Appendix III).[16] Adjacency is certainly not a general requirement in reduplication; in languages as diverse as Chukchee (Krause 1980), Madurese (Stevens 1985; McCarthy & Prince 1995a), and Umpila (Harris & O'Grady 1976; Levin 1985b), for example, the reduplicant is truncated to the initial portion of the word being doubled, yet surfaces *after*, not before, the nontruncated copy (thus, for example, from Chukchee, *nute-nut* 'earth' or, from Umpila, *maka-l-ma-* 'die, go out (fire)').

It is beyond the scope of this study to determine why internal reduplication is apparently more restricted in this way. One speculation, however, drawing on work by Inkelas 1990, is that the generalization may follow from the impossibility of discontinuous prosodic constituents. In a case like Eastern Kadazan, where a doubled word has an internal Proot (e.g. *in{dad}anpo*), an output in which the two Proots were not adjacent would violate continuity: *{da}in{dad}anpo*, cf. the actual output *in{da}{dad}anpo* (which perhaps resolves to *in{dadad}anpo*). We leave this issue for future work on infixation to illuminate.

5.3   Morphological opacity outside of reduplication

In containing no reduplication-specific elements, the MDT analysis of reduplicative opacity predicts parallel opacity effects outside of reduplication. It has long been known that morphology–phonology layering, of the sort intrinsic to our cophonological construction model, is a potential source of opacity. Indeed, Kiparsky (2000) has gone so far as to claim that all opacity results from this type of layering. This claim is almost surely too strong, as there are clear cases of opacity derived within a single cophonology (see, for example, the case of Turkish velar deletion, discussed in Sprouse 1997). However, it is clear that reduplication has no corner on the opacity market. We briefly examine two cases here that resemble our reduplication examples in the type of opacity they exhibit but do not involve reduplication themselves.

5.3.1   *Opacity by truncation*

Just as truncation in reduplication can render opaque otherwise transparent phonology, we find truncation outside of reduplication producing the same effects. A well-known example from the recent literature is English nickname formation. As documented in Benua 1997, in a certain dialect of American English, [æ] is prohibited before tautosyllabic /r/, though [æ] may precede /r/ if it ends an open syllable.[17] This distribution is violated in nickname formation; names with heterosyllabic [ær] sequences can truncate to syllables ending in [ær]: *Larry* [læri] → *Lar* [lær], etc. Benua treats the *Larry-Lar* relationship as word-to-word (Output–Output) rather than input–output, though she does have to stipulate a "Base-Identity" principle whereby *Larry*, as the morphological "base," is privileged over *Lar*. That is why markedness constraints are satisfied in *Larry* but violated in *Lar*. We find it more plausible to set up, as does Weeda 1992 for parallel phenomena, an input–output relationship between *Larry* and *Lar* such that the output of *Larry* [læri], a form obeying the distributional restrictions on [æ], serves as input to truncation. The output of truncation, *Lar* [lær], violates the ban on [. . . ær] syllables but is faithful to the input.

(41)   *Lar* [lær]
    | ⇐ truncation:[æ] opaque but faithful to input
   Larry [læri]
    | ⇐ [æ] transparently OK
   /lAri/

In its details this analysis is almost exactly parallel to the analysis of Javanese laxing. What can be thought of as an æ → ɛ rule seems to underapply in the output of truncation, but that is simply because the output is faithful, in its vowel quality, to the input, where the rule is transparently not conditioned. A similar example involving place of articulation is *Gram* [græm]; for those speaker who pronounce the word *Grandma* as [græmma], the place of articulation in the final consonant of *Gram* can be explained only by assimilation to the following *-ma* of *Grandma*, its morphological base. Numerous other examples can be found in Weeda 1992; see especially pp. 78ff., where Weeda discusses cases of vowel tensing in Madurese and New York English that closely parallel Benua's data and involve clearly productive alternations.

5.3.2   *Opacity by infixation*
Just as it does in reduplication, infixation can induce opacity outside of reduplication. Sundanese is a well-known case in which morphological infixation (Robins 1959:368) renders an otherwise transparent phonological alternation opaque (Cohn 1990; Benua 1997). Sundanese is subject to rightward nasal harmony, triggered by a nasal consonant and affecting following vocoids. It is blocked by supralaryngeal consonants. The singular forms in (42a) show nasal harmony applying transparently. In the plural forms in (42b), the plural infix

-al- ~ *-ar-*, which follows the first consonant, renders nasal harmony opaque. Harmony appears to overapply to the right of the infix, where it is not conditioned on the surface; the final liquid of the infix is the type of consonant that blocks harmony.

(42)   Singular Plural   Gloss

    a. ŋãũr   ŋãlãũr   'say'
    b. ŋãĩãn   ŋãrãĩãn   'wet'
    c. mĩãsih   mãrĩãsih   'love'
    d. ŋũliat   ŋãrũliat   'stretch'
    e. mãrios   mãlãrios   'examine'
    f. ŋãluhuran ŋãrãluhuran 'be in a high position'
    g. mãwur   mãlãwur   'spread'

Standard accounts of Sundanese nasal harmony appeal to the cycle (Cohn 1990) or its equivalent (Benua 1997; see also Anderson 1974:150–51). The idea, in MDT terms, is that Nasal Harmony is part of the cophonology of the stem that the plural infix combines with as well as the cophonology of the stem that the plural infix produces. Nasal Harmony therefore applies to the input as well as to the output of plural infixation, producing the attested surface forms. The layered analysis of Sundanese plural infixation in (43) combines two constructions: the singular stem-forming construction in which Nasal Harmony applies to the singular root, and the plural stem-forming construction in which Nasal Harmony applies, again, to the output of plural infixation.

(43)   [ŋãrũliat]

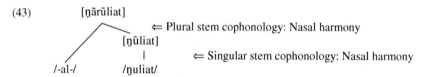

                     ⇐ Plural stem cophonology: Nasal harmony
          [ŋũliat]
            | ⇐ Singular stem cophonology: Nasal harmony
   /-al-/   /ŋuliat/

5.4   MDT vs. Coerced Identity theories

Even though its occurrence may be more common – or simply more noticeable – in reduplication, opacity is clearly not a reduplication-specific effect. Nonetheless, the literature has seen the development of a number of theories designed precisely to handle opacity (over- and underapplication) in reduplication, all of which treat opacity as resulting from phonological identity requirements on base and reduplicant. Wilbur (1973) proposed the Identity Principle, which has been given new life in the notion of BR correspondence in Optimality Theory. Both Mester (1986) and Clements (1985) propose representations specific to reduplication which have the effect of requiring the phonological outputs of base and reduplicant to be the same; their insights, too, can be seen in the BR correspondence proposal. Other reduplication-specific proposals for handling reduplicative opacity include those in Raimy 2000 and Frampton 2003.

What all of these proposals have in common is the claim that the reduplicant is derived, by some phonological duplication mechanism, from the base, and that either structural or correspondence relations keep the base and reduplicant from diverging too far. The underlying empirical premise is that reduplicative opacity keeps base and reduplicant more similar than they otherwise would be. In this section we show this premise to be unfounded. Our discussion will make reference to the most influential of the theories based upon it, namely BR correspondence theory, which enforces surface identity between reduplicant and base even in face of pressures to the contrary from markedness constraints.

Consider, for example, the case of Javanese suffix ablaut, seen in §5.1.2, and exemplified by the pair *apeq* 'prayer,' with underlying /e/, vs. *apiq + apiq-an* (reduplicated, nominalized), with ablauted [i] in both copies. In BRCT, the identity in root vowels across base and reduplicant in *apiq-apiq-an* is achieved using the ranking BR-FAITH, ABLAUT » IO-FAITH, IR-FAITH, as shown below:

(44)

	RED-apeq-an	BR-FAITH	ABLAUT	IO-FAITH	IR-FAITH
a.	apeq-apeq-an		*!		
b.	apeq-apiq-an	*!		*	
☞ c.	apiq-apiq-an			*	*
d.	apiq-apeq-an	*!	*		*

On the BRCT analysis, the opaque application of Ablaut in the reduplicant, which in MDT we attributed to the transparent application of Ablaut in the input suffixed stem, is attributed to its transparent application in the base, which is followed by an overt triggering suffix. The ranking Ablaut » IO-FAITH forces ablaut to apply in the base; BR-FAITH forces the base and reduplicant to be identical, thus resulting in the observed "overapplication" effect.

Underapplication has a similar provenance in BRCT. Consider the example of underapplication from Javanese, in which closed syllable laxing of /i/ to /ɪ/ opaquely fails to apply in the reduplicant of *murid-murid-e*, though it does apply to the same root ("student") in isolation and in unsuffixed reduplication:

(45)

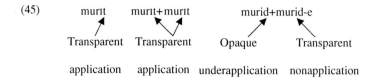

| murɪt | murɪt+murɪt | murid+murid-e |

Transparent   Transparent   Opaque   Transparent

application   application   underapplication   nonapplication

The transparent failure of Laxing to apply in the base of reduplication, /*murid-e*/, is attributed to the ranking *TENSE/Closed syllable » *LAX, IO-FAITH, which requires laxing in closed syllables but prevents it from applying in open syllables. The opaque failure of Laxing to apply in the reduplicant is due to BR-IDENT, which is ranked above *LAX, the ban on lax vowels.

(46)

	RED-murid-e	*TENSE/CLOSED	BR-IDENT	*LAX	IO-FAITH
☞ a.	mu.rid-mu.ri.d-e				
b.	mu.rid.-mu.rɪ.d-e		*!	*	*
c.	mu.rɪd.-mu.rɪ.d-e			*!*	*
d.	mu.rɪd-mu.ri.d-e		*!	*	

BRCT and MDT might appear to work equally well for these Javanese examples of over- and underapplication – although, as argued in §5.5.3, MDT makes stronger predictions than BRCT regarding which alternations will show overapplication and which will show underapplication.

We add to this argument in the next several sections of this chapter, showing other ways in which MDT provides a better account of reduplicative opacity than does BRCT in general. We make three points:

- Not all reduplicative opacity increases BR identity; therefore BRCT is not sufficient
- BRCT predicts kinds of identity effects that don't occur; thus BRCT overgenerates
- MDT can handle the apparent identity effects that do occur; thus BRCT is not necessary

Opacity in MDT derives from morphological structure; MDT is therefore more explanatory than theories of opacity which do not take internal hierarchical structure into account.

5.4.1   Opacity does not always increase identity

Although the work of Wilbur (1973) and McCarthy and Prince (1995a) has highlighted those instances of reduplicative opacity in which BR identity is increased, not all cases of opacity are of this kind. To take one example, the Chamorro infixing reduplication analyzed in §5.2.1 creates opacity that has nothing to do with increasing identity. Recall examples like the following:

(47)   Plain form: hugándo
        Reduplicated form: hugágando

What is opaque about the reduplicated form is the location of stress, which is normally penultimate in Chamorro. But this "displacement" of stress does not result in the base and reduplicant being more identical than they otherwise would be; if stress were penultimate in the reduplicated form, giving us *hugagándo*, base and reduplicant would be no less similar.

MDT can handle both the effects in Chamorro, in which identity clearly plays no role, and those in Javanese, in which identity could be said to play a role, in the same manner. By contrast, BRCT has no light to shed on Chamorro. BRCT would presumably also have to appeal to cyclicity in some guise and would therefore derive the opacity the way MDT does; BR correspondence would play no role.

5.4.2   Distribution of opacity

The predictions of Morphological Doubling Theory and Identity theories are very clearly distinguished in the area of junctures. MDT limits the scope of reduplicative opacity to mother–daughter relationships. The daughter cophonologies can render the phonology of their inputs opaque; the mother cophonology can render the phonology of its daughters opaque. Overapplication effects occur when conditioning environments triggering an alternation in a lower cophonology are obscured by some operation in a higher cophonology; underapplication effects occur when an alternation that would apply in a lower cophonology cannot because the conditioning environment is absent, even though a higher cophonology provides it. We have seen examples of both kinds already in this chapter. (Klamath, discussed in Chapter 4, is another instance of the latter type.)

What a cophonology cannot do is render opaque phonological effects conditioned in morphological constituents over which the cophonology does not have scope. The cophonology of one daughter in reduplication cannot influence the outcome of the cophonology of the other daughter; similarly, no cophonology in reduplication can influence the phonological outcome of morphemes outside the morphological constituent produced by reduplication.

The effects of the cophonological structure of MDT can be summed up in the following prediction:

(48)   Scopal Opacity Prediction (SOP): cophonologies can render only the phonology of their inputs opaque

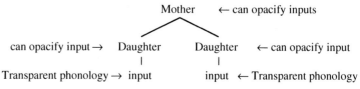

The SOP does not follow from BRCT. As a result, BRCT makes dramatically different predictions regarding phonological opacity in reduplication. Below we survey three types of phonological alternations which in BRCT are predicted to participate in over- or underapplication. We will show that only one of these types of effects actually does participate, namely stem-internal phonology, precisely as MDT predicts.

5.4.2.1 Stem-internal phonology
Both MDT and BRCT predict the possibility that a phonological alternation whose applicability is determined solely in input should be able to over- or underapply in reduplication, as below:

(49)   a. Overapplication (h-deletion)
           /bədah-e/ bəda-bədae (vs. *bədah-bədae)
         b. Underapplication (closed-syllable laxing)
           /gilik-e/   gilig-gilige (vs. *gilɪk-gilige)

We have already seen how MDT and BRCT handle such cases; (a) is discussed in the section on Javanese *h*-deletion (§5.1.5), and (b) is discussed in the section on Javanese laxing (§5.1.6).

5.4.2.2 Internal junctural alternations
While BRCT and MDT both predict the possible opacity of over- or underapplication of daughter-internal (for BRCT, base-internal) phonology in reduplication, BRCT predicts additional types of opacity that MDT does not. The first of these involves phonology applying across the base-reduplicant juncture. Consider the hypothetical opaque internal junctural alternation below. "NPA" stands for nasal place assimilation, the hypothetical alternation at hand:

(50)   bihan → biham-biham
         tarem → taren-taren

At the internal base-reduplicant juncture, the nasal ending the first copy assimilates in place to the consonant beginning the second copy; this alternation is then reflected in the second copy.

MDT cannot describe this effect. There is no cophonology that could assimilate the final segment of the second copy to the first segment of itself or of the preceding copy. MDT predicts (50) not to occur. By contrast, BRCT can easily describe it. Let us assume for the sake of exposition that in (50) the second copy is the reduplicant. Letting "NPA" in (51) stand for the constraint(s) responsible for requiring nasal-stop clusters to agree in place, the ranking NPA » IO-IDENT-PLACE ensures that NPA will take place generally in the language, and therefore in bases of reduplication as well. Satisfaction of IO-IDENT-PLACE compels the reduplicant-final consonant to be identical to the base, yielding overapplication of a BR-juncture effect:

(51)

		/bihan-RED/	NPA	IO-IDENT	BR-FAITH
a.		biham-bihan		*	*!
b.	underapplication	bihan-bihan	*!		
☞ c.	overapplication	biham-biham		*	

The BRCT analysis of this case is actually formally parallel to the BRCT treatment of the actual opaque stem-internal Javanese alternations analyzed in §5.4.2.1, above. The problem with this is that cases like *bihan* → *biham-biham* do not exist. McCarthy and Prince (1995a), discussing parallel hypothetical but unattested examples, are able to offer no formal explanation for the gap (pp. 327–28).[18]

5.4.2.3 External junctural alternations

A third possible type of opacity, which MDT rules out but BRCT predicts possible, is exemplified by the hypothetical alternation below, in which consonant assimilation, triggered by a suffix external to the reduplicated stem, is propagated long distance to both members of the reduplicated stem to which the suffix attaches. Assume, for the sake of argument, that the second copy is the base:

(52) a. Total reduplication   tapan → tapan-tapan
       b. Suffixation to reduplicated stem: tapan-tapan + -la → tapal-tapal-la

In (52b), total assimilation of the base-final nasal to the following suffix-initial /l/ is reflected in the reduplicant, where it is not conditioned. If such effects occur, MDT is in trouble and BRCT is supported, since only BR correspondence could produce this result. BRCT can easily describe the hypothetical situation in (52b):

(53)

		/[RED-tapan]-la/	BR-FAITH	ASSIMILATION	IO-FAITH
a.	transparent	tapan-tapal-la	*!		*
☞ b.	overapplication	tapal-tapal-la			*
c.	underapplication	tapan-tapan-la		*!	

To our knowledge, effects like these do not occur. However, the analysis BRCT offers of these hypothetical data is formally completely parallel to the opaque stem-internal alternations above, predicting that they should be equally common. BRCT misses a major cross-linguistic generalization in generating, with equal facility, overapplication effects for phonology applying stem-internally (which occurs often), phonology applying across the BR-juncture, and phonology applying across junctures external to reduplication (neither of which occur reliably).

The statement that cases like those in (50) and (52) do not occur does not mean that there are no data which superficially resemble these patterns, as seen already in the discussion of Javanese in §5.1. To take another example, the data from Tawala (Austronesian; Ezard 1997:38), below, might initially appear to instantiate overapplication of an external junctural effect (as in (52)). All of these words exhibit CVCV reduplication, which marks durative aspect. Data from the reduplication of long roots shows that the first copy is the truncated one (e.g. *geleta* 'to arrive,' *gele-geleta* (durative); Ezard 1997:41). As seen below, suffix-induced vowel change in the second copy is replicated in the first copy as well.

(54)   a. dewa-dewa-ya /dewa-dewa-ya/ '...-3SG'
        b. dewe-dewe-ya /dewa-dewa-e-ya/ '...TRV-3SG'
        c. dewi-dewi-yai /dewa-dewa-iyai/ '...-1PL.EXCL'

Whether this qualifies as overapplication of an external junctural alternation depends entirely on one's morphological analysis. If what is being reduplicated is the bare root, then the double vowel-raising effects require explanation; if what is being reduplicated is a stem consisting of root plus suffixes, then the double vowel-raising effects are unremarkable. The input to reduplication in (54b) is *deweya*, which reduplicates, as expected, as *dewe-deweya*. There is reason to believe this latter analysis is correct for Tawala.

The two suffix types whose effect on a preceding root vowel is replicated in reduplication are the transitivizing suffix "TRV" shown in (54b), and the six object agreement suffixes, one of which is illustrated in (54c). As a derivational suffix, the transitivizer is expected to occur closer to the root, hierarchically speaking, than inflection, which includes object agreement and aspect. Cross-linguistic expectations about inflectional affix ordering, e.g. Bybee 1985, hold that object agreement is generally closest to the verb root, followed by aspect; tense and subject agreement are even farther from the verb root. Thus the null hypothesis for Tawala would be that durative reduplication operates on a stem including the verb root, any derivational morphology, and object agreement. On this hypothesis the data in (54) are completely expected.[19]

Eastern Kadazan, seen earlier in §5.2.2, might also appear at first glance to involve overapplication of an external junctural effect between prefix and redu-plicant. As argued in §5.2.2, however, morphology again explains the pattern: the opacity in Eastern Kadazan is due to infixation. The alternation in question – adjunction of a prefix-final consonant into an otherwise vowel-initial Proot – is stem-internal.

Two other examples like Eastern Kadazan, namely Tagalog and Chumash, have in fact been analyzed in the BRCT literature as instantiating the overappli-cation of an effect at the external juncture between prefix and reduplicant. It is argued in Chapter 6 that the opacity in Tagalog and Chumash should be under-stood in a parallel fashion to that of Eastern Kadazan: independent evidence exists that both languages have internal reduplication, and that the juncture in question is internal to the stem being reduplicated.

5.4.2.4 Summary

MDT makes restrictive predictions about what kinds of phonological effects can over- or underapply in reduplication; BRCT predicts a much wider range of reduplicative opacity. The predictions of MDT are borne out in the data, while those of BRCT are not. Observations parallel to ours about the apparently false predictions of BRCT are also made in Kiparsky (1997), in the context of a discussion of Sanskrit reduplication.

5.5   Case study: Fox

We turn now to a case study of Fox which illustrates, more fully than any of our previous studies, the different behavior of stem-internal vs. stem-external alternations in reduplication, confirming the predictions of MDT in this regard. Our discussion is based on Dahlstrom 1997. Reduplication in Fox targets a well-defined potentially morphologically complex constituent which we will call the stem. Fox has both stem-internal and stem-external phonology. The former is subject to overapplication effects; the latter applies transparently in reduplication. This is exactly as MDT (but not BRCT) predicts.

The more productive of Fox's several reduplication patterns, disyllabic pre-fixing reduplication marks what Dahlstrom characterizes as iterative aspect (repeated action or action distributed over group of subjects or objects); see Conathan and Wood 2003 for further elaboration of the semantics of the construction. As can be seen in the data in (55b), vowel length is preserved in the first syllable of the reduplicant but is lost in the second. Similarly, in (55c), coda consonants are preserved in the first syllable of the reduplicant but not in the second. Dahlstrom (p. 218) relates both these facts to the phonotactics of Fox words, which must end in light (CV) syllables. The reduplicant, in boldface, is thus best understood as a disyllabic (minimal) prosodic constituent; following Dahlstrom, we will call it a minimal Pword.[20]

(55) a. pye:taw-e:wa   **pye:ta**-pye:tawe:wa   'he brings it for him'   217
          kʷi:nom-e:wa   **kʷi:no**-kʷinome:wa   'he longs for him'   217
          ni:škesi-wa   **ni:ške**-ni:škesiwa   'he is overburdened'   217
          ki:hpoče:-wa   **ki:hpo**-ki:hpoče:wa   'he eats his fill'   217
      b. we:ne:haki   **we:ne**-we:ne:haki   'who (pl)?'   218
                                *****we:ne:**-we:ne:haki
          mayo:-wa   **mayo**-mayo:wa   'he cries'   218
                                *****mayo:**-mayo:wa
          po:swe:kesi-wa   **po:swe**-po:swe:kesiwa   'he cries louder'   218
                                *****po:swe:**-po:swe:kesiwa
      c. nenehke:nem-e:wa   **nene**-nenehke:neme:wa   'he thinks about him'   218
                                *****neneh**-nenehke:neme:wa
          nakiškaw-e:wa   **naki**-nakiškawe:wa   'he meets him'   218
                                *****nakiš**-nakiškawe:wa
          kokʷa:ške:-wa   **kokʷa**-kokʷa:ške:wa   'he is jerked'   218
                                *****kokʷaš**-kokʷa:ške:wa

Disyllabic reduplication is sandwiched morphologically between inflectional suffixation, which is present in the input to reduplication, and inflectional pre-fixation, which is not.

The data in (56a) illustrate that inflectional suffixal material can reduplicate if it falls within the first two syllables of the stem. The forms in (56b) show that inflectional prefixes are not in the scope of reduplication. The claim that reduplication operates inside of prefixation is reinforced by (56c), *nesi*, a word consisting only of prefixes because its root 'say' is phonetically null. The word *nesi*, lacking any overt root or suffix material, cannot reduplicate at all:

(56) a. mi:n-e:wa   mi:ne-mi:ne:wa   'he gives it to him'   208
         kot-aki   kota-kotaki   'he swallows it; conjunct'   219
      b. ne-mi:n-a:wa   ne-mi:na-mi:na:wa   'I give it to him'   220
         ke-nepa   ke-nepa-nepa   'you sleep'   220
      c. ne-s-i-<u>Ø</u>   —   'I say'   220

Based on these facts, we follow Dahlstrom in positing the following structure for a Fox word containing prefixes and suffixes:

(57)

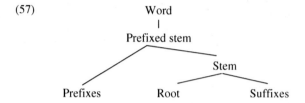

Reduplication operates on Stems – thus "outside" of suffixation – but "inside" of prefixation. Layering reduplication in this manner accounts for why *nesi*, a word in which the Stem is phonetically null, cannot overtly manifest reduplication. It also accounts for why suffixes but not prefixes can be doubled in reduplication. A word containing reduplication, prefixation, *and* suffixation will have the structure below; we assume that prefixes can combine either with Stems or with Rstems, where 'Rstem' is the product of reduplication:

(58)

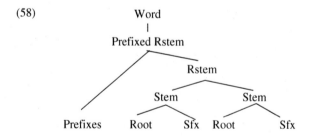

This layered morphological structure also makes predictions about the reduplicability of the effects of phonological alternations conditioned within Stems versus those conditioned solely in Rstems or Words. Stem-internal alternations are predicted on this Morphological Doubling Theory analysis to be reduplicable, in the sense that they apply within both daughters of the Rstem. However, alternations applying only within Rstems or Words are not expected to be doubled. These predictions are completely supported by the data.

5.5.1   *Stem-internal alternations: opaque overapplication by truncation*

Dahlstrom (1997) describes a number of alternations which we know to be stem-internal because they are conditioned by individual suffixes. Because Fox disyllabic reduplication targets the (suffixed) stem, we expect all of these stem-internal alternations to be reflected in both copies of the reduplication construction. This prediction is borne out. Opacity arises in just those cases in which the triggering suffix is truncated but the affected segments are not.

The first example involves the root 'say,' which has two suppletive allomorphs: /en/ and /Ø/. The choice of root allomorph is determined by the immediately following suffix. /Ø/ is used before the inflectional suffixes -ek^w- "inverse theme sign," -ek^wi- "inanimate subject," and -en(e)- "2nd person object." As shown below, when stems formed from the root for 'say' are subject to disyllabic reduplication, the same suffix-triggered root allomorph is present in both copies. Because the root is so short, the first syllable or two of the suffix always surfaces in the reduplicant, making the root allomorphy transparent:[21]

(59) a. ne-t-<u>en</u>-a:wa   ne-t-**ena**-h-**ina**:wa   'I say to him'   220
          ke-t-<u>en</u>-a:wa   ke-t-**ena**-h-**in**-a:wa   'you say to him'   220
          <u>in</u>-e:wa   **ine**-h-**ine**:wa   'he says to him (O B V)'   220
      b. ne-t-<u>Ø</u>-ek^{w}a   ne-t-**ek^{w}a**-h-**ik^{w}a**   'he says to me'   221
          ke-t-<u>Ø</u>-ek^{w}a   ke-t-**ek^{w}a**-h-**ik^{w}a**   'he says to you'   221
          <u>Ø</u>-ik^{w}a   **ik^{w}a**-h-**ik^{w}a**   'he (O B V) says to him'   221

Below we sketch several other instances in which stem-internal phonological alternations appear in each copy in reduplication. The alternations are all clearly stem-internal; they are morphologically conditioned to affect a root-final segment in the environment of suffixes.

(60)

		No reduplication	Reduplication	
a.	Root-final /n/ → /š/ before /i/ (in some roots)			
	/ke-t-en-ipena/	ke-t-eš-ipena	ke-t-eši-h-išipena	223
	'you say to us'			
b.	Root-final /Cw/-e → C-o			
	/amw-ekoči/	amokoči	amo-h-amokoči	223
	'he [obv.] eats him'			
c.	Root-final /aw/-e . . . → o: (where *e* is part of certain inflectional suffixes)			
	/ke-na:**taw-ene**/	ke-na:to:ne	ke-na:to-na:to:ne	224
	'I go after it for you'			
d.	Umlaut: root-final a: → e: before independent indicative 3rd person suffixes			
	/nepa:-wa/	nepe:-wa	nepe-nepe:wa	224–225
	'he sleeps'			
	/na:k^w**a:**-waki/	na:k^{w}e:-waki	na:k^{w}e-na:k^{w}e:waki	224
	'they leave'			

Not all suffixes trigger these root-final effects; compare, for example, the examples in (61) to those in (60d). The Umlaut alternation is triggered by independent indicative third person suffixes (Dahlstrom 1997:224); the examples in (61), with second person (a) or conjunct paradigm (b) suffixes, do not show any alternation in the root-final vowel:

(61) /ke-nepa:-pwa/   ke-nepa:-pwa ke-nepa-nepa:pwa   224–25
      'you (pl) sleep'
      /na:kʷa:-waki/   na:kʷa:-wa:či na:kʷa- na:kʷa:wa:či 224
      'they leave; conjunct'

As they are suffix-specific, the alternations in (60) are necessarily Stem-level processes:

(62)

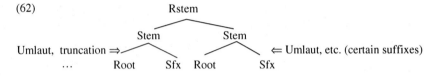

Alternations like Umlaut therefore apply internal to the stem that is doubled and (in the first instance) truncated in reduplication. Insofar as reduplicative truncation obscures the suffixal triggers for these processes, they apply opaquely. As Dahlstrom puts it (p. 223), "bisyllabic reduplication copies the output of the rule but not the environment which triggers the rule." This is precisely the description of daughter-internal opacity in MDT.

5.5.2 Juncture alternations: normal application

Morphological Doubling Theory predicts "overapplication" effects *only* in the case of alternations triggered within both daughters of the reduplication construction. Alternations triggered outside of one daughter, which happen to affect that daughter, are not expected to overapply to the other daughter (unless independently conditioned there). Fox provides clear illustration of the different behavior of daughter-internal phonology and junctural phonology in regard to overapplication. Having already seen cases of daughter-internal phonology in Fox, we turn next to cases of junctural phonology, looking at phonological alternations triggered by prefixes external to reduplication and at alternations triggered at the base-reduplicant juncture.

5.5.2.1 Prefix-Rstem junctures

"Initial Change" is an ablaut process marking certain inflectional categories (Dahlstrom 1997:221); when it applies to reduplicated words it affects only the initial consonant, rather than both copies. Equating Initial Change formally with prefixation, Dahlstrom observes that it is outside, not inside, the scope of reduplication. Initial Change turns initial /a/, /e/, /i/ to /e:/, and initial /o/ to /we/. The examples below illustrate Initial Change in its function of marking conjunct participle inflection in reduplicated words. As seen, Initial Change affects the initial vowel in the word, resulting in phonological divergence between the two copies of the root:

(63)   /amw-/   e:mwa-h-amw-a:čihi   'the ones whom they (repeatedly) eat'   222
        /ašam-/   e:ša-h-ašam-a:či   'that which he (repeatedly) feeds him' 222
        /kanawi-/ ke:na-kanawi-ta   'the one who gives speeches'   222

In Morphological Doubling Theory, Initial Change is handled in the cophonology of the prefixal construction creating conjunct participles:

(64)

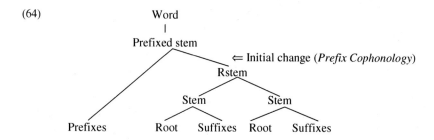

Initial Change applies external to the stem and is therefore not present in the input to reduplication; we correctly predict no "overapplication" in those cases where Initial Change happens to affect the first of the two daughters in the reduplication construction.

A second alternation applying at the Prefix-Rstem juncture is /t/-epenthesis, triggered by VV sequences across the Prefix-Stem or Prefix-Rstem juncture:

(65)   ne-t-en-a:wa   'I say to him'   220
        ke-t-en-a:wa   'you say to him'   220
        ke-t-a:čimo   'you tell a story'   220
        ne-t-ekʷa   'he says to me'   221

As a Stem-external junctural rule, /t/-insertion must be handled by a cophonology higher than the Stem, namely the Prefix cophonology:

(66)

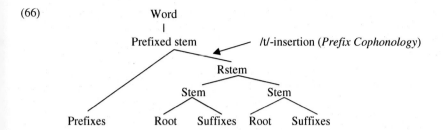

Morphological Doubling Theory predicts strongly that, like Initial Change, /t/-insertion will apply transparently to the output of the Rstem created by reduplication. This prediction is correct, as shown by the reduplicated form below (Dahlstrom 1997:220), with only one instance of /t/-insertion.

(67) ne-t-amw-aːwa 'I eat him' ne-t-amwa-**h**-amw-aːwa (*ne-t-amwa-t-amw-aːwa)

5.5.2.2 Rstem internal juncture

The /h/ at the juncture between the two copies in (67) is due to a separate pattern which inserts /h/ between vowels at the base-reduplicant juncture. This is illustrated further below:

(68) aškʷat-amwa aškʷa-h-aškʷat-amwa 'he has [food] left over' 217
      aːmiː-wa   aːmi-h-aːmiːwa   'he moves camp'   218
      opyeːni   opye-h-opyeːni   'slowly' (preverb)   218
      amw-eːwa   amwe-h-amweːwa   'he eats him'   219
      ay-oːyaːni   ayo-h-ayoːyaːni   'I use it; conjunct'   219
      i-wa   iwa-h-iwa   'he says'   219

Many prefixed reduplicated forms show both /t/- and /h/-epenthesis (see, for example, (59) and (67); neither alternation over- or underapplies in the service of greater base-reduplicant identity. This is exactly as MDT predicts; neither inserted /t/ nor inserted /h/ is present in the input to reduplication, i.e. within either daughter of the Rstem. Because it is a junctural alternation, /h/-insertion has to be handled higher up, either at the Rstem or, as argued below, at the Word cophonology.

5.5.2.3 Word-level alternations

Short /e/ is raised to /i/ in absolute word-initial position; thus the root /enaːpi-/ 'look [there]' surfaces with /e/ when prefixed (*ne-t-enaːpi* 'I look [there]') but with /i/ when initial (*inaːpi-wa* 'he looks [there]' (Dahlstrom 1997:215–16)). Because /e/ → /i/ is conditioned by word-initial position, we expect it to be a Word-cophonology alternation and to apply to the output of reduplication. This prediction might seem to be contravened by the data in (69), in which /e/-raising applies to both copies of a reduplicated root.

(69)

Root	Unreduplicated	Reduplicated		
/ena:pi-/	ina:pi-wa	ina-h-ina:piwa	'he looks [there]'	216
/enowe:-/		ino-h-inowe:-wa	'he says [thus]'	216
/ešawi-/		iša-h-išawi-wa	'he does [thus]'	216

This might be interpreted as an instance of overapplication of a Word-level alternation in service of base-reduplicant identity, but the data in (70) argue against an identity-driven overapplication analysis. In these similar forms, the reduplicated root is prefixed, rendering the first copy non-initial in the word. As a result, /e/-raising does not apply to the first copy. But it still applies to the second copy:

(70)

/ena:pi-/	ne-t-ena:pi	ne-t-ena-h-ina:pi	'I look [there]'	216
/ešawi-/		ne-t-eša-h-išawi	'I do [thus]'	216
/enowe:-/		ne-t-eno-h-inowe	'I say [thus]'	216

Here, the apparently opaque application of /e/-raising in the second copy serves to differentiate the two copies of the root, not to make them more similar. Base-reduplicant identity is clearly irrelevant to the application of /e/-raising. We instead adopt Dahlstrom's view (p. 216) that /e/-raising applies within phonological words (Pwords), and that the daughters of reduplication are separate Pwords. Prefixes incorporate into the following Pword, explaining why root-initial /e/-raising is blocked by prefixation.[22]

The question then arises: why doesn't junctural /h/ syllabify with the root, in the above examples, make it consonant-initial? Our proposal is that both /h/-insertion and /e/-raising apply at Pword boundaries in the Word cophonology, and interact in a counterbleeding fashion. (On approaches to counterbleeding in Optimality Theory, see, for example, McCarthy 1996; Sprouse 1997; McCarthy 1999.)

5.5.3　Summary of Fox

We have seen three types of junctural phonological alternations in Fox, summarized below:

- Root-sfx junctural alternations: *reduplicated*
- Prefix Stem junctural alternations: *not reduplicated*
- Word Level, at phonological word junctures: *not reduplicated*

MDT correctly predicts the reduplicability of these alternations. Those applying internal to stems will be doubled when the stems are doubled; those triggered in cophonologies external to the morphological constituent created by reduplication will apply transparently (relative to reduplication). The morphology of the Fox word, plus the assumption that cophonologies are associated with morphological constituent types, correctly predicts the scope of a given phonological alternation. It is only when morphology is ignored that overapplication of the kind we have seen in Fox becomes a mystery and requires extra theoretical mechanisms to describe.

5.6   Conclusion: morphology underlies opacity

We have seen in all of the case studies in this chapter that morphology often explains what phonology alone cannot. Once the role of morphology–phonology layering is recognized in reduplication, the need for special mechanisms like BR-FAITH vanishes. Not only is BR-FAITH unnecessary; it has in fact become an impediment to understanding the nature of reduplicative opacity, in that it predicts unattested types of opaque reduplicative phonology.

It is sometimes claimed, though without supporting evidence, that opacity (over- and underapplication) is much more common in reduplication than in other kinds of constructions. The MDT approach is in many ways similar to the rule-ordering approach to reduplicative opacity discussed in, for example, Wilbur 1973, Dudas 1976, and other sources of that era. In those approaches, a given phonological rule could be ordered after reduplication, in which case it would apply transparently, or before reduplication, potentially giving rise to overapplication or underapplication effects. Kenstowicz (1981), comparing such approaches unfavorably to Wilbur's Identity Principle in generating over- and underapplication, writes that ordering theories

> [do] not provide an explanation for why reduplication should have this tendency to late ordering while other morphological processes such as suffixation, infixation, etc. typically apply before most if not all phonological rules. The reason appears to be the "iconic" nature of reduplication.   (p. 441)

Since the writing of this passage, of course, many cases have been documented of phonology applying to the inputs to affixation and other morphological processes; indeed the entire literature on cyclicity is of this kind. It is difficult, however, to evaluate Kenstowicz's claim that opacity is more common in reduplication than elsewhere. Even if this is true, it is still not obvious that a grammatical BR-identity requirement is responsible. The prevalence of opacity in reduplication could simply be due to the historical development of truncation in partial reduplication, from which, it is our impression, most cases of synchronic opacity result. Blevins (2004) lays out a detailed historical explanation of the development of C duplication from CV reduplication, but the diachronic pathway to more severe truncation is not well enough understood to make speculation on this matter fruitful here (see, however, Niepokuj 1997).

5.7   The question of backcopying

As seen in this chapter, MDT makes more restrictive, and accurate, predictions regarding the opacity of junctural phonological effects in reduplication than does BR correspondence theory. In this section we examine one last prediction that distinguishes BRCT from MDT: the question of mutual influence between base and reduplicant.

Possibly the most striking claim of BRCT is that the output form of the reduplicant can influence the output form of the base via BR correspondence, a predicted phenomenon referred to as backcopying (McCarthy & Prince 1995a). We examined, and rejected, one potential case of backcopying underapplication in Klamath in Chapter 4. A schematic example of backcopying overapplication is presented in (71). This hypothetical language laxes vowels in closed syllables, as shown in (a). CVC reduplication of a CVCV stem, as shown in (b), results in one copy (the reduplicant) which consists of a closed syllable, and another (the base) which consists of two open syllables. The transparent application of vowel laxing would result in a lax vowel in the reduplicant and a tense vowel in the base. BRCT, however, makes it possible for the reduplicant to influence the base: if the constraint requiring closed syllable laxing (LAX) and BR-IDENT both outrank IO-FAITH, the result is a lax vowel in the base as well, as shown in (b):

(71)   Backcopying of internal alternation
   a. Language has closed syllable laxing:
      /kem-ta/   → [kɛmta]   LAX » IO-FAITH
   b. Laxing overapplies to open syllable in base (backcopying)
      /RED-kema/ → kɛm-kɛma BR-FAITH, LAX » IO-FAITH

Coupling the possibility of backcopying with the possibility, predicted in BRCT, that internal or external junctural phonology may be rendered opaque by BR correspondence, derives an even more dramatic set of predicted opacity effects. In the example in (72), also from a hypothetical language with CVC reduplication, nasal place assimilation (NPA) applies across prefix-root junctures (a). NPA also applies at the reduplicant-base juncture, as in (b). Here, we see that by virtue of the ranking BR-FAITH, NPA » IO-FAITH, assimilated place features of the reduplicant-final nasal are backcopied to the corresponding nasal in the base.

(72)   Backcopying of internal junctural alternation
      a. Language has NPA:
        /in-kana/   → [iŋkana]
      b. Internal BR juncture, backcopying overapplication
        /RED-kana/ → [kaŋ-kaŋa] BR-FAITH, NPA » IO-FAITH

In a similar vein, BRCT can derive the backcopying of junctural phonological effects triggered at the juncture between the reduplicant and another affix. To illustrate this predicted phenomenon we modify our hypothetical language slightly so that it has VC suffixing reduplication, as shown in (73a). In (b) we see the word in (a) followed by the suffix *-ta*, to which the reduplicant-final nasal assimilates in place. Backcopying, resulting from the ranking BR-FAITH, NPA » IO-FAITH, causes the base-final nasal to take on the assimilated features of the reduplicant-final nasal:

(73)   External juncture backcopying
      a. /pekam-RED/   → [pekam-am]
      b. /pekam-RED-ta/ → [pekan-an-ta] NPA, BR-FAITH » IO-FAITH

MDT strongly predicts these effects not to occur in morphological reduplication.

5.7.1   *Lack of evidence for backcopying in morphological reduplication*

Backcopying in morphological reduplication appears rare, if not nonexistent. To our knowledge there have been no claimed cases of stem-internal backcopying (71). Two examples of apparent internal junctural backcopying (72) have been described in the literature, namely Johore Malay (Onn 1976) (note 18, this chapter) and Chaha (Kenstowicz & Petros Banksira 1999), discussed below in §5.7.2. Alleged cases of external junctural backcopying (73) are the most numerous in the literature, and we will focus on these here.

Thus far we have in fact already seen two cases that superficially appear to meet the description of External Juncture backcopying. One was the purported instance of underapplication in Klamath (McCarthy & Prince 1995a), which we reanalyzed (following Zoll 2002) in Chapter 4. Rather than instantiating backcopying underapplication, Klamath is a case of non-application;

the mother node cophonology associated with reduplication fails to impose a syncope alternation which some other prefixes in the language trigger.

The other case is Eastern Kadazan, analyzed earlier in §5.2.2, which also could be described in terms of backcopying overapplication. Recall forms like the following, from (34), above (Hurlbut 1988:107):

(74)   UR of unreduplicated stem   Reduplicated stem
         _____
         /m-pi-siN-alud/   misi**ngang**alud

The fact that the prefix-final consonant, "ng," is doubled along with the following root-initial vowel in this example could be described as a case of backcopying overapplication. In fact, McCarthy and Prince (1995a) give precisely such an analysis to parallel phenomena in Chumash and Tagalog. Using Eastern Kadazan data in place of Chumash or Tagalog, their analysis would situate the reduplicant immediately preceding the root and require the reduplicant to be a light syllable, as below:

(75)   /m-pi-siN-RED-alud/   RED $= \sigma_\mu$

Since its base is *alud*, the reduplicant might be expected to be *a*. However, because of universal syllabification constraints, the preceding prefix-final consonant ('ng') must syllabify with the vowel of the reduplicant. McCarthy and Prince (1995a:310) propose for a different case, Chumash, that resyllabification results in morphological reaffiliation; the prefix-final consonant acquires a morphological affiliation with the reduplicant morpheme, which in the Eastern Kadazan case in question would consequently consist of the well-formed syllable *nga*. Backcopying from reduplicant to base results in the "ng" segment being duplicated at the left edge of the base, yielding *m-i-si-nga-ngalud*.

As seen in §5.2.2, however, there is independent evidence to support a completely different account of Eastern Kadazan in which reduplication is a late infixing construction, targeting an internal prosodic constituent (Proot) within potentially complex words. The prefix-root juncture in (75) is internal to the stem that is the subject of reduplication, and its internal syllable structure is respected by the infixing process that produces a CV copy of the Proot.

Chapter 6 argues that this same analysis is in fact the correct one for Tagalog, and Chumash as well. Involving both infixation and truncation, Eastern Kadazan, Tagalog, and Chumash perfectly illustrate the factors which we have argued in this chapter lead to reduplicative opacity. Their analysis does not require backcopying.

5.7.2 Backcopying as phonological assimilation

Although we contend that there are few or no viable cases in which BR identity results in backcopying of the types discussed above, it is undeniable that in some cases the constituent called "base" can assimilate phonologically to the one labelled "reduplicant," giving the superficial appearance of backcopying. However, as has been documented by Zuraw (2002), the types of assimilation involved are not specific to reduplication but are found in nonreduplicative contexts as well. There is no need to appeal to BR identity to force their existence. This point is illustrated, below, by an example in which base assimilates to reduplicant in morphological reduplication, followed by an example in which source assimilates to copy in phonological duplication. Both examples yield to a similar analysis in which BR correspondence per se plays no role. What is instead involved is phonologically mandated string-internal correspondence between similar segments. Walker (2000a), Hansson (2001), and Rose and Walker (2001) have variously proposed, in their analyses of long-distance consonant interactions, that segments in the same word can be required to correspond if they meet specified proximity and similarity thresholds (the closer together and more similar two segments are, the likelier they are to correspond); corresponding segments can then be compelled to be identical (or non-identical) in certain respects, yielding harmony (or dissimilation). String-internal correspondence is purely phonological, unrelated to BR correspondence.

5.7.2.1 Chaha biliteral roots

As described by Kenstowicz and Petros Banksira (1999), a near-allophonic alternation between [k] and [x] in Chaha exhibits apparent backcopying effects in reduplication. The general rule in Chaha is that the velar obstruent surfaces as [x] unless a fricative follows, in which case it surfaces as [k]. (Some exceptions to this generalization in certain cells of verbal paradigms derive from historical or abstract gemination of [x], yielding opaque [k].) We follow Kenstowicz and Petros Banksira in assuming that the velar is underlyingly [x], though a representation unspecified for [continuant] is also plausible. The relevance for backcopying is the following: when a biliteral root such as /xt/ 'cut' is reduplicated to flesh out a CVCCVC template, the velar fricative in the second copy feeds hardening, to [k], of the velar in the first copy, and the velar in the second copy consequently hardens sympathetically to [k], producing, for the root /xt/, the output [kətkɨt]. In such forms Kenstowicz and Petros Banksira analyze the first copy as the reduplicant and the second as the base, making this, in their view, an instance of backcopying of an internal junctural effect in reduplication. The relevance of this particular example to the question of BR identity hinges, however, on whether or not the attested hardening and assimilation processes can be independently motivated outside of a reduplicative context. Kenstowicz and Petros Banksira cite data showing that an initial velar obstruent in a (nonreduplicated) triliteral root must surface as [k] if either the second or third root consonant is a fricative; for example, 'hash,' a root they analyze underlyingly as /xtf/, surfaces with [k] in the jussive: *yə-ktif* (p. 575). Thus for an input /xt-xt/ we independently expect hardening of the first /x/ to [k]. The question is then how to analyze the hardening of the second /x/ to [k] even though no fricative follows. Our perusal of Kenstowicz and Petros Banksira 1999 shows no words – reduplicated or not – in which a [k] is followed in a word by [x], or indeed any words in which the two different allophones co-occur. This distributional generalization easily follows if we assume a surface correspondence relation between velars (in this case, velars in adjacent onsets), subject to a typical phonological agreement constraint, entirely independent of reduplication, which requires velar obstruents to agree in [continuant]. Constraints such as this are needed independently to handle everyday, nonreduplicative consonantal co-occurrence restrictions of the sort discussed in Hansson 2001 and the many references cited therein; see especially the discussion of stricture harmony (p. 137).

In summary, requiring [continuant] agreement of velars in Chaha obviates the need for BR correspondence in the analysis of Chaha [k] ~ [x] alternations and relates the facts to the well-known typology of consonant harmony.

5.7.2.2 Hausa participle formation

Hausa forms adjectival participles by adding to a verbal base a suffix consisting of the vowels *a* and *eː*, separated by a geminate consonant which is featurally identical to the root-final consonant (Newman 2000:19):

(76)   Verb   Participle

dafàː	dàf-affeː	'cook/cooked'
cikàː	cìk-akkeː	'fill/full'
gasàː	gàs-as ssheː	'roast/roasted'

An autosegmental analysis would spread a root node (or all of the features it dominates) to the suffixal consonant position. In Optimality Theory, a variety of approaches exist to accomplish the same representational end. One possibility is to rank DEP, the ban on feature insertion, higher than the ban on multiple indexation of output features, which would favor feature sharing (copying) over the insertion of a completely new set of consonant features. The other possibility is to hand the task of copying over to the constraints compelling string-internal correspondence (Walker 2000a; Hansson 2001; Rose & Walker 2001) between segments meeting specified thresholds of similarity and proximity.[23] Either approach will result in a representation like that in (77), in which the suffix consonant features are co-indexed with those of the root-final consonant:

(77) $d_i af_j$-aff$_j$eː

In the representation in (77), root-final *f* and suffixal *ff* correspond to each other. This is precisely the relation that, in reduplication, BRCT predicts to give rise to backcopying (although here, of course, the correspondence is driven by the phonology, not by a special BR-identity imperative). There is indeed evidence in Hausa that phonological alternations affecting the copy consonant can be replicated on the root-final consonant. Hausa palatalizes coronals before front vowels (e.g. /saːt-eː/ 'steal-pronoun_object' → [sàːtʃeː], /oːfîs-n/ 'office-def' → [oːfîʃin], etc.; see Newman 2000:307, 414ff., 627ff.). The participial suffix has a front vowel, setting up the palatalization environment in case the root it combines with copies a coronal consonant into the suffix. As noted in McCarthy 1986; Newman 2000:417, the palatalization which, as expected, targets a suffixal coronal is occasionally extended to the stem-final consonant, resulting in the overapplication of palatalization:

(78)   fasàː → [fàs-aʃʃeː] ~ [fàʃ-aʃʃeː] 'roast/roasted'

In summary, the phonological interaction between similar segments in the same string is not restricted to cases of morphological reduplication. String-internal correspondence is, according to Walker, Rose, and Hansson, implicated in all phonological harmony (or dissimilation) effects. There is no reason to expect reduplication to be any different from reduplicative morphology in its susceptibility to harmony.

As the Hausa example shows, phonological duplication is itself an extreme effect of long-distance phonological correspondence, the situation in which the quality of an essentially epenthetic consonant is determined by surface correspondence.

Consonant harmony, speech errors (to which Hansson explicity links consonant harmony), and phonological duplication all involve the same mechanism. BR correspondence is not required; rather, only sufficient similarity (featural and positional) and proximity are needed for the segments to affect each other.

5.7.3   *Implications*

Most of the examples of backcopying in morphological reduplication cited in the BRCT literature turn out instead to be reanalyzable in one of two directions. Either the phenomenon in question is actually close-range phonological assimilation of a type attested outside of reduplication (and therefore not reducible to BR identity), or the phenomenon in question is illusory, the result of morphological misanalysis. Chapter 6 is devoted to demonstrating the latter for two famous cases of apparent backcopying, and to arguing that for these, as well as for the cases discussed in this chapter, morphological doubling, sans BR-identity constraints, is the right analysis of morphological reduplication.

6 Case studies

This chapter presents case studies of partial reduplication in Tagalog and Chumash, two languages which have been cited in the BRCT literature in support of backcopying overapplication. As we saw in Chapter 5, backcopying is not a possible phenomenon in MDT, and it is therefore incumbent on MDT to provide superior alternative analyses of both cases.

Our investigations have succeeded in doing so. Closer inspection of the morphological properties of Tagalog and Chumash reduplication reveals an infixing pattern exactly comparable to that of Eastern Kadazan, discussed in Chapter 5. All three languages exhibit apparent overapplication of phonological effects occurring at the juncture between a prefix and a preposed reduplicant. The reason is that the alternation applies internal to the morphologically complex stem which is reduplicated. Part of the opacity in Tagalog and Chumash results from the fact that, as in Eastern Kadazan and Javanese, the reduplicant is truncated to (some portion of) the Proot, which closely corresponds to but does not exactly match the morphological root. This near match has led to the understandable, but mistaken, assumption in past BRCT analyses of Javanese, Tagalog, and Chumash that reduplication targets the morphological root.

The apparent overapplication effects in Tagalog and Chumash result from a conspiracy of three factors: a mismatch between the morphological root and the Proot; truncation; and infixation. We have seen all three factors at work in reduplicative opacity in Chapter 5. They are sufficient to account for the opacity in Tagalog and Chumash as well. The increased power of backcopying in BRCT is not justified by these cases.

6.1   Tagalog

Like many other Austronesian languages, Tagalog has partial reduplication in the vicinity of the root, as well as a phonological process of nasal fusion operating at prefix junctures. The interaction of these two phenomena creates opacity in reduplication.

McCarthy and Prince (1995a) cite the forms in (1) in support of BRCT's prediction of backcopying overapplication. Nasal fusion, conditioned by some ŋ-final prefixes, converts a sequence of /ŋ/ + /p,k,t,s/ to a single nasal consonant at the relevant place of articulation (/m,ng,n,n/); nasal fusion also optionally collapses /ŋ-b/ to /m/ and /ŋ-ʔ/ to /ŋ/).[1]

(1)   a. pa-mu-mutul   'a cutting in quantity' MP95:255
          cf. pa-mutul < /paŋ-putul/   'that used for cutting'
          cf. putul   'cut (n.)'
       b. na-ŋi-ŋisda   'is/are going fishing'[2] MP95:308, SO:364
          cf. maŋ-isda   'go fishing'   SO:364

McCarthy and Prince (1995a) take the position, consistent with descriptions in the primary sources (e.g. Schachter & Otanes 1972; marked "SO" above) that Tagalog has root reduplication. They assume morphological inputs of the type in (2):

(2)   /paŋ-RED-putul/
       /naŋ-RED-isda/

Given these inputs, McCarthy and Prince are naturally concerned with the fact that the prefix affects the shape not only of the reduplicant, which it immediately precedes, but also the base, to which it is not adjacent. In (1a), the result of nasal fusion at the reduplicant-base juncture is reflected in the base as well, and in (1b), the final consonant of the prefix is actually doubled, serving as onset not only to the reduplicant vowel but also to the base.

McCarthy and Prince's (1995a:60) solution to the doubling problem is back-copying: the reduplicant interacts transparently with the prefix and, as a result of BR identity, the phonological results are mirrored in the base: /paŋ-RED-putul/ → [pa-mu-mutul].

6.1.1   Alternatives to backcopying

Given the morphological analysis in (2), backcopying would seem to be the only analytical option. However, a number of researchers – Carrier-Duncan 1984; Aronoff 1988; Lathroum 1991; Booij & Lieber 1993; Cole 1994, as well as French 1988 – have proposed an alternative account: essentially, reduplication, which is internal, applies to the output of prefixation. The morphological analysis on this account is very different from that assumed by McCarthy and Prince, as shown below for the same two forms considered above:

(3)

Input to reduplication:	[pamutul] (< /paŋ-putul/)	[naŋisda] (< /naŋ-isda/)
	↓	↓
Output of internal reduplication:	[pa-mu-mutul]	[na-ŋi-ŋisda]

Because reduplication operates on prefixed stems, the output of nasal fusion is thus present in the input to reduplication. The fact that its effects are doubled is not a mystery.[3]

6.1.2   Prefixation vs. infixation

Three arguments, all derived from close study of reduplicated stems bearing the prefix *maŋ-* (on which there is abundant data), support the infixation + normal application analysis in (3) over the prefixation + backcopying analysis in (2).

First, reduplication appears to be dependent on prefixation, in that in most cases an independent *maŋ-*stem (with a transparently related meaning) exists, while an independent reduplicated stem, with a meaning such that it could serve as the input to *maŋ-*prefixation in these words, does not. Illustrative examples from English's (1986) Tagalog–English dictionary are provided in (4); forms or glosses also cited by Schachter and Otanes (1972:103) are marked "SO".[4]

(4)

	Stem	Unreduplicated *maŋ-*Stem	Reduplicated *maŋ-*Stem
a.	bayan 'town,' 'country' (SO)	ma-mayan 'to live or reside in a town'	ma-<u>ma</u>-mayan 'resident of a city or town' 'citizen' (SO)
b.	ibig 'love, fondness'	ma-ŋibig 'to court, to be a suitor'	ma-<u>ŋi</u>-ŋibig 'beau, suitor,' 'lover' (SO)
c.	tahi 'sew'	ma-nahi 'to engage in sewing'	ma-na-nahi 'one who sews; tailor, seamstress . . .,' 'dressmaker' (SO)
d.	sayaw 'dance (n.)'	ma-nayaw 'to take up dancing as a profession'	ma-<u>na</u>-nayaw 'a professional dancer'
e.	dambon 'loot, plunder (n.)' 'armed robbery' (SO)	man-dambon 'to loot, plunder'	man-<u>da</u>-rambon 'looter, plunderer, pillager,' 'bandit' (SO)
f.	kalakal 'merchandise, commodity,' 'business' (SO)	ma-ŋalakal 'to engage in trading or commerce'	ma-<u>ŋa</u>-ŋalakal 'trader, merchant, businessman'

These data suggest that the *maŋ*-stem is a subconstituent of the word containing both *maŋ*- and reduplication, whereas the bare reduplicated stem is not.

The second, semantic, argument supports this conclusion. Although the semantic evidence is not always cut-and-dried, in examples like those in (4) the meaning of the word with both reduplication and *maŋ*- is based on the meaning of the *maŋ*- stem in a way that supports treating the *maŋ*-stem as a subconstituent of the word. The prefixed stem *ma-mayan* means 'to reside in a town'; *ma-ma-mayan* is the nominalization of that verb. The same relationship holds between *maŋibig* (< /maŋ-ibig/) 'to court, be a suitor' and its nominalized counterpart *ma-ŋi-ŋibig* 'beau, suitor.'

The third argument in favor of infixation is phonological. Some stems containing disyllabic prefixes, when subject to reduplication, show variation between stem reduplication and second syllable reduplication (which happens to target the prefix). The data below are taken from Schachter and Otanes 1972:370:[5]

(5)

Basic form	Contemplated aspect		
UR, no reduplication	Stem reduplication		Second syllable reduplication
a. /ika-takbo/	ika-ta-takbo	∼	i-ka-katakbo
'cause to run'		'will cause to run'	
b. /ipag-linis/	ipag-li-linis	∼	i-pa-paglinis
'clean for'		'will clean for'	
c. /maka-halata/	maka-ha-halata	∼	ma-ka-kahalata
'notice'		'will notice'	

Second syllable reduplication is clearly infixing, showing that infixation has to play some role in Tagalog reduplication; this lends plausibility to an infixing analysis of reduplication in other cases as well.

If we accept infixation as the right analysis for Tagalog prefixation generally, the question then becomes one of mechanics: to what is the infixing reduplication being infixed in the case of stems with monosyllabic prefixes (e.g. *maŋ*-)? Aronoff (1988) proposes that reduplication looks into the word for the morphological head. Booij and Lieber (1993), Cole (1994), and Downing (1998d) all propose, with minor variations, a prosodic solution for the mismatch between the morphological root and what actually reduplicates: essentially, reduplication targets not the root but a prosodic constituent which corresponds closely but in some cases imperfectly to the morphological root. We build on this proposal in developing an analysis similar to what we proposed in Chapter 5 for Javanese and Eastern Kadazan: reduplication truncates the word down to the first CV of

its Proot. In Tagalog, the Proot consists of the morphological root plus a preceding prefix-final consonant to serve as a syllable onset, where needed. An
analysis of an apparent overcopying example, *maɲiŋibig* 'suitor,' is provided
below. This structure is composed of three independent constructions: prefixation, which produces *maŋ*-stems, truncation (which produces the truncated stem
type called for in the first daughter), and reduplication:

(6)

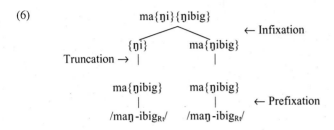

Once it is recognized that prefixes are present in the input to reduplication and
that the reduplicant is a truncated version of the Proot, which can include prefixal
material, the doubling of onsets and of nasal fusion in Tagalog reduplication
is no longer a mystery. Rather, it is normal application of phonology, rendered
opaque by truncation. No backcopying is required.

6.2   Chumash

Chumash, like Tagalog, has been described as exhibiting root reduplication
with opaque overcopying of prefix material to the left of the reduplicative
prefix (McCarthy & Prince 1995a). Our investigations have revealed a very
different picture: instead, as we found for Tagalog and, in Chapter 5, for Eastern
Kadazan, Chumash exhibits infixing reduplication which targets the Proot of a
morphologically complex word. Our conclusions echo those of Cole (1994) and
Downing (1998d), both of whom also recognize the role of the prosodic stem in
Chumash reduplication. Downing, in particular, observes that an infixing Pstem
analysis makes McCarthy and Prince's backcopying analysis unnecessary.

Our sources for Chumash data are Applegate 1972; 1976, on the Ineseño
dialect, and Wash 1995, on the Barbareño dialect. We will refer to these data
sources in examples as A72, A76, and W95, respectively.[6] Most discussions in
the literature are based on the Ineseño dialect; any examples from Barbareño
will be explicitly identified.

The data in (7) illustrate the apparently prefixing stem reduplication in
nouns and verbs. Reduplication pluralizes nouns and renders verbs repetitive,

distributive, intensive, or continuative (Applegate 1972:383). To assist in parsing these complex words, roots are in bold in unreduplicated forms, and reduplicants are in bold in reduplicated forms:[7]

(7)

čʰ**umaš**	'islander'	čʰ**um**+čʰumaš 'islanders'	A76:273
k-ni-**č'eq**	1SUBJ-TRANS-tear	kni+**č'eq**+č'eq 'I'm tearing it up'	A76:282
k-wi-**č'eq**	1SUBJ-BY_HITTING-tear	kwi+**č'eq**+č'eq 'I pound it to pieces'	A72:387

Chumash stem reduplication has played a prominent role in the BRCT literature because of data like those in (8). McCarthy and Prince (1995a:308) cite these forms, taken (apparently via Mester 1986) from Applegate (1976:279), as manifesting backcopying overapplication in reduplication, a signature prediction of BRCT:[8]

(8)

	Plain	Reduplicated		
a.	s-**ikuk**	**sik**+sikuk	'he is chopping, hacking'	(cf. *s-ik-ikuk)
b.	s-iš-**expeč**	**ši**+**šex**+šexpeč	'they two are singing'	(cf. *š-iš-ex-expeč)
c.	k-**ʔaniïš**	**k'an**+k'aniïš	'my paternal uncles'	(cf.*k-ʔan-ʔaniïš → k'anʔaniïš)

In the forms in (8), an alternation conditioned at the prefix-reduplicant juncture is reflected in the base, where it is not conditioned. In (8a) and (8b), the alternation consists of syllabifying the prefix-final consonant into the onset of the syllable containing the VC reduplicant. It is the doubling of this onset consonant after the reduplicant, where it surfaces as onset to the base-initial syllable that McCarthy and Prince (1995a) analyze in terms of backcopying. In (8c), the relevant alternation consists of fusing the prefixal consonant with the reduplicant-initial glottal. This alternation appears to overapply in that the fused consonant appears following the reduplicant, at the beginning of the base, where it is not expected.

Similar phenomena occur in Barbareño Chumash (Wash 1995). As in Ineseño, a sequence of identical stops or fricatives across a morpheme boundary is converted to a single, aspirated consonant.[9]

(9) /s-šuphuč/ → šʰuphuč 'it is full of earth/dirt' W95:98
     /k-kutiy-šaš/ → kʰutiyšaš 'I saw myself [in the mirror]' W95:98

Aspiration appears to overapply in the Barbareño forms in (10), where a sequence of identical stops across the prefix-reduplicant boundary reduces to a single, aspirated stop. In such cases, aspiration is reflected in the base of reduplication as well. Surface forms and glosses are taken from Wash 1995 (pp. 31–32, 167):

(10)

		Plain stem	Reduplicated	
/s-/ prefix (3SG subject)	a.	/s-suʔnan/ → sʰuʔnan	sʰun+sʰuʔnan 'he would continue'	W95:32
	b.	/s-šutowič/ → šʰutowič	šʰut+šʰutowič 'he was very quick'	W95:167
/k-/ prefix (1SG subject)	c.	/k-kalaš/ → kʰalaš	kʰal+kʰalaš 'I am breathing'	W95:31
/p-/ prefix (2SG subject)	d.	/p-paš-/ → pʰaš	pʰaš+pʰaʔš 'You are vomiting'	W95:32

6.2.1 Alternatives to backcopying

McCarthy and Prince (1995a), who discuss the Ineseño forms in (8), develop a backcopying overapplication analysis, driven by a requirement that reduplicant and base begin with identical segments. Their analysis crucially relies on the assumption that CVC reduplication targets the morphological stem, schematized again below:

(11)   Prefixation analysis: /Pfx-R ED-Stem/

In situations in which the prefix-final consonant interacts with the reduplicant, base-reduplicant faithfulness constraints require the effects of this alternation to be duplicated on the corresponding segments of the base. Below, three possible outputs for the input /s-iš-R ED-expeč/ (8b) are evaluated for well-formedness and BR identity:

(12)   *   si.še.x-ex.peč   ONSET satisfied, but BR identity violated (š ≠ e)
        *   siš.ex.-ex.peč   ONSET violated, though BR identity maintained (e=e)
        ☞   si.š ex.-šex.peč ONSET satisfied *and* BR identity maintained (š = š)[10]

Insofar as backcopying of effects from reduplicant to base can only be described if reduplicant and base segments are in correspondence, effects such as this are clear support for Correspondence Theory and its family of BR-FAITH constraints.

But linear or hierarchical order is never straightforward to determine for morphological constructions consisting of prosodic operations, and the logically possible alternative to (11) is that Chumash CVC reduplication is infixing. As in Tagalog, reduplication could be targeting the stem – or, more accurately, the Pstem – inside of a morphologically complex word:

(13)

Input to reduplication:	[si.šex.peč]	(> /s-iš-expeč/)	[k'aniiš]	(> /k-?aniiš/)
	↓		↓	
Output of internal reduplication:	[si-šex-šexpeč]		[k'an-k'aniiš]	

On the infixing account, by contrast, all the relevant phonological alternations are transparently conditioned, if we assume that, as in Tagalog, what Chumash reduplication targets is a prosodic constituent which matches the morphological stem but can be mismatched in case a preceding prefix ends in a consonant and the stem begins with a vowel. Indeed, this very Pstem proposal has already been made by Downing (1998d), who observes that if the PStem is the domain of reduplication, backcopying becomes unnecessary in the analysis of overcopying effects. In the MDT account, reduplication operates after, or on the output of, prefixation; the prefix-final consonant is adjacent to the stem-initial segment in the input to reduplication. Thus any doubling of effects at the prefix-stem juncture are the result of normal application of Chumash syllabification rules. No overcopying, and crucially no backcopying, takes place.

The infixation account also corresponds closely to the account favored by Applegate (1976), who writes (p. 278) that "CVC reduplication is a very low-level phonological process which applies to the output of the main block of phonological rules."

The choice between the prefixing and infixing alternatives is highly significant to Morphological Doubling Theory, which lacks the descriptive power of backcopying. If Morphological Doubling Theory is to be able to account for Chumash, it must adopt the infixing hypothesis in (13). The Morphological Doubling Theory account would look something like (14), in which the input to reduplication – the input to each daughter in the construction – contains all the morphemes involved in the phonological alternations in question. Each stem thus contains (in its input) the context for the resyllabification/fusion alternation, even though truncation of the reduplication renders this context opaque:

(14)   Infixation analysis, in Morphological Doubling Theory

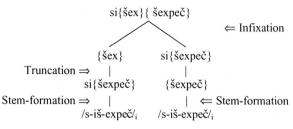

Two different morphological hypotheses about Chumash reduplication are now in competition, one (Prefixing) which motivates backcopying and therefore BRCT, and one (Infixing) which is compatible with the more restrictive MDT approach. Is Chumash stem reduplication strictly prefixing, in which case backcopying is entailed, or is it infixing, in which case the phonological doubling effects are simply ordinary reduplication? Our answer, that infixation is the correct analysis, requires some background in Chumash morphology to explain.

6.2.2   *Chumash verb morphology*
A detailed description of Ineseño Chumash morphology is found in Applegate's (1972) PhD dissertation, based primarily on the field notes of J. P. Harrington, in which he discusses six types of reduplication in Ineseño Chumash. Of these only the most well-known, CVC prefixing reduplication, is discussed here. Wash (1995) provides a thorough survey of productive CVC prefixing reduplication in Barbareño Chumash, allowing for comparison between the two dialects.

Although Applegate (1972) is the best source of information about the morphological structure of complex words, most theoretical discussions of (Ineseño) Chumash rely on Applegate's short (1976) paper on reduplication, in which morpheme breaks are not given. Such discussions are thus not informed by the morphological evidence to be presented here.

Chumash verbal morphology is heavily prefixing (there are also a small number of suffixes, both derivational and inflectional). Applegate (1972) partitions verb prefixes into three main classes: Inner, Outer, and Personal, with inner prefixes occurring closest to the root and outer prefixes, farthest away:

(15)   Outer prefixes – Personal prefixes – Inner prefixes – [root – suffixes]$_{Stem}$

Outer prefixes mark things like negative, tense, nominalization/relativization, clause subordination, and sentential adverbs. Personal prefixes mark person and number of subject. Inner prefixes are quite various, including aspectual, instrumental, action classifiers, spatial orientation, verbal force, and other things (see Applegate 1972:301ff.).

This segregation accords closely with the level ordering system for affixes proposed by Wash for Barbareño. According to Wash, Level 1 includes derivational suffixes; Level 2 includes derivational prefixes (including classifier prefixes, causative, and diminutive); Level 3 includes inflectional suffixes and prefixes (including tense, aspect, reflexive, stativizer/nominalizer, pronominal suffixes, venitive, desiderative, and habitual); and Level 4 prefixes, which Wash analyzes as clitics, include tense, indefinite, subordinate, plural, emphatic, article, deictic, pronominal, and connectives.

The difference between Inner prefixes and all other prefixes is relevant to reduplication. Where possible, we will use a hyphen "-" to mark Inner prefixation boundaries and an equals sign "=" to mark Outer and Personal prefixation boundaries. Reduplication boundaries are marked with a plus sign "+".

6.2.3   *Which prefixes can contribute an overcopying final C?*

In Ineseño, it appears that *any* preceding prefix will contribute its final C to a V-initial reduplicating syllable or fuse its final consonant, as appropriate, with the initial consonant of the reduplicating syllable.[11]

(16)

Gloss	Unreduplicated	Reduplicated	Source
a. 'he is naked'	s=ʔamɨn' → s'amɨn'	s'am+s'amɨn'	A72:389, A76:279
b. 'they two are singing'	s=iš-ex-peč	ši+šex+šexpeč	A76:279
c. 'they are doing it'/ 'they are making . . .'	s=iy-eqwel	si+yeq+yeqwel	A72:386/ A76:279
d. 'basket-maker'	ʔal-aqnɨp'	ʔa+laq+laqnɨp'	A72:210

In Barbareño, a Morpheme Integrity Constraint (as in Kinande or Javanese) appears to prevent the comparable phenomenon, although consonantal prefixes are amenable to reduplicating along with a following root. See Wash 1995 (especially Chapter 4) for discussion.

6.2.4   *Inner (Level 2) prefixes in the reduplication domain*

As seen earlier, Applegate's (1976) characterization of Chumash CVC reduplication as stem reduplication plays a central role in McCarthy and Prince's (1995a) prefixing analysis. In fact, however, as Applegate (1972) is especially careful to document, reduplication often targets Inner prefixes as well: "With the exception of a few prefixes which regularly shift reduplication to the following morpheme . . . CVC reduplication falls on the first CVC sequence following person-number markers" (Applegate 1972:386). This is a highly significant fact, since it dispels any notion that the reduplicant simply targets the morphological root. Reduplicating prefixes are part of the Pstem, whose initial CVC portion is what the reduplicant is truncated down to.

Examples from Ineseño and Barbareño in which an Inner prefix is included in the reduplicant are given in (17). In (17a–b), the Causative *su-*, an Inner prefix, is part of the string of which the initial CVC is reduplicated. In (17c), the agentive prefix *ʔal-* is doubled; in (17d), the reduplicant is instantiated by material from the prefix *wi-* 'apart.' Curly brackets in the unreduplicated forms demarcate the Pstem; Pstem-internal Inner prefixes are shown in boldface.

(17)

		No reduplication	Reduplication	
Ineseño	a.	k={**su**-pše?}	k+šup+šupše?	A76:282
		1SUBJ-CAUS-to‗be‗extinguished	'I'm putting out (a fire)'	
	b.	k={**su**-towič}	k+šut+šutowič	A76:282
		1SUBJ-CAUS-?	'I'm doing it fast'	
	c.	{**ʔal**-aqša+Vn+?}	ʔal+ʔalaqšan'	A72:210
			'the dead'	
	d.	s-{**pil**-kowon}	s+pil+pilkowon	A76:281
			'it is spilling'	
Barbareño	d.	{**wi**-phatatan}	wih+wiphatata?niš	W95:128
		OF‗HITTING-fall‗apart =	'pieces'	
		to destroy, take apart'		

A difference between Ineseño and Barbareño, attributed above to Morpheme Integrity, is that in Barbareño, the reduplicant apparently cannot partially truncate two different morphemes (Wash 1995:128). In (17b), an /h/ is inserted to supply the reduplicant with a final C, rather than taking the initial stem C for a coda, as Ineseño would do. (See Downing 1998d for further discussion of the significance of the dialectal difference for the BRCT approach to reduplication.)

Forms in which reduplication targets a Pstem containing a prefix, which appear to be common in both dialects, show clearly that the Prefixation picture in (11) cannot be right. Reduplication is not targeting the morphological root, and cannot therefore be treated as a morphological prefix to the root; instead, reduplication is targeting a potentially morphologically complex constituent, the Pstem.

6.2.5 *A split among Inner prefixes in Ineseño*

Although some Inner prefixes are Pstem-internal, as seen above, others are not. As part of his comprehensive inventory of verbal affixes, Applegate (1972) classifies each Inner prefix according to whether or not it can reduplicate.[12] Building on the analysis developed so far, this split corresponds to whether an Inner prefix is Pstem-internal or Pstem-external. According to Applegate (1972), "the great majority" of Inner prefixes are Pstem-internal (p. 387). Below are a number of examples containing Pstem-external Inner prefixes (in boldface) that do not reduplicate.[13]

(18)

Without reduplication	With reduplication	Gloss	Source
a. k=**wi**-{č'eq}	kwi+č'eq+č'eq	'I pound it to pieces'	A72:387
1SUBJ-BY‑HITTING-tear			
b. s=**uti**-{lip'in}	suti+lip+lip'in	'the ground is uneven'	A72:390
c. s=**wati**-{k'ot}	swati+k'ot+k'ot	'is broken to pieces'	A72:384
/s=**wati**-{lok'in-š}/	šwati+lok+lok'ič	'it falls apart'	A72:388
d. s=**pili**-{paq'}	spili+paq+paq'	'a travelling company splits up'	A72:389
e. s=**ni**-{wɨy}	šni+wɨy+wɨy	'he is cutting notches on it'	A72:384
k=**ni**-{č'eq}	kni+č'eq+č'eq	'I'm tearing it up'	A76:282
ni-{pʰat}	ni+pʰat+pʰat	'to break to pieces'	A72:390
f. s-am=**ti**-{lok'in}	samti+lok+lok'in	'they cut it off'	A72:387
g. s=**akti**-{kuti}	sakti+kut+kuti	'he comes to wash'	A72:387

The same word can contain both Pstem-external and Pstem-internal Inner prefixes. As expected, reduplication targets the Pstem, duplicating the Pstem-internal, but not the Pstem-external, Inner prefixes. Inner prefixes are, as before, in boldface in the unreduplicated forms:

(19)

Without reduplication	With reduplication	Gloss	Source
a. k=**sili**-{**pil**-wayan}	ksili+piw+piwayan	'I want to swing'	A72:387
b. s-iy=**ak**{**t-aqu**-smon}	siyak+taq+taqusmon	'they come to gather it'	A72:388
< /s-iy-akti-{aqu-smon}/			

The form in (19b) shows that the final consonant of a Pstem-external prefix will incorporate into the Pstem, as expected, in case the Pstem would otherwise be V-initial.

When more than one Inner prefix is present in a word, the Pstem contains the leftmost Inner prefix and all following material. In (20), the root is preceded by a string of up to three Inner prefixes, each independently known to be Pstem-internal. The reduplicant (in bold) is the initial CVC portion of this Pstem. The form in (20c) shows that Pstems which include Inner prefixes behave in the same way as those based on roots. If the Pstem would be vowel-initial but is preceded by a consonant-final prefix (subject to the dialectal conditions discussed above), the consonant joins the Pstem. In the unreduplicated form, Inner prefixes are shown in boldface and the Pstem is delimited with curly brackets:

(20)

Without reduplication	With reduplication	Gloss	Source
s={**max**-keken}	s+mex+mexkeken	'he is spreading it open'	A72:387
{s=**ali-max**-keken}	sal+salimexkeken	'he is stretching it out'	A72:387
{s=**uti-ali-max**-keken}	sut+sutalimexkeken	'he suddenly gives it a stretch'	A72:387

6.2.6   Implications of the split among Inner prefixes

The split between reduplicating and nonreduplicating prefixes is easy to model on the Infixation account, as seen above: reduplication, a late morphological process, calls for two instances of the entire word, truncating the first copy down to the first CVC portion of its Pstem. Reduplicating Inner prefixes are within the Pstem; nonreduplicating Inner prefixes are not.

The split in the behavior of Inner prefixes is much more difficult to capture on the Prefixing account crucially underlying McCarthy and Prince's (1995a) backcopying analysis. On the Prefixing account, the R E D morpheme immediately precedes the string whose first (C)VC it copies. To distinguish reduplicating from nonreduplicating Inner prefixes on this account, it would have to be the case that reduplicating Inner prefixes are linearly ordered closer to the Stem than nonreduplicating Inner prefixes, and that reduplication is ordered in between the two prefix classes:

(21)   Nonreduplicating Inner prefixes – R E D – Reduplicating Inner prefixes – Stem

The Prefixation hypothesis, with ordering as its only possible account of the split behavior of Inner prefixes, makes a striking morphological prediction: all reduplicating Inner prefixes should be ordered after (inside, closer to the stem than) all nonreduplicating Inner prefixes. The Infixation hypothesis makes no such prediction, as it draws no structural morphological distinction between Pstem-internal and Pstem-external Inner prefixes.

The ordering prediction of the Prefixation account appears to be inconsistent with the information provided by Applegate on the relative linear order of the Inner prefixes. Applegate partitions Inner prefixes into position classes which correlate roughly with syntactic function and semantic transparency. Although there are not as many examples containing both types of Inner prefixes as one would like, the forms that do exist give the clear impression that there is no fixed linear ordering between reduplicating and nonreduplicating Inner prefixes.

Example (19) illustrates words in which nonreduplicating Inner prefixes precede reduplicating Inner prefixes. These data are consistent with the Ordering hypothesis. But Inner prefixes also occur in the opposite order, contrary to the Ordering hypothesis. The examples in (22) illustrate the ubiquitous, highly productive Causative prefix *su-* seen earlier in (17), (20). A Pstem-internal, reduplicating prefix (see, for example, (17)), *su-* can precede other prefixes which Applegate classifies as nonreduplicating or, in the terms used here, Pstem-external. In (22), reduplicating (Pstem-internal) prefixes are subscripted as "R"; nonreduplicating (Pstem-external) prefixes (on which see (18)) are subscripted as "N". One or two of the Inner prefixes in (22) are unclassified, due to a lack of sufficient data.

(22)

a. /maq$_R$-su$_R$-ni$_N$-apay$_{Rt}$/ maqsunapay 'to raise a line, string a bow' A72:379
   /wi-su$_R$-ni$_N$-apay$_{Rt}$/ wisunapay '[sea] to cast ashore' A72:383
b. /k=su$_R$-wati$_N$-lok'in$_{Rt}$/ ksuwatilok'in 'I cut it in passing A72:368
   (I'll be back for it later)'
c. /su$_R$-ti$_N$-wɨy$_{Rt}$/ sutiwɨy 'to sing a charm, spell' A72:324
   /su$_R$-waš$_R$-ti$_N$-aq-pey$_{Rt}$/ šuwešteqpey 'to mend, fix' A72:383

When verbs like these are subject to reduplication, the leftmost Pstem-internal prefixes define the left edge of the Pstem, which includes all following material, including Inner prefixes that would otherwise be Pstem-external. This can be seen in example (23), in which the Pstem-internal prefix *xul-* precedes the Pstem-external transitive prefix *ni-* (see (18e)). The reduplicant is *xun*, which consists of the prefix *xul* plus the initial consonant of *ni-*, with which the final *l* of the prefix fuses.[14]

(23)

	Plain	Reduplicated	Source
	/k=xul$_R$-ni$_N$-yɨw/ → k{xuniyɨw}	k+xun+xuniyɨw	A72:384
	'1SUBJ=?-TRANS-?'	'I am looking all over for it'	

The inescapable conclusion from examples like (22) and (23) is that the split in reduplicability within Inner prefixes is not reflected in their ordering relations; both reduplicating > nonreduplicating and nonreduplicating > reduplicating orders are well-attested in Ineseño Chumash. Furthermore, a normally nonreduplicating prefix can be "promoted" to a reduplicating prefix if it is sandwiched between a reduplicating prefix and the stem. This behavior follows naturally from the Pstem analysis; it is contrary to the predictions of the Prefixation account, and therefore supports the Infixation account of reduplication.[15]

Although evidence from semantics is not strong, it tends to support the claim of the Infixation account that reduplication is a late morphological process targeting whole words, rather than having scope over only stems (as the Prefixation account would predict). Applegate (1972) describes CVC-verb reduplication as endowing the verb with "a repetitive, distributive, intensive, or continuative force" (pp. 383–84). Examples like the following are consistent with the prediction of the Infixation account that reduplication should have semantic scope over the whole verb:[16]

(24)

	Plain	Reduplicated	Source
a. /s={**tal**-memen}/ 3SUBJ=OF_GRASPING-?	štelmemen 'he touches it'	š+tel+telmemen 'he [is] groping around'	A72:384
b. /s=**wati**-{k'ot}/ 3SUBJ=OF_DISINTEGRATION-?	swatik'ot 'is broken'	swati+k'ot+k'ot 'is broken to pieces'	A72:384
c. /**ni**-{pʰat}/ TRANS-?	nipʰat 'to take apart'	ni+pʰat+pʰat 'to break to pieces'	A72:390

Consider the nonreduplicating Inner prefix *wati-* in (24b). Although it is not reduplicated phonologically, its meaning appears to be affected by reduplicative semantics. According to Applegate *wati-* means 'apart, of disintegration,' which is transparent in the unreduplicated word *swatik'ot* 'is broken.' Judging by the meaning of the reduplicated verb with *wati-*, i.e. *swatik'otk'ot*, reduplication is acting semantically on the prefixed verb. The meaning 'is broken to pieces' is the expected result of applying a distributive suffix to a form meaning 'is broken.' This is exactly as the Infixation account would predict. By contrast, the Prefixation account would predict *wati-* to attach after reduplication, and therefore to be outside its semantic scope. (It would of course help to know what *k'ot* means.)

6.2.7   Summary

In Chumash, as argued above, the whole word is subject to reduplication; the first copy is truncated to the initial CVC portion of its Pstem, which is then infixed before the Pstem of the second copy. The Pstem contains the stem and any Pstem-internal prefixes (as well as other prefixes sandwiched in between). Because of consonant fusion and onset requirements, Pstems can also contain the final consonant of a preceding prefix which is otherwise Pstem-external. The potential mismatch between Pstem and morphological constituent is what gives rise to the appearance of onset overcopying, or overapplication of consonant fusion. However, both effects are normal application within the MDT analysis, for which we have provided independent support from Chumash morphology.

This analysis is, interestingly, very close to Applegate's own characterization of reduplication as "a very low-level phonological process which applies to the output of the main block of phonological rules" (Applegate 1976:278); "Reduplication occurs only after all other applicable rules have determined the final shape of the terminal CVC sequence to be reduplicated" (Applegate 1976: 279).

Chumash is a clear illustration of the theme sounded throughout this book. Understanding the phonology of reduplication requires a solid understanding of the morphology of reduplication. In Chumash, as in Tagalog, Eastern Kadazan, Fox, Javanese, Klamath, and many of the other case studies in this book, morphology explains phonological phenomena which would be puzzling from a purely phonological perspective, and which in some cases have prompted the introduction of reduplication-specific technologies which are unnecessary in a theory which approaches reduplicative phonology from the broader perspective of morphologically conditioned phonology.

7 Final issues

A fundamental claim of Morphological Doubling Theory is that reduplication involves semantic, rather than phonological, identity. If this is true, then wholesale, potentially long-distance phonological string copying, developed expressly to account for reduplication (see, for example, Marantz 1982; Clements 1985; Mester 1986; Steriade 1988, inter alia), is not needed in phonological theory. As argued in Chapter 1, however, there is still motivation for small-scale, proximal, phonologically motivated phonological copying, both within and outside of reduplication. This chapter returns to the distinction between morphological duplication and phonological copying, firming up the defining criteria and exploring the potential for interaction between the two types of duplication.

7.1 Criteria distinguishing phonological copying from morphological reduplication

The four criteria distinguishing between phonological copying and morphological reduplication, originally presented in Chapter 1, are given below:

(1) Phonological copying | Morphological reduplication
1. Serves a phonological purpose | Serves a morphological purpose
2. Is phonologically proximal | Is not necessarily phonologically proximal
3. Involves single phonological segments | Involves morphological constituents
4. Is driven by phonological identity imperative | Is not driven by phonological identity imperative

7.2 The purpose and nature of phonological copying

Accounting for phonological assimilation is central to any theory of phonology. In autosegmental phonology, assimilation is viewed as spreading; well-formedness constraints on autosegmental association ensure that assimilation is proximal, meaning that a target segment will assimilate to the closest eligible trigger, not (for example) the farthest. Recent work in Optimality Theory has cast assimilation in terms of correspondence; for Walker 2000a; b; Hansson 2001; Walker to appear, assimilation occurs when a grammar imposes identity requirements on corresponding segments; a key component of the theory is that segment-to-segment correspondence is established in the first place only among segments that are sufficiently similar *and* sufficiently proximal in the input. In this approach, as in the autosegmental approach, assimilation can occur at a distance only if it also occurs locally; assimilation is therefore always proximal. In Turkish vowel harmony, for example, a harmonic suffix agrees with the closest root vowel, not the farthest, as can be demonstrated with disharmonic roots: thus *anne* 'mother' is *anne-ler* and *elma* is *elma-lar*. There is no language with vowel harmony in which these plurals could be *anne-lar* and *elma-ler* (unless dissimilation is involved, but then the identity of the initial vowel would be irrelevant).

The view of phonological segment copying adopted in this book is that phonological copying is an extreme form of phonological assimilation. It conforms to the same generalizations about proximity, and it is handled with the same theoretical mechanisms. What distinguishes phonological copying from ordinary epenthesis of a default segment is the phonological correspondence established between the introduced segment and its nearest comparable neighbor. Zuraw (2002) has observed that phonological correspondence itself can be a desideratum; where faithfulness to input features is not an issue, an epenthetic segment which corresponds to another is, from that perspective, more desirable than one which does not.

To illustrate the ways in which phonological segment copying patterns with phonological assimilation, rather than with morphological reduplication, we may fruitfully contrast Hausa noun pluralization (2a) and Ponapean prefixation (2b) with Madurese noun pluralization (2c):

(2)   a. fensir-oːriː   'pencils'
          moːt-oːciː   'cars'
          teːbur-oːriː   'tables'
       b. ak-pwung   → akupwung   'petty'
          ak-dei   → akedei   'to engage in a throwing contest'
          ak-tantat   → akatantat   'to abhor'
       c. w̃ã-mõw̃ã   'faces'
          ỹãt-nẽỹãt   'intentions'
          wɣ-kʰuwɣ   'caves'

The Hausa requirement that syllables begin with consonantal onsets leads to consonant epenthesis in the plural suffix.[1] As discussed in Chapter 1, phonological copying derives from the need for this consonant to be featurally specified; as expected in phonological assimilation, it draws all of its features from the nearest consonant. In a similarly cross-linguistically common pattern, Ponapean inserts an epenthetic copy vowel when "an impermissible consonant cluster is created through the process of affixation" (in these examples, involving the prefix *ak-*, meaning 'to make a demonstration of') and the following syllable is heavy (Rehg 1981:70, 92). The epenthetic vowel takes on the quality of the vowel in the immediately following syllable. Proximity of this kind is typical of phonological copying generally. It is not, however, a requirement of morphological reduplication, as illustrated by the "opposite-edge" morphological reduplication occurring in Madurese (Stevens 1985, via McCarthy & Prince 1995a:278), where, as mentioned in Chapter 5, the first copy in plural noun reduplication is truncated to its last – not its initial – syllable. Although opposite-side effects are a minority pattern in reduplication, the important point is that they exist at all; opposite-edge effects never occur in phonological assimilation.[2]

In summary, phonological copying serves a phonological purpose; it involves single segments, and when copying is involved, the copying is proximal. In all of these ways, phonological copying is distinct from morphological copying, which involves morphological constituents – often long strings, not single segments – is potentially nonproximal, and serves a morphological purpose.

Despite being different – or perhaps *because* they are different – phonological copying and morphological reduplication are not mutually exclusive. For example, Hausa pluractional formation (discussed in Chapters 1 and 4) involves both phenomena. Pluractional verbs are formed in Hausa by doubling the verb stem and truncating the first copy to CVC. This is morphological reduplication.

(3)

	Plain stem	Reduplicated stem
'open mouth widely'	waːgèː	waw-wàːgeː
'step on'	taːkàː	tat-tàːkaː
'oppress'	dannèː	dad-dànneː
'go out'	fìtá	fìf-fìtá
'sell'	sayar	sas-sayar

The final consonant of the truncated first copy, however, is subject to a form of phonological copying: it assimilates totally to the following consonant, under appropriate conditions discussed in Chapter 4. This is phonological copying.

7.3   The morphological purpose of reduplication

In saying that morphological reduplication serves a morphological purpose it is important to understand that morphological reduplication need not always be associated with a specific meaning, as it is in Hausa pluractional reduplication in (3). Morphological reduplication can also serve a morphological purpose by creating a stem type that is called for by other morphological constructions. For example, the Bella Coola diminutive (4a) selects for reduplicated stems (see Raimy 2000:61), as do many Ilokano affixes, including the adjective intensifying prefix illustrated in (4b) (Rubino 2001).

(4) a. Bella Coola diminutive suffix /i~yi/ (Nater 1984:109)
          qwtulh   qw-tulh-tlh-i   'cradle basket'   108
          kwpalh   kw-palh-plh-i   'liver'   108
          sum   su-sum-ii   'trousers'   109
          qlhm   q-lhm-lhm-ii   'black cod'   109
     b. Ilokano adjective intensification (Rubino 2001)
          naángot   smelly   naka-ang-ángot   'stinking very much'
          nasakít   'sore'   naka-sak-sakít   'very sore'
          katáwa   'laughter' naka-kat-katáwa   'funny'

The Roviana construction deriving instrumental or locational nouns from verbs, discussed in Chapter 4, is another such case; the construction is instantiated simultaneously by reduplication and the suffix *-ana* (Corston-Oliver 2002:472–80). Thus, for example, *ha^{m}bo* 'sit' nominalizes as *ha^{m}bo-ha^{m}botuana* 'chair' (p. 469). Reduplication without suffixation has a completely different meaning (verb affect intensification); the reduplication seen with *-ana* serves no semantic function which can be distinguished from that of *-ana*, and is best analyzed as a requirement of the suffix.

In MDT, morphologically required reduplication of this sort is handled by positing a semantically null reduplication construction whose only morphological function is to create stems of a type that certain constructions call for.

(5)   Stem-forming reduplication:

Just like semantically null affixation, semantically null reduplication is constrained by structural economy constraints (e.g. *STRUC) from occurring within words unless required; in the cases seen just above, the requirement is an instruction on the part of affixation constructions that their stem be of type "x," where "x" is the arbitrary name of the stem type issuing from the semantically null reduplication construction.

Occasionally morphological reduplication is recruited to bring a stem up to the minimal size required for it to participate in another morphological construction, as in Chukchee.[3] The absolutive singular is marked in Chukchee by root reduplication, which truncates the second copy of the root to its initial CVC portion. Interestingly, this contentful reduplication construction is recruited, minus its absolutive singular connotation, in absolutive plurals, which are normally marked with the suffix -*t*. Exactly when the root is CVC in shape, the absolutive plural shows the same reduplication found throughout the absolutive singular (Krause 1980):

(6)

Root shape	Absolutive singular	Absolutive plural	
CVCV	nute-nut	nute-t	'earth'
	tala-tal	tala-t	'pounded meat'
CVC	čot-čot	čot-čot-te	'pillow'
	tam-tam	tam-tam-ət	'growth'

Krause (1980) and Kiparsky (1986) attribute the phonologically conditioned plural reduplication to a prosodic minimality condition on noun roots; to be inflected (e.g. with plural -*t*), a noun stem should be larger than CVC. Some languages might epenthesize a vowel in this situation; Chukchee appeals instead to semantically null reduplication.

The fact that reduplication is obligatory in the absolutive singular makes a morphological analysis of the plural reduplication particularly plausible. If, as is commonly assumed, absolutive is the unmarked case and singular is the unmarked number, there are already grounds to propose that the morphologically required reduplication construction generating absolutive singular stems is semantically vacuous. It is therefore available to be recruited to assist CVC roots in satisfying the disyllabicity requirements of the plural suffix. Morphological reduplication in Chukchee functions, in the absolutive plural, like the semantically empty affixes in Ndebele, Chichêwa, and other languages discussed in Chapter 2. It serves the ultimately morphological purpose of building a stem of the type for which some other morphological construction selects.

7.4   CV reduplication

Although for the majority of examples it is clear whether phonology or morphology is driving the observed duplication, it is inevitable that there will be cases where the two analyses are similarly compelling, without a good way to choose between them. The area of greatest potential ambiguity involves duplication of strings small enough to be manageble phonologically but large enough to be plausible as truncated morphological constituents – in particular, CV reduplication. CV reduplication has generally been analyzed as morphological in this work (see, for example, Paamese, in Chapter 2, Roviana and Tawala, in Chapter 3; Tohono O'odham and Chamorro, in Chapter 4; Eastern Kadazan, in Chapter 5, Tagalog, in Chapter 6, and others). In some of these cases, e.g. Paamese, there is evidence from allomorphy that the process is clearly morphological reduplication; in other cases, we have simply made the assumption that morphological reduplication is taking place, in the absence of evidence to the contrary.

It is theoretically possible that, in the unusual event that vowel and consonant epenthesis are conditioned simultaneously and copy epenthesis is preferred to default segment epenthesis, CV duplication could be derived phonologically. In Miya, for example, pluractional stems are formed in a variety of ways which Bissell (2002) unifies under the analysis of mora prefixation. As described by Schuh (1998), CaC roots form the pluractional via vowel lengthening, e.g. *tlakə* → *tláakə* 'scrape' (p. 176), while for all other CVC roots the pluractional is formed through Ca- prefixation, where the C is a phonological copy of the root-initial consonant, e.g. *pa-pə́rà* 'cut' (p. 175), *kwa-kwíyà* 'catch' (p. 176). The lengthening evident in *tláakə* could be seen as copy vowel epenthesis, while the prefix consonant in *pa-pə́rà* could be seen as copy consonant epenthesis. If both happened to co-occur in the same syllable, purely phonological processes could add up to what appears to be CV reduplication. A similar phenomenon occurs in the English construction Yu (2003) terms "Homeric infixation," in which the infix -ma- follows a metrical foot: *saxophone* → *saxa-ma-phone*, *secretary* → *secre-ma-tary*. The infix imposes another condition, however, which is that at least one syllable must follow. Thus in cases such as *music* or *tuba*, which consist of only one foot, consonant duplication *and* schwa (spelled "a") insertion take place to satisfy the demands of the infix: *mu-**sa**-ma-sic*, *tu-**ba**-ma-ba*. This instantiates the phonological insertion of a CV syllable; it is not exactly CV duplication, since the vowel is fixed, as in Miya, but, like Miya, it comes close.

The potential for CV duplication to occur for phonological reasons is consistent with the essential bifurcation we have argued for between phonological duplication and morphological reduplication. The ambiguous nature of CV duplication is also consistent with evidence from language change. Niepokuj (1997) has argued for four stages in the diachronic evolution of reduplication. Stage 1 is total; in Stage 2, one copy is reduced. In Stage 3, reduplication is affixal (= partial), and by Stage 4, the reduplicant is so reduced as to be realized as gemination. Although Niepokuj does not have evidence from reconstructions to support all aspects of this schema, she does cite two cases that strongly support the diachronic path from Stage 3 CV prefixing reduplication to Stage 4 consonant gemination, possibly by way of CV prefixing reduplication (with a reduced, nonreduplicated vowel). A larger body of similar cases is also discussed in Blevins (2004), in the context of the evolution of geminate consonants. Thus, for example, where Nez Perce (representing the more conservative CV stage) forms distributives through CV prefixing reduplication (7a), its sister language Sahaptin geminates the initial consonant (7b). Where proto-Micronesian exhibited CV prefixing reduplication, modern Trukese geminates initial consonants (7c) (Goodenough 1963, via Niepokuj 1997:63 and Blevins 2004:169, 172). Bellonese exhibits synchronic CV ∼ V variation, associating CV reduplication with a slower speech rate and C gemination with a faster speech rate (7d) (Elbert 1988, via Blevins 2004:37, 45, 50).

(7)   a. Nez Perce (simplex/distributive)   tílu   ti-tílu   'big'   N34
      b. Sahaptin (simplex/distributive)   k'aiwá   k-k'aiwá   'short one'   N35
      c. Proto-Micronesian > Trukese   *ca-canu   > ccen   'watery/wet'
      d. Bellonese (slow/fast)   βa-βaŋe   β-βaŋe   'to play'
                                            sa-saka   s-saka   'to beg'
                                            ha-hatu   h-hatu   'to untie'

It stands to reason that if CV reduplication can change into Cə reduplication or C gemination, there is likely to be a stage in which a part or all of the CV reduplicant is analyzed as a phonological copy segment. Our assumption is still that the null hypothesis, for duplication above the level of the segment, should be morphological reduplication, but we leave open the possibility that in certain cases where it is phonologically plausible, a phonological analysis may also be considered. The analysis of phonological copying is, of course, possible only when the duplication is proximal and involves single instances of phonological structure types. Chaha CVC reduplication, discussed in Chapter 5, is potentially a case of this kind. CVC roots double to flesh out a CVCCVC template. This could be analyzed either as semantically vacuous double root selection, of the kind discussed in §7.3, or as copy epenthesis (with the epenthetic onset matching the existing onset feature for feature, and the same for the epenthetic coda; see note 2). In this case there is no empirical evidence that could shed light on the question.

7.5   The question of rhyme

The final criterion in (1) is phonological identity. It has been argued extensively in this book that phonological identity is not a requirement in morphological reduplication. Phonological identity plays a direct role only in phonological copying, although it may exert an auxiliary effect on elements in a morphological reduplicant that sit in close enough proximity to be subject to surface correspondence of the type described in Walker 2000a; b; Hansson 2001; Rose & Walker 2001; Walker to appear.

This stance departs sharply from the position of Yip (1999), who, extending observations by Kiparsky 1973b and Holtman 1996, has argued that reduplication is formally identical to, and should be analyzed in the same terms as, rhyme, alliteration, and related devices (such as those summarized in Fabb 2002). As Yip (1999) puts it, "humans have both an aptitude and a taste for creating repetitive sequences" (p. 4). For Yip, then, phonological surface identity requirements of the type utilized in language art are also strongly ensconced in language proper.

Allowing the grammar of a language to require morphological constituents to alliterate, or rhyme, or exhibit assonance or consonance, goes far beyond the usual assimilatory principles according to which phonetically similar things become more similar, formalized as string-internal output correspondence in Walker 2000a; b; Hansson 2001; Rose & Walker 2001; Walker to appear and, in a somewhat different guise, by Zuraw 2002. Evidence that phonological agreement can be imposed by fiat on any kind of word or pair of words, regardless of their original phonetic similarity, would be evidence for the kind of phonological correspondence imposed by BRCT and, therefore, evidence against MDT.

While alliteration and rhyme clearly seem to play a role in processing and are aesthetically pleasing, the evidence suggests that rhyming, alliteration, and other similar correspondences do not play a significant role in productive morphology. If rhyming constraints were part of grammar, we would expect to find phenomena like the following: suppletive root allomorphy whose distribution is governed by rhyme with preceding prefixes or following suffixes; suffixal allomorphs distributed according to alliteration with the stem-initial consonant; words in which all primary or secondary stressed syllables must alliterate; and so forth. Setting aside language games, this does not occur. The cases Yip discusses are ambiguous between rhyme and reduplication. However, unambiguous cases of rhyme, alliteration, assonance, and so forth are not found in morphological derivation.

There are several exceptions that prove this rule by virtue of how extraordinary they are and by virtue of the fact that none actually crosses the threshold of rhyme, alliteration, etc., despite seeming to come close.

Rhyme sometimes plays a role in nickname formation, a morphological phenomenon which can cross the boundary into language play, where rhyme is known to figure prominently (see, for example, Bagemihl 1988; Weeda 1992). Watson (1966:79) describes nickname formation in Pacoh as follows: "A

Pacoh nickname is formed by choosing two words which are commonly used together . . . the second of which rhymes with the given name of the person being nicknamed. The appropriate sex-title, *ku* 'male' or *kán* 'female' is then chosen to precede the paired words and the given name."

(8)   Ku-tur kânsíng Kíng   'male cobra's back King'
      Kán sêl târla Pa   'female peel potatoes Pa'

This example, while compelling in its illustration of the aesthetic role rhyme plays for humans, does not pass the substitution test: it would be very surprising to find a pattern which phonologically resembled the Pacoh nickname construction but instead formed, for example, agentive compounds. Our take on the Pacoh construction is based on an observation made by Ourn and Haiman 2000, namely that in some cases, instances of a particular grammatical construction that happen to rhyme are preferred stylistically to ones that do not.

Apte (1968), for example, describes a productive construction in Marathi which couples words whose meanings are the opposite of each other and which rhyme, e.g. *jewha-tewha* 'every now and then, lit. when-then' (p. 54). Alliteration is common in synonym compounds, as well, e.g. in the Khmer examples in (9) (from Ourn & Haiman 2000, discussed in Chapter 2); alliteration is not, however, an absolute requirement of the construction.

(9)   treek   'enjoy'   +   traʔaal   'enjoy'   'enjoy'   503
      sruəl   'easy'   +   sranok   'easy'   'easy'   503
      cuəp   'meet'   +   cum   'meet'   'meet'   502
      proət   'depart' +   praah   'depart' 'depart' 502

Rhyme can function as a stylistic filter on stylized constructions, e.g. choosing the best nickname for a given individual. Rhyme should not be expected to function as a filter on, or precondition for, truly general grammatical constructions like noun-noun compounding, verb serialization, causativization, and so forth.

The conclusion that rhyme and reduplication are not the same thing does not, however, require the complete abandonment of Yip's generalization that the structural elements involved in versification (onsets, rimes, feet) are similar to those involved in reduplication. As argued extensively in Kiparsky 1973b; Hanson & Kiparsky 1996, inter alia, versification in any particular language is intimately connected to the structures in use in that language's grammar. The connection between reduplication and rhyme is that both make use of the same structural alphabet. It does not have to follow from this that both are regulated by the same constraints.

A truly grammatical phenomenon which comes close to the threshold of rhyme, but significantly does not cross it, is so-called "alliterative concord," which Dobrin (1998) explicitly relates to reduplication (p. 60). Dobrin (1998; 1999; see also Aronoff 1992; 1994) analyzes a system of agreement in Arapeshan dialects originally described by Fortune (1942). According to Dobrin, Arapeshan requires agreement, on the part of various syntactic elements, with a noun's final consonant. Dobrin cites examples like the following:

(10)   a. ulubu**n**   šaku-šaku-**n**   b. anauwip-i**h** ñmine**h**
           hardwood‗palm(6) small-small-6   six-13.pl   day(13.pl)
           'small hardwood palm'   'six days'

In (10a), the modified noun 'hardwood palm' ends in the consonant *n*; the agreeing adjective takes an *n* suffix as well. Were it modifying a noun ending in a different consonant, it would end in the corresponding consonant. In (10b), the head noun 'days' ends in *h*; the concord element in the preceding adjective ends in the consonant *h*.

The concord elements in (10) are assigned numbers in morpheme glosses. These numbers represent noun classes. Dobrin makes the important point that the concord in Arapeshan is mediated, to a very high degree, by noun class, as analyzed by Aronoff (1992; 1994). Following Fortune (1942), Aronoff and Dobrin posit thirteen noun classes in Arapeshan. Masculine and feminine human nouns are assigned to fixed classes (7 and 4, respectively), regardless of the final consonant they end in. Most other nouns have class membership consistent with their final consonant.

(11)

Class	Final	phonological string of singular noun	
I	b^y	ahoryb^y	'knee'
II	bør	wabør	'village'
III	g	aijag	'leg'
IV	k^u	babwek^u	'grandmother'
V	Vm	daudam	'spider'
VI	n	lawan	'tree snake'
VII	n	ašuken	'older brother to a man'
VIII	ñ	abotiñ	'long yam'
	V	sumo	'flying fox'
	C	pas	'taro pounder'
IX	p^u	ilup^u	'feast'
X	r~l	awhijar	'bat'
XI	t	nybat	'dog'
XII	uh~^{uh}	bawe^{uh}	'mountain road'
XIII	a^h~u^h	ata^h	'ear'

Aronoff and Dobrin present a variety of convincing reasons for thinking of the agreement system as noun class agreement, rather than as a phonological requirement that final consonants of nouns and their agreeing elements be identical. First, for masculine and feminine human nouns there is no consonance. Masculines fall into class 7 regardless of final consonant; feminines fall into class 4. Any phonological agreement pattern operating at the phrase or utterance level would have to be sensitive not only to part of speech but also to properties of gender and humanness, properties to which postlexical phonological rules or constraints have not independently been shown to have access. Second, some nouns are exceptional. The noun *kwoǰar*, though it ends in *r* and would be expected to trigger class 10 concord, instead takes default class 8 concord (Dobrin 1998:65). This pattern is inexplicable phonologically but is easily captured morphologically by prespecifying the noun root as morphological class 8, instead of letting the grammar assign it to class 10 on phonological principles.

Setting aside exceptional nouns and human nouns, there are still serious barriers to a phonological account of the apparent consonance effect. First, the size of the phonological string shared by agreeing elements varies considerably. In some cases it is a single consonant; in other cases it is a syllable, e.g. *bør* (class 2) or a syllable rime, e.g. *Vm* (class 5). No single statement of phonological identity could cover all of these cases. Second, the phonological position of the agreeing string does not fall in the same phonological location in the various types of words with which a noun agrees. Dobrin, citing Fortune, provides a templatic description of all the concord elements in Arapeshan, in which "C" stands for the constant phonological string. For example, the possessor noun suffix is *-iC* with final "C," e.g. *polisipepimin-it musket* 'the policeman's rifle,' *eguh-ib tinab* 'cans of fish' (Dobrin 1998:66). The demonstrative pronoun used in 'near me' contexts, *aCuda?*, has a medial "C," e.g. *aguda dybarig amwi-eg* 'whose garden is this?' (Dobrin 1998:63). In yet other cases, e.g. the adjective ending *-Cali*, the "C" is morpheme-initial, as shown in (12), an example which illustrates the wide range of phonological positions in which the agreeing "C" is found (Dobrin 1998:67).

(12) əgɨdak nebe-**g**-ali   tra**g**
       this(3)   big-3-lasting_quality   truck(3)
       'this big truck'

Again, no single phonological identity statement could cover all of these cases.

A third phonological barrier to a phonological agreement analysis, and an argument in support of a noun class analysis, is that vowel-final nouns pattern with nouns ending in *ñ* in triggering *ñ*-based concord, e.g. *taia ñ-etemu ɔmañ* 'tire(8) 8-be heavy-8 = the tire was heavy' (Dobrin 1998:67). If agreement were essentially phonological, we would instead expect to find a vowel, or simply nothing, in place of "C" in the words agreeing with vowel-final nouns. *ñ*-based concord makes no sense in terms of phonological identity, but it makes perfect sense in terms of morphological concord, as Dobrin herself observes. Class 8 is the default class; it happens to be instantiated, on agreeing elements, by *ñ*.

As Aronoff and Dobrin make clear, a noun class system is independently needed anyway in order to capture generalizations about the relationship between the singular and plural form of any given noun. The plural form of any given noun is generally predictable from the singular, though plurals and singulars do not agree phonologically. Rather, there is simply a set of often arbitrary correspondences between the endings of singulars and plurals of the sort that noun class is designed to capture. Class 1 singular nouns, which end in b^y, end in *bys* in the plural: *ahoryb^y* ~ *ahorybys* 'knee(s)'; class 2 singular nouns, which end in *bør*, end in *ryb* in the plural: *wabør* ~ *waryb* 'village(s).' The correspondences can be quite arbitrary, as the class 2 forms show; moreover, some noun classes admit a variety of plural forms. Thus class 3, whose singulars all end in *g*, have two options for plurals: *s* and *gas*, which Aronoff allocates to the subclasses 3a and 3b: for each singular noun, which subclass of 3 it belongs to must be learned, e.g. *aijag* ~ *aijas* 'leg(s)' (class 3a); *nubarig* ~ *nubarigas* 'garden(s)' (Class 3b). For some other classes there is an even greater number of subclasses.

What gives the system the appearance of grammatically enforced "alliteration" (for which "consonance" would be a more accurate term) is, primarily, the fact that the set of agreement markers for any given noun class tends to intersect in the phonological string ending singular nouns of that class. This intersection presumably has a historical explanation of the kind that has been offered for similar patterns in Bantu languages, in which the use of a particular head-modifying morpheme was extended to other syntactic elements, resulting in agreement. Dobrin provides two arguments that the phonological consonance generalization, while overridable, should nonetheless be a part of the synchronic grammar of Arapeshan. The first argument is that borrowed nouns ending in a consonant not found finally in native nouns have spawned a new agreement pattern. Borrowings from Tok Pisin which end in *s* cannot (or could not, originally) simply be slotted into an existing class for *s*-final nouns, as none occur natively in Arapeshan. What has happened is that such nouns take *s*-agreement. The "C" position in words agreeing with *s*-final nouns is instantiated with *s*.

(13)   ənan-is   kes   Dobrin 1998:68
              PRO.7-POSS suitcase
              'his suitcase'

But this pattern does not demand a phonological agreement analysis. An equally viable approach would be to view the pattern as the result of morphological analogy, or backformation, which occurred in the recent history of the language, setting up a new noun class and set of associated concord markers along the lines of those for existing classes.

Dobrin's second argument that consonance is phonologically enforced comes from an alternation specific to class 3 nouns and agreeing elements. The class 3 plural ending, *s*, optionally alternates with *ʔ* when word-final. According to Dobrin, "the glottal stop does not appear in place of *s* on agreeing elements unless it appears in place of *s* on the noun; nor [does *s* appear] on final agreeing elements when the noun itself is pluralized with glottal stop." Intriguing as this is, it still supports a noun class analysis. Class 3a has two subclasses, call them 3ai and 3aii, in either of which a class 3 noun may be realized. If a noun is optionally realized as 3ai, it must take the 3ai singular ending and 3ai agreement; likewise for 3aii. Crucially, as Dobrin points out, only class 3a *s* behaves in this manner; the plural *s* of other classes do not. This is strong evidence that noun class, not phonology, plays the central role. If Arapeshan really were using consonance in the way it is used in versification, all nouns ending in *s* would trigger *s*-consonantism in their modifiers; *s*-consonantism would be in a fixed location, e.g. initial or final. This is not the case. By coming close to but not achieving the description of consonance, Arapeshan is an exception which proves the rule that rhyme, alliteration, consonance, and assonance are not viable grammatical principles.

As mentioned above, Kiparsky has often made the point that the connection between rhyme and reduplication is their mutual use of the phonological structures that the language independently makes available (Kiparsky 1973b; Hanson & Kiparsky 1996). This is not, however, license to equate the two phenomena. Reduplication is morphological, and rhyme is phonological; close inspection shows their manifestations to be sharply different. In a larger context, this is the same point made in Chapter 5 about morphological reduplication vs. phonological duplication. Though there is a small set of data for which the two analyses converge, in general the criteria for morphological vs. phonological identity are sharply different, and a good theory must treat them separately.

7.6   The question of anti-identity

Anti-identity effects are just as relevant as identity effects to the question of whether grammars can enforce phonological identity across morphemes or words. Any grammar with the power to compare phonological strings across morphemes and words has the power to enforce either identity or anti-identity. It is our view that anti-identity is no more integral in morphology than is identity; anti-identity effects do not support the need for generalized phonological correspondence between morphological constituents.

One apparent type of anti-identity effect in morphology is classified under the Repeated Morph Constraint (Menn & MacWhinney 1984), a ban on the occurrence of consecutive homophonous morphemes. It is true that some such sequences are banned in particular languages. However, the problem with attributing such bans to anti-identity is that languages also often ban the occurrence of adjacent morphemes which are not homophonous, and it is far from clear whether the bans on homophonous morphemes have any special status. Turkish highlights this issue particularly dramatically. In Turkish, the third possessive suffix (e.g. *oda-sı* 'room-3poss') and the suffix marking productive compounding (*yemek oda-sı* 'dining room-sfx') are homophonous: following a vowel, both surface as *-sI* (with a harmonic high vowel). Compound nouns can be possessed. However, it is not possible to have two *-sI* suffixes in a row; the possessed form of 'dining room' is homophonous with the nonpossessed form: *yemek oda-sı*. The doubly marked **yemek oda-sı-sı* is ungrammatical. This might seem to be an ironclad case of the RMC. However, looking at the example in the broader context of Turkish morphology shows that the generalization is not, in fact, anti-identity-driven. The first piece of evidence is that both the compound marker and the third person possessive suffix have two suppletive allomorphs, *-sI* and *-I*, which occur after vowels and consonants, respectively (thus *oda-sı* 'his/her/its room', *okul-u* 'his/her/its school').[4] A compound ending in *-I* cannot take a third person possessive *-sI*, and vice versa; thus, even when identity is not at issue, forms containing both suffixes in sequence are ungrammatical (*kılıç balığ-ı* 'sword fish' = 'his/her/its sword fish,' **kılıç balığ-ı-sı* 'his/her/its sword fish'). Even more significantly, the ban on the third possessive suffix following compound-marking *-sI~-I* is only a small part of a larger picture: Turkish also prevents the compound-marking suffix from co-occurring with any other possessive suffixes; thus 'my dining room' is *yemek oda-m*, not **yemek-oda-sı-m*. This ban cannot be attributed to the RMC. Further afield, even certain affixes which are altogether outside the possessive paradigm are unable to co-occur with compound markers. One example is the 'with' suffix /-lI/: *yemek-oda-lı* 'endowed with a dining room,' not *yemek oda-sı-lı. What these facts show is that the constraint barring *yemek oda-sı-lı cannot be a prohibition on adjacent identical morphs; it is something more arbitrary and unrelated to phonological form. Given that languages can ban arbitrary sequences of morphemes (as position class languages attest in the extreme), careful statistical analysis would have to be undertaken to show that the RMC is not an illusion, the result of linguists paying attention to morpheme co-occurrence constraints when the morphemes are identical, and not paying as much attention otherwise. Another window onto the psychological reality of the RMC could be reanalysis; if languages that used to allow sequences of identical morphs start banning them, it could be that the RMC has reared its head. According to Yoquelet (2004), however, synchronic instances of what appears to be the RMC tend strongly, if not universally, to derive historically from morphemes that have acquired multiple functions but retain the distributional properties of their shared ancestor. If Yoquelet is right, then the RMC is not a real grammatical constraint even diachronically.

Anti-identity effects have been claimed to hold elsewhere in morphology as well. Kurisu (2001) argues that much nonconcatenative morphology can be reduced to an anti-identity requirement holding between words, where one word is the morphological base of the other. If no overt affixation marks the derived word, anti-identity requires some other modification to take place. Kurisu proposes that the ranking of anti-identity requirements in the markedness hierarchy determines what modification will be performed: truncation, ablaut, metathesis, stress shift, etc. Even if we set aside the cases in which homophony does occur in paradigms, however, Kurisu's approach cannot account for cases in which truncation, ablaut and other effects co-occur with overt affixation which itself is sufficient to ensure non-homophony between related words. Further, Kurisu's approach incorrectly predicts that words in which anti-identity forces modification should differ minimally, in being less marked along some single dimension, from their nonderived counterparts. In any event, all of Kurisu's data can be handled by input–output dissimilation; it is universally recognized in generative phonology (including Optimality Theory) that there is phonological correspondence between inputs and outputs.

It is beyond the scope of this chapter to review all of the claims in the literature to the effect that the synchronic grammar acts to avoid identity across related words, a topic that has recently come into focus (see, for example, Crosswhite 1997; 1999; Suzuki 1999). We can only suggest that such claims be strongly scrutinized.[5] Opening the door to phonological correspondence, whether used to enforce or to prohibit identity, endows the theory with a great deal more descriptive power, much of which is clearly unnecessary, e.g. the ability to describe overapplication of junctural effects (see Chapter 5, §5.5.2), backcopying (see Chapter 5, §5.8), and other unattested phenomena.

7.7   Beyond reduplication

The natural next step for the MDT approach to reduplication, a construction whose daughters are required to be semantically identical, would be to extend the approach to morphological and syntactic constructions whose daughters are in a different, but equally obligatory, semantic relationship. Chapter 4 opened the door to this possibility by observing that reduplication forms a natural class with antonym constructions.

One clear area for future research, which our framework predicts possible, is that a construction could require sisters to be in a semantic or morphological subset relationship, where one sister is more specific than the other in some way. For example, the formation of reciprocal verbs in Malay calls for two verb stems, one consisting of the bare verb root and the other prefixed with *meng-*, a prefix which marks agent focus on transitive verbs and patient focus on intransitives (Mintz 1994:130–32). Data are from Mintz 1994:275:

(14)   tulis-menulis   'to write to one another'
        tolong-menolong   'to help one another'
        pandang-memandang 'to observe one another'

A neutral description of this construction would be that the second daughter is specified for thematic role focus, while the first is unspecified. This kind of relationship, where one copy of the relevant constituent is unspecified relative to the other, is probably very common; indeed, a number of the examples of syntactic doubling discussed in Chapter 1 were of this kind. Noun incorporation is a likely area in which to find more. So-called "classifier incorporation" (Mithun 1984; Rosen 1989; Mithun 2000) can involve two copies of a head noun, one, which is uninflected for case and number, in the verb, and the other, fully inflected, heading the corresponding noun phrase in the syntax.

We have argued in this book that reduplicative phonology is best understood in the larger context of morphologically conditioned phonology. The same principle applies to reduplication as a morphological construction. Further investigation into parallelism in grammar is sure to shed further light on the small corner of morphology we have investigated here.

Notes

1   Introduction

1. Weber (1989) characterizes the meaning of adverbial clause reduplication as "repetition of the event referred to by the reduplicated element" (p. 323).
2. The Hausa data are taken from Newman 2000 (p. 424); the Amele data are from Roberts 1991 (p. 135), and the Warlpiri data are based on Nash 1986 (p. 130).
3. On the quality of the prefixal vowel, see Akinlabi 1993; Pulleyblank 1998; Alderete et al. 1999.
4. Other languages cited by Landau as having similar verb copying effects include Haitian, Vata, Yoruba, Brazilian Portuguese, Yiddish, and Russian.
5. See Raimy 2000; Frampton 2003 for a phonological approach to reduplication that does not invoke a RED morpheme.
6. One exception is the literature on a-templatic reduplication, which offers criteria for distinguishing templatic from a-templatic morphological reduplication. See, for example, Gafos 1998b; Urbanczyk 1998; Hendricks 1999, as well as Zuraw 2002. We return to this issue in Chapter 7.
7. Following McCarthy and Prince 1995a, this conviction has been bolstered by renewed attention to apparent identity effects described by Wilbur 1973; Moravcsik 1978; Marantz 1982; Clements 1985; Kiparsky 1986; Mester 1986; Steriade 1988; McCarthy and Prince 1993; 1995a; 1999b, and elsewhere. These will be discussed at length in subsequent chapters.
8. Chechen data are presented in the practical orthography developed by Johanna Nichols; for more information, see http://socrates.berkeley.edu/~chechen.
9. See Chapter 2 for a fuller discussion of Sye and other cases of divergent allomorphy. The same general phenomenon (in Sanskrit and other languages) is also discussed in Saperstein 1997.
10. Blust (2001) argues, with examples from Thao (Formosan), that triplication often does have an iconic function of intensifying whatever meaning is associated with ordinary reduplication.
11. For recent overviews of Optimality Theory, see Kager 1999; McCarthy 2002b. It is important to note that the use of Optimality Theory in this work differs from standard implementations in two ways: (a) some practitioners of Optimality Theory reject the use of cophonologies, though all admit morphologically conditioned phonology in some guise, and (b) the Base-Reduplicant Correspondence Theory (BRCT) developed for Optimality Theory by McCarthy and Prince 1995a is not used here; MDT

is intended as an alternative to BRCT. Cophonologies are highlighted in Chapters 3 and 4; BRCT is addressed most directly in Chapters 4, 5, and 6.

12. These roots come from forms with underlying schwa, which has undergone a process of unstressed vowel deletion. See Black 1996 for discussion.

2   Evidence for morphological doubling

1. Piñon demonstrates that reduplicated preverbs behave differently from conjoined preverbs in respect to the word orders allowed in sentences containing them and suggests that preverb reduplication may occur in the syntax. If so, then Hungarian provides further evidence for the kind of syntactic reduplication discussed in Chapter 1.

2. Roberts (1987) and Roberts (1991) use slightly different transcription systems for Amele; the forms cited here reflect these differences. In the forms taken from Roberts 1987, "c" = [ʔ] and "q" = ĝb.

3. Some roots, instead of reduplicating, lengthen a following vowel instead. These are not shown here; see Roberts 1987:254–55, Roberts 1991 for discussion.

4. Double reduplication of affix and root, with the same overall meaning as reduplication of just one of those constituents, would appear to violate general principles of morphological economy; see, for example, §2.2.1.

5. Compare to the distinction drawn by Bloomfield (1933) (and also, more recently, Saperstein 1997), who associated partial reduplication with affixation and total reduplication with compounding.

6. GTT was developed not so much to capture generalizations about root and affix size as to avoid the necessity to directly stipulate the prosodic shape of any given reduplicant. The reason for avoiding such statements is the so-called "Kager–Hamilton" problem, discussed in more detail in Chapter 3.

7. We are grateful to Galen Sibanda for discussion of Ndebele; his dissertation paints a much fuller picture of all of the phenomena discussed here.

8. For further discussion of this suffix, see Chapter 7. We are grateful to Orhan Orgun for help with our understanding of Turkish phonology and morphology.

9. Rice and McDonough analyze the inserted material as phonologically epenthetic, rather than as constituting a lexically listed empty morph, the approach we have taken to such data in this chapter. It is not always easy to decide whether a given segment-zero alternation is morphologically conditioned epenthesis or due to the presence vs. absence of a semantically empty, lexically listed morph. The fact that Ndebele has two distinct phonological strings alternating with zero supports an empty morph analysis for at least one of them.

10. Our approach also has important points of contact with the Enriched Input theory of Sprouse 1997, originally designed to handle phonological opacity. Enriched Input theory provides competing phonological inputs based on a single underlying form.

11. Srichampa 2002, citing various data sources, describes a number of other rhyme-replacing reduplicative constructions in Vietnamese; this particular one is not mentioned.

12. Transcriptions are converted, using Bosson's romanization (p. 11), from the Cyrillic.

13. See Saperstein 1997 for an earlier proposal which allows the two daughters in reduplication to differ in stem type.
14. Steriade (1988:76), citing Wiesemann 1972, describes a similar process in Kaingang, where pluralization can be marked by g-insertion, raising a penultimate vowel, and/or reduplication.
15. *-eʔ* and *-oʔ* are infinitive suffixes; *-doʔ* is a combination of object marker (*-do-*) and infinitive suffix. See Roberts 1987:272, 281ff. for discussion of the generalizations over which vowels will be replaced by which other vowels.
16. Tier replacement is the analysis given in Inkelas 1998 of "consonant extraction" in Modern Hebrew (see, for example, Bat-El 1994 and references therein) and is also arguably involved in the well-known Javanese habitual-repetitive construction, about which Yip has written extensively (see, for example, Yip 1997; 1998), and in which a particular vowel in one of the copies is replaced; thus *eliŋ* → *elaŋ-eliŋ* 'remember,' *tuku* → *tuka-tuku* 'buy,' *udan* → *udan-uden* 'rain' (Yip 1997).
17. For an analysis in this same spirit of Sanskrit reduplication in terms of different stem allomorphs, see Saperstein 1997.
18. Crowley notes (p. 199) that verb roots beginning with *t* and *k* exhibit allomorphy only in the active, not in the stative.
19. We are grateful to Terry Crowley for discussing the Sye data with us.
20. Crowley (1982) notes (p. 155) that for verbs which participate in both CV- and CVCV- reduplication, it is typical for CV- reduplication to be associated with habitual/random or habitual/uninterrupted semantics, and for the CVCV- variant to be associated with detransitivizing or habitual/interrupted meanings. However, this association does not hold for verbs which reduplicate in only one way.
21. Singh calls these "partial reduplication"; however, as no truncation appears to be associated with the process, we use the more standard term of "echo reduplication." This particular pattern of echo reduplication, in which the onset of the second member is replaced by a labial, occurs throughout Asia; see Abbi 1991 for a typological overview, and §2.2.4 for discussion of echo formation as Melodic Overwriting.
22. See also Malkiel's (1959) discussion of the semantics of irreversible binomials.

3   Reduplicative phonology: daughters

1. Donca Steriade, in unpublished work, has recently argued that there are outside-in effects in which the phonology of derived words can influence, synchronically, the phonology of words serving as their bases; similarly, Bochner (1992) has argued for treating morphological backformation on a par with other morphological derivation. We agree that sporadic outside-in and backformation phenomena exist but, following Kiparsky 1982c, view them as diachronic events, rather than as patterns regulated by synchronic grammar.
2. Some verbal or nominal suffixes impose different patterns, such that only a subset of verb stem-forming affixes are in fact associated with the cophonology in (9a); similarly, only a subset of noun stem-forming suffixes are associated with the cophonology in (9b). The fact that we are simplifying the picture here should not

detract from our basic observation that different morphological constructions can be associated with different cophonologies.

3. Some reduplication constructions combine bare morphemes, not derived stems, and thus do not have cophonologies associated with the daughters; see especially the discussion of affix reduplication in Chapter 2. The construction in (11) should be understood as the maximally complex reduplication construction.

4. Only full-grade forms are shown here. Zero-grade allomorphs of the root may exhibit other differences between the two copies, which Steriade (1988) argues to be a consequence of differences in the syllabification of full vs. zero grades. See also Saperstein 1997 for an analysis more in line with MDT's double stem selection approach.

5. Transcriptions are based on Weeda 1992: 162–63. "HBC" stands for the Hooper Bay/Chevak dialect; other forms are from the General Central Alaskan Yupik complex of dialects.

6. Alderete (1999; 2001) invokes input–output anti-identity constraints to drive accentual dominance effects, but the phenomenon he is analyzing is one of neutralization (accent deletion), rather than dissimilation proper.

7. Hausa data are presented in Hausa orthography, with three exceptions: vowel length is marked with a colon rather than a macron; following Newman 2000, tapped /ř/ is marked with a tilde to distinguish it from retroflex /r/; following Hausa linguistic tradition and Newman 2000, Low tone is marked with a grave accent (High is unmarked).

8. The coronals /z/ and /dʒ/ are related via coronal palatalization, which applies before front vowels.

9. Truncation and vowel raising do not occur in polysyllabic bases. Niepokuj (1997:24ff.) takes this as evidence that monosyllabic and polysyllabic reduplication are different morphological constructions (prefixing and suffixing, respectively).

10. A possible alternative analysis, after Downing 2004, might be to analyze the Tarok pattern as the result of the base melody being mapped, via the regular left-to-right association algorithm of the language, to the prosodic word which contains both base and reduplicant. However, for monosyllabic Low-toned bases the tone pattern in reduplication is Low-Mid; according to Sibomana 1980:201, Low-Mid is not a legal result of regular tone distribution.

11. In response to similar ranking paradoxes in reduplication in other languages (e.g. Kwakwala and Lushootseed), Struijke (2000a; 2000b) has proposed Existential Faithfulness (∃-Faith), which differs from standard input–output faithfulness in being satisfied as long as input structures have correspondents anywhere in the output; they could be in the reduplicant or in the base. While ∃-Faith would permit BRCT to describe the Tarok facts, it is argued on other grounds in Chapter 4 that ∃-Faith is not a generally viable approach to reduplicative phonology.

12. The adoption of reduplicant-specific markedness constraints, e.g. *V:]$_{RED}$, might seem to be another alternative, but it is also essentially identical to introducing cophonologies and just as incompatible with the foundational assumptions of BRCT.

13. In any case, nothing in BRCT, even with GTT, could rule out the reduplication of, for example, a truncated nickname (e.g. *Jonathan* → *Jon* → *Jon-Jon*), which is

surface identical to directly truncating reduplicant and base (*Jonathan* → *Jon-Jon*). MDT predicts both scenarios to be possible.
14. Our source for the Stanford truncations is our personal knowledge as well as the website http://www.stanford.edu/dept/undergrad/uac/freshmen/glossary.htm. Our source for the English truncations is the website http://ccat.sas.upenn.edu/plc/echo.
15. Healey, Isoroembo, and Chittleborough (1969:35) describe the semantics of reduplication as follows: "The stem of a verb may be modified to indicate a repetitive action or (if transitive) a plural object by the use of a reduplicative prefix or a suffix or both."
16. On infixing reduplication in MDT see Chapters 5 and 6.
17. One possible example of base-dependence occurs in Ponapean, where the prosodic quantity of reduplicants and bases appears to be (inversely) correlated; see McCarthy and Prince 1999b for an overview. The facts are more complicated than this, but in any case any sort of prosodic relationship between reduplicant and base could also be analyzed as a relationship between the input and output forms of each daughter.
18. A minority pattern is to reduplicate both vowels: *daona* 'long (verb)' → *dao-daona* 'long (adj.),' *gao* 'gap' → *gao-gao* 'week.' Note the semantic irregularity of these forms; this set also includes apparently lexically reduplicated roots like *woe-woe* 'to paddle' (Ezard 1997:42).

4   Reduplicative phonology: mothers

1. See §4.4 below for more discussion of Lushootseed reduplication. The transcription system used here is that of Urbanczyk 1996; "X" represents a uvular fricative.
2. The presentation here is highly simplified for purposes of illustration. For a full discussion of the morphophonemics of Japanese accent, see, for example, McCawley 1968; Poser 1984.
3. For similar reasons, Kim (2003) proposes construction-specific constraints to explain suffix-specific requirements on the shape of their base in Nuu-chah-nulth.
4. On cophonologies, see, for example, Itô and Mester 1995b; 1996b; Mester and Itô 1995; Orgun 1996; Inkelas, Orgun, and Zoll 1997; Orgun 1997; Inkelas 1998; Inkelas and Orgun 1998; Orgun 1999; Yu 2000; on morphologically specific output–output correspondence constraints, see Downing 1998a, 1998b; also Downing 1997; 1999a,b; 2000; 2001; on indexed constraints, see, for example, Benua 1997; Smith 1997; Alderete 1999; Itô and Mester 1999; Alderete 2001; on affix-specific correspondence relations, see Alderete 1999; 2001. A detailed comparision of constraint indexation and cophonologies can be found in Inkelas and Zoll 2003; the issue is also discussed in Chapter 3.
5. Dakota allows a variety of onset clusters. See Patterson 1990:67 for details.
6. The absence of the final vowel is not a special property of the reduplication construction. The final vowel fails to appear whenever a consonant-final stem is the first member of a lexical compound or whenever a consonant-final noun is incorporated into a verb (Shaw 1980:119). Notice that this vowel is also not subject to stress (Shaw 1980:32).

7. Since dissimilation occurs only at the juncture, a full account of this effect in any framework must include a mechanism to restrict the alternation to derived environments. On derived environment effects, see Mascaró 1976; 1982b; 1993 and, more recently, Burzio 1997; Lubowicz 1999; Inkelas 2000; Anttila in press; Cho in press.

8. A potential alternative to this ranking paradox, ∃-FAITH, is discussed and rejected in §4.4.

9. Cohn and McCarthy's (1998) more detailed account of Indonesian stress utilizes the following constraint on the relationship between two PrWds (after Chomsky & Halle 1968) to force stress subordination in compounds:

NUC-STR
In $PrWd_1 PrWd_2$, $PrWd_2$ is more prominent

A general CULMINATIVITY constraint is sufficient for the argument here, but see their paper for justification of NUC-STR.

10. Kenstowicz (1995) and Cohn and McCarthy (1998) use a comprehensive BR-MAX constraint.

11. One might wish to account for the seeming typological oddity of the opposite pattern, whereby stress demotion would occur in reduplication but not in compounds. At present, however, its existence is predicted possible by any theory, including BRCT, which could derive it as a standard TETU effect by changing the relative ranking of BR-FAITH and IO-FAITH with respect to markedness. Ruling it out would require as yet undiscovered meta-constraints on constraint indexation/reranking.

12. Another potential contributing factor to underapplication is opaque interactions between daughter and mother cophonologies; we discuss a case from Javanese in Chapter 5.

13. "TETU" stands for "The Emergence of the Unmarked," the phenomenon whereby a low-ranking markedness constraint M can have an effect when a higher-ranking constraint, obedience to which normally prevents satisfaction of M, is itself necessarily violated in some context, permitting satisfaction of M. See McCarthy and Prince 1994a; Alderete et al. 1999.

14. The candidate *bukú-bukú-ña*, where stress shifts in both RED and BASE, is ruled out by a constraint favoring initial stress. See Kenstowicz 1995 and Cohn and McCarthy 1998 for details.

15. Not all cases previously described as underapplication will yield to the same analysis as Klamath. See Chapter 5 for cases of underapplication in Javanese which have a different origin.

16. This process, described in detail by Barker 1963; Barker 1964, has been discussed extensively in the linguistics literature; see, for example, Kisseberth 1972; Kean 1973; White 1973; Thomas 1975; Feinstein and Vago 1981; Clements and Keyser 1983, inter alia.

17. Transcriptions of Klamath throughout this discussion follow Barker, except for phonetically reduced symbols in brackets; uppercase letters represent voiceless sonorants.

18. The "Intensive" has a variety of meanings. Barker (1964: 120) states that it can signify repeated action, such as "twinkling, flickering, trembling," or "emotional and bodily conditions which persist: e.g., being nauseated, feeling bad, burning (in taste), etc."

19. See Raimy 2000 for discussion of Southern Paiute, cited in McCarthy and Prince (1995a) as exhibiting identity-induced underapplication. As Raimy and, independently, Gurevich (2000) demonstrate, consideration of additional data from Sapir 1930 shows the effect to be nonexistent.

20. "REDUCE" stands for the constraint(s) driving reduction; see Urbanczyk 1996; Struijke 2000b for a detailed Optimality Theory account of the specifics of vowel reduction.

21. Hausa data are presented in Hausa orthography, with three exceptions: vowel length is marked with a colon rather than a macron; following Newman 2000, tapped /ř/ is marked with a tilde to distinguish it from retroflex /r/; following Hausa linguistic tradition and Newman 2000, Low tone is marked with a grave accent (High is unmarked).

22. See the detailed discussion of Lushootseed in Park 2000 as well.

23. On derived environment effects, see Mascaró 1976; 1982b; 1993 and, more recently, Burzio 1997; Lubowicz 1999; Inkelas 2000; Anttila in press; Cho in press.

24. Fitzgerald (2002), a response to Yu 2000, focuses on theoretical objections to cophonologies; for discussion of the issues Fitzgerald raises, see Chapter 3 and Inkelas and Zoll 2003.

25. CVCV reduplication is attested in nouns, adjectives, and verbs; in the case of verbs, it is intensifying (Corston-Oliver 2002:470, 483).

26. Prefixes also attract stress. Corston-Oliver states that roots of three or more syllables are stressed on the first and second syllables, an observation which suggest that "stress" in Roviana may either consist of, or be accompanied by, tone.

27. The suffix -*ana* derives instrumental or locational nouns from verbs; it is always accompanied by verb root reduplication (Corston-Oliver 2002:472). Otherwise, verb root reduplication "indicates intensive affect" (p. 480). See Chapter 7 for further discussion.

28. For discussion of compound reduction in another Tibeto-Burman language, see Nagaraja 1979 on Khasi.

29. In pluractional CVG verbal reduplication (G = gemination of following consonant), the reduplicant agrees in tone with the following syllable; however, in CVG-reduplication deriving adjectives of sensory quality, the reduplicant is uniformly L toned, e.g. *zurfi:* 'heat' → *zùz-zurfa:* 'very deep' (Newman 2000:511). Both patterns are non-tone-integrating.

5 Morphologically driven opacity in reduplication

1. Javanese has a ten-vowel surface inventory (i, ɪ, e, ɛ, ə, a, ɔ, o, ʊ, u; see, for example, Dudas 1976:5). Transcriptions of Javanese consonants are orthographic. 'tj' = [ts]; 'dj' = [dz]; 'q' = [ʔ], 'nj' = [ɲ], 'ng' = [ŋ]; 'j' = [j]. Conversions are as follows; 't' and 'd' are dental; 'ṭ' and 'ḍ' are alveolar.

2. The issue of whether the /a/~/ɔ/ alternation is one of /a/-raising or /ɔ/-lowering is extensively discussed by Dudas (1976). Although we follow Dudas in adopting a raising analysis, we note that the opacity arguments would be similar if the alternation were reanalyzed as /ɔ/ lowering.

3. A parallel situation occurs in Warlpiri, as documented by Nash (1986). Verb reduplication, in which the first copy is truncated to the first two syllables of the verb, lends "speed, vigor or distributivity" to the meaning of the verb (p. 136). Nash shows that inflectional suffixes surface in the first copy only when they are needed to satisfy disyllabicity, thus *yirra-ka* 'put-IMP' → *yirra-yirra-ka* (p. 136) vs. *pu-ngka* 'hit-IMP' → *pungka-pungka* (p. 137). Warlpiri has a process of anticipatory vowel harmony by which root /i/ vowels assimilate to suffixal /u/. This process affects both syllables of reduplicated disyllabic verb roots even though the triggering inflectional suffix surfaces only after the second copy, thus, for example, *pangi-pangi-rni* 'dig (reduplicated)-NPAST' vs. *pangu-pangu-rnu* 'dig (reduplicated)-PAST' (p. 142). The opaque harmony in the first copy follows naturally from an account in which reduplication targets suffixed stems; the suffix is truncated in most cases by the general process reducing the first copy to two syllables.

4. A few roots retain their final vowel before *-an*, e.g. *gawe-an* 'work, activity' (H123).

5. Horne (1961:127) documents double *-(a)n* suffixation in some cases of reduplication, e.g. *aŋɔ-n-aŋɔ-n-an* (nominalization of *aŋɔ* 'use, wear').

6. Sumukti (1971:98) cites two intriguing examples in which the Nominalizer shows up (in its [-n] form) on both vowel-final members of compounds: *kakɔ-n + atɛ-n* 'hot tempered,' cf. *kaku* 'stiff,' *ati* 'heart'; and *gugɔ-n + tuhɔ-n* 'superstitious,' cf. *gugu* 'to obey,' *tuhu* 'earnest.' Although it is not clear to us whether semantically nominalization would be expected to occur before or after compounding, these data do suggest that the Nominalizer can be present in the input to compounding, just as it can in the input to reduplication. Phonological identity is an unlikely explanation for double nominalization within compounds.

7. Dudas and Horne differ in their characterization of liquid-initial stems; according to Horne, the active prefix is *nge-* or *me-* in such cases, while according to Dudas, it is *nge-* or *ng-*. Horne (1961:103) reports that monosyllabic roots take a syllabic allomorph of the prefix (*nga-* or *nge-*).

8. Cole's analysis is more like the one sketched here, in that for Cole, the Pstem is what reduplicates. For Downing, such conscription represents a misalignment between reduplicant and prosodic structure.

9. This could be seen as an anti-opacity effect; since causative allomorphy is sensitive to whether the root ends in a consonant or a vowel, /h/-deletion would render allomorph selection opaque.

10. Horne (1961) provides the same form, with glosses, but transcribes the vowels differently (p. 71): *ḍajoh* 'guest,' *ḍajoh-ḍajoh* 'guests,' *ḍaju-ḍaju-e* 'the guests.'

11. We have no explanation for the discrepancy in the medial consonants in the two copies in this form; it may be an aberration in the data, but in any case does not affect the issue at hand.

12. Stressed CV reduplication serves a variety of functions, including nominalization and the marking of continuative aspect. Final CV reduplication intensifies adjectives, negatives, and directional adverbs (Topping 1973:183). Topping marks only irregular stress; in addition, regular penultimate stress is marked on all relevant forms here.

13. Klein (1997) proposes a BRCT analysis of final CV reduplication in which the opaque antepenultimate stress pattern is attributed to BR identity; penultimate stress, on Klein's analysis, would make base and reduplicant metrically unequal. As discussed in Chapter 4, however, Klein's analysis founders once the facts of stressed CV reduplication are considered.

14. Lexical items are taken from sentences in Hurlbut 1988, who provides interlinear glosses for morphemes but not for words; therefore word glosses are not attempted here.

15. Hurlbut 1988 does not gloss the prefix *to-*; however, she mentions the existence of a root *ruol* (p. 60) and cites, in the glossary, the forms *o-ruol* 'be painful' and *poko-ruol* 'curse, lit. cause pain' (p. 133).

16. The counterexamples to this generalization all involve single-segment reduplication, which, as argued in Chapter 7, falls under the category of phonological duplication, rather than morphological reduplication.

17. See Kiparsky 2000:9 for critical discussion of Benua's analysis of this example; Kiparsky's objections, however, do not affect the point made here.

18. There are two reported examples, to our knowledge, of overapplication of a BR-juncture effect. One, in Chaha, is reanalyzed in §5.7 as phonological agreement, not necessarily reduplication-specific. The other is a case from Malay, discussed in Kenstowicz 1981; McCarthy and Prince 1995a. In Malay, nasality spreads rightward from a nasal consonant to any following vowel or glide; it is blocked by nonglides. In forms like *hamã* → *hãmã-hãma*, nasal harmony applies across the BR juncture (*hamã-hamã* → *hamã-hãmã*) and is then apparently reflected to the first vowel of the first copy (→ *hãmã-hãmã*), even though it is not transparently conditioned there. This dramatic example of overapplication has attracted much attention in the literature. To our knowledge Onn 1976 is the only source of this data, which has not been replicated in any other publication.

19. For a parallel example, see the discussion of Warlpiri in note 3.

20. As Richard Rhodes has pointed out to us, the first form in (55c) exhibits double reduplication; the initial *ne* of *nenehkememeːwa* is an instance of monosyllabic reduplication, a less productive pattern than the disyllabic reduplication discussed here. On double reduplication in Fox, see Dahlstrom 1997.

21. The /e~i/ alternation in the roots in (59a) and the suffixes following the null roots in (59b) is due to "Initial Change" discussed in §5.5.2.1. The /e/ vowel is underlying; /i/ is derived.

22. An alternative view is offered by Burkhardt 2002, who proposes output-output faithfulness as a means of handling the overapplication of /e/-raising.

23. Zuraw (2002) develops what is in many ways a similar theory, though gives a base-reduplicant analysis to the corresponding strings. Her view is that learners reanalyze words containing similar segments or sequences as reduplicative, which then leads them to make the strings in question even more similar (hence the name for her theory, namely "Aggressive Reduplication"). However, since the effect of the reanalysis (increased similarity) is comparable to what is yielded by the purely phonological correspondence analyses of Hansson 2001 and Rose and Walker 2001, it seems unnecessary to posit a reduplicative morpheme as part of the process.

6   Case studies

1. These data are taken from McCarthy and Prince 1995a. The rest of the data cited in our discussion come from Bloomfield 1933; Schachter and Otanes 1972; English 1986; French 1988. Data are orthographic, except for 'ng,' which is converted to [ŋ]. Stress and vowel length, not represented in orthography, are not represented here either, despite being marked in some of the sources.

2. This form, whose gloss comes from Schachter and Otanes 1972:364, is the imperfective of *maŋ-isda* 'go fishing.' According to Schachter and Otanes, imperfectives of verbs beginning with *m*-initial prefixes are formed by a two-part operation: reduplication and replacement of *m* with *n*.

3. Another alternative is offered by Saperstein (1997), who suggests a possible process of reanalysis by which stems such as *putul* have developed nasal-initial allomorphs (e.g. *mutul*), for which reduplication selects.

4. On the predictable d ~ r alternation illustrated in (4e), see Schachter and Otanes 1972.

5. In some cases, e.g. *magpa-kain* → *mag-pa-pakain*, second syllable reduplication is the *only* option.

6. Both Applegate and Wash use as their data source the field notes of J. P. Harrington; Wash, in addition, draws from tape recordings made by Madison Beeler.

7. Applegate does not typically provide morpheme glosses. Applegate 1972 contains extensive discussion of Chumash affixational morphology, and with work one can usually identify the affixes in a given verb. However, there is enough homophony among the affixes to make this tricky in some cases. We have supplied morpheme glosses here and there, but have not yet attempted to do this for every form.

8. The glosses in (8) are taken directly from Applegate 1976; some minor typographical data errors in Mester 1986:204, carried over in McCarthy and Prince (1995a:308, 313), are also corrected here.

9. Wilbur (1973:17) says that geminate aspiration applies transparently in Chumash, citing the form /k-kut-kuti/ → *kʰutkuti* 'to look.' We have not been able to confirm this form in Applegate's work.

10. Note that this analysis requires the prefix-final consonant to switch morphemic allegiance from prefix to reduplicant, a transformational process which could not occur in MDT.

11. A CV or CVʔ stem will have a CVh reduplicant.

12. For only a minority of cases is supporting evidence given in the dissertation. However, there are examples to back up all of the crucial arguments made here.

13. The prefix in (18a) does reduplicate in Barbareño; see (17d). In (18f) we correct an apparent typographical error by Applegate, whose surface form omits the vowel in the first syllable.

14. As elsewhere, Applegate does not gloss these individual morphemes. There is a prefix *qili-/qulu-* 'of seeing, vision' (p. 362) that could be the source of *xul-*. The consonants /q/ and /x/ alternate freely in Chumash, and the final /i/ of *qili-/qulu-* could be epenthetic (see p. 327), rather than underlying.

15. In an affix-ordering chart, Applegate (1972:380) indicates that *ni-* precedes *su-*, a claim consistent with such examples as

/ni-su-wal-tun/ [nisuwatun] 'to put something over something else' A72:332
/ni-su-tap/   'to put into; to stuff (e.g. a doll)'   A72:332

The prefixes *ni-* and *su-* thus occur in both orders. Several explanations are possible – free variation, different orderings with different meanings, two different *su-* prefixes, or two different *ni-* prefixes – but it is impossible to decide among these on the basis of the available data. A similar discrepancy involves *su-* and *wati-*, occurring below in the opposite order from what is exhibited in (22):

/wati-su-axsil-š/ [watišaxšilš] 'to go fishing every now and then' A72:383

16. The surface form of 'my arm is broken' is constructed from Applegate's underlying representation.

7 Final issues

1. On Hausa, see Newman 2000. Another recently discovered example of onset-driven phonological copying occurs in American English "Homeric" infixation examples, discussed by Yu 2003.
2. Proximal assimilation includes the possibility of onset-to-onset assimilation (possibly across an intervening coda) or coda-to-coda assimilation (possibly across an intervening onset); Temiar, recently the subject of several insightful studies by Gafos (1998a; 1998b), appears to be a case of the latter type.
3. Two other such cases occur in Kinande (Mutaka & Hyman 1990) and Nancowry (Radhakrishnan 1981). The Kinande facts are amply discussed by Mutaka and Hyman, and we will not repeat them here. Nancowry has been described by Hendricks 1999 as a system in which reduplication of monosyllabic roots occurs "to create a stem that is usable for other processes, such as inflection" (p. 251), though in fact only one affix (the causative, which is derivational) selects for reduplicated roots. There is no general requirement that the base of affixation must be disyllabic. In his grammar of Nancowry, Radhakrishnan 1981 discusses five different affixes, three of which have two suppletive allomorphs, making a total of eight lexically listed affixes. Five of these eight affixes are able to combine directly with monosyllabic roots; in fact the possessive *-u* (e.g. *kan-u* 'possessing [married to] a woman'; p. 65), the objective *-a* (e.g. *wiʔ-a* 'a thing made'; p. 66), the causative *ha-* (e.g. *ha-káh* 'to cause to know'; p. 54), and the instrumental *-an-* (e.g. *s-an-ák* 'spear'; p. 61) combine *only* with monosyllabic roots. Two of the affixes, causative *-um* (e.g. *p-um-ʔʹy* 'to cause to have bad smell,' cf. *paʔʹy* 'smell'; p. 54) and instrumental *-in-* (e.g. *t-in-kuác* 'tracer,' cf. *takuác* 'to have a trace'; p. 62), combine only with lexically disyllabic roots; reduplication of a monosyllabic root is not an option for these. But it is for one prefix, the /ma-/ allomorph of the agentive. This prefix combines only with reduplicated monosyllabic roots (p. 58), thus /ʔáp/ 'to be closed' → *m-up-ʔáp*

'one that is closed,' where *up-ʔáp* is the reduplicated root. (On the phonology of Nancowry reduplication, see Steriade 1988; Alderete et al. 1999; Hendricks 1999.)

4. Following standard practice in the literature on Turkish, we use uppercase letters (e.g. "I") for vowels whose specifications for [back] and [round] are predictable from the context.

5. For example, Alderete (1999; 2001) invokes anti-identity constraints in analyzing accentual dominance effects; anti-identity is used only to accomplish tone deletion, not actually to toggle the values for tones or to insert tones into toneless bases. Simple tone deletion (as proposed for the same data in Inkelas 1998) might be a more straightforward analysis. Crosswhite (1997; 1999) invokes anti-identity constraints to prohibit homophony within inflectional paradigms in Bulgarian and Russian. For example, the suffix vowel in the Russian verb /stávʲ-at/ 'place-3PL' reduces to /ə/ (*stávʲət*), rather than the expected /i/, ostensibly in order to avoid homophony with the third singular form *stávʲit*. As Alan Timberlake (personal communication) points out, however, other suffix /a/ vowels also reduce to /ə/ in the same phonological context even when homophony is not at issue; the target of reduction appears to be morphologically conditioned, making anti-homophony unnecessary as a causal factor.

References

Abbi, Anvita. 1991. *Reduplication in South Asian languages: an areal, typological and historical study*. New Delhi: Allied Publishers Limited.

Akinlabi, Akinbiyi. 1985. Tonal underspecification and Yoruba tone. PhD thesis, University of Ibadan.

Akinlabi, Akinbiyi. 1993. Underspecification and the phonology of Yoruba /r/. *Linguistic Inquiry* 24:139–60.

Alderete, John. 1999. Morphologically governed accent in Optimality Theory. PhD thesis, University of Massachussets, Amherst.

Alderete, John. 2001. Dominance effects as transderivational anti-faithfulness. *Phonology* 18:201–53.

Alderete, John, Jill Beckman, Laura Benua, Amalia Gnanadesikan, John McCarthy, and Suzanne Urbanczyk. 1999. Reduplication with fixed segmentism. *Linguistic Inquiry* 30:327–64.

Anderson, Stephen R. 1974. *The organization of phonology*. San Diego: Academic Press.

Anderson, Stephen R. 1992. *A-morphous morphology*. Cambridge: Cambridge University Press.

Anttila, Arto. 1997. Deriving variation from grammar. In Frans Hinskens, Roeland Van Hout, and W. Leo Wetzels (eds.), *Variation, change and phonological theory*. Amsterdam: John Benjamins, 35–68.

Anttila, Arto. 2002. Morphologically conditioned phonological alternations. *Natural Language and Linguistic Theory* 20:1–42.

Anttila, Arto. In press. Derived environment effects in Colloquial Helsinki Finnish. In Kristin Hanson and Sharon Inkelas (eds.), *The nature of the word: essays in honor of Paul Kiparsky*. Cambridge: MIT Press.

Anttila, Arto and Young-mee Yu Cho 1998. Variation and change in Optimality Theory. *Lingua* 104:31–36.

Applegate, Richard. 1972. Ineseño Chumash grammar. PhD thesis, University of California, Berkeley.

Applegate, Richard. 1976. Reduplication in Chumash. In Margaret Langdon and Shirley Silver (eds.), *Hokan Studies*. The Hague: Mouton, 271–83.

Apte, Mahadeo. 1968. *Reduplication, echo formation and onomatopoeia in Marathi*. Poona: Deccan College Post-Graduate and Research Institute.

Arnott, David W. 1970. *The nominal and verbal systems of Fula*. Oxford: Oxford University Press.

Aronoff, Mark. 1988. Head operations and strata in reduplication: a linear treatment. *Yearbook of Morphology* 1:1–15.

Aronoff, Mark. 1992. Noun classes in Arapesh. *Yearbook of Morphology* 1991:21–32.

Aronoff, Mark. 1994. *Morphology by itself: stems and inflectional classes*. Cambridge: MIT Press.

Austin, Peter. 1981. *A grammar of Diyari*. Cambridge: Cambridge University Press.

Bagemihl, Bruce. 1988. Alternate phonologies and morphologies. PhD thesis, University of British Columbia.

Barker, Muhammad Abd-al-Rahman. 1963. *Klamath Dictionary*, University of California Publications in Linguistics, vol. 31. Berkeley and Los Angeles: University of California Press.

Barker, Muhammad Abd-al-Rahman. 1964. *Klamath grammar*. University of California Publications in Linguistics, vol. 32. Berkeley and Los Angeles: University of California Press.

Barnes, Jonathan. 2002. Positional neutralization: a phonologization approach to typological patterns. PhD thesis, University of California, Berkeley.

Bat-El, Outi. 1994. Stem modification and cluster transfer in Modern Hebrew. *Natural Language and Linguistic Theory* 12:571–96.

Bates, Dawn. 1986. An analysis of Lushootseed diminutive reduplication. In N. Nikiforidou, M. VanClay, M. Niepokuj, and D. Feder (eds.), *Proceedings of the Berkeley Linguistics Society 12*. Berkeley, CA: Berkeley Linguistics Society, 1–13.

Bates, Dawn and Barry F. Carlson. 1998. Spokane (Npoqi'nis&cn) syllable structure and reduplication. In Ewa Czaykowska-Higgins and Dale Kinkade (eds.), *Salish languages and linguistics: theoretical and descriptive perspectives*. Trends in Linguistics: Studies and Monographs 107. Berlin: Mouton de Gruyter, 99–123.

Bates, Dawn, Thom Hess, and Vi Hilbert. 1994. *Lushootseed dictionary*. Seattle: University of Washington Press.

Benua, Laura. 1997. Transderivational identity: phonological relations between words. PhD thesis, University of Massachusetts.

Bhaskararao, Peri. 1977. *Reduplication and onomatopoeia in Telugu*. Poona: Deccan College.

Bissell, Teal. 2002. "Avoidance of the marked" in Miya pluractional allomorphy. In Aniko Csirmaz, Zhiqiang Li, Andrew Nevins, Olga Vaysman, and Michael Wagner (eds.), *Phonological answers*. Cambridge, MA: MITWPL, 1–42.

Black, Deirdre. 1996. The morphological and phonological structure of Spokane lexemes. PhD thesis, University of Montana.

Blevins, James. 2003. Stems and paradigms. *Language* 79:737–67.

Blevins, Juliette. 1996. Mokilese reduplication. *Linguistic Inquiry* 27:523–30.

Blevins, Juliette. 1999. Untangling Leti infixation. *Oceanic Linguistics* 38:383–403.

Blevins, Juliette. 2004. *Evolutionary phonology: the emergence of sound patterns*. Cambridge: Cambridge University Press.

Bloomfield, Leonard. 1933. *Language*. New York: Henry Holt.

Blust, Robert. 2001. Thao Triplication. *Oceanic Linguistics* 40:324–36.

Boas, Franz and Ella Deloria. 1941. *Dakota Grammar*, vol. 23, part 2: Memoirs of the National Academy of Sciences.

Bochner, Harry. 1992. *Simplicity in generative morphology*. Publications in Linguistic Sciences 37. Berlin: Walter de Gruyter.

Booij, Geert. 1984. Coordination reduction in complex words: a case for prosodic phonology. In H. van der Hulst and N. Smith (eds.), *Advances in non-linear phonology*. Dordrecht: Foris, 143–60.

Booij, Geert. 2000. Morphology and phonology. In Geert Booij, Christian Lehmann, and Joachim Mugdan (eds.), *Morphologie – morphology*. Berlin: Walter de Gruyter, 335–43.

Booij, Geert and Rochelle Lieber. 1993. On the simultaneity of morphological and prosodic structure. In Sharon Hargus and Ellen Kaisse (eds.), *Phonetics and phonology 4: studies in lexical phonology*. San Diego: Academic Press, 23–44.

Bosson, James E. 1964. *Modern Mongolian: a primer and reader*. The Hague: Mouton & Co.

Bowen, Donald J. 1969. *Beginning Tagalog: a course for speakers of English*. Berkeley: University of California Press.

Breen, Gavan and Rob Pensalfini. 1999. Arrernte: a language with no syllable onsets. *Linguistic Inquiry* 30:1–25.

Broselow, Ellen. 1983. Salish double reduplications: subjacency in morphology. *Natural Language and Linguistic Theory* 1:317–46.

Bruening, Benjamin. 1997. Abkhaz mabkhaz: m-reduplication in Abkhaz, weightless syllables, and base-reduplicant correspondence. In Benjamin Bruening, Yoonjung Kang, and Martha McGinnis (eds.), *PF: papers at the interface*. Cambridge, MA: MIT Working Papers in Linguistics, 291–330.

Burkhardt, Petra. 2002. Multiple faithfulness relations in Fox (Central Algonquian) reduplication. In Marjo van Koppen, Joanna Sio, and Mark de Vos (eds.), *Console X*. University of Leiden, 33–48.

Burzio, Luigi. 1997. Cycles, non-derived environment blocking, and correspondence. In Joost Dekkers, Frank van der Leeuw, and Jeroen van de Weijer (eds.), *The pointing finger: conceptual studies in Optimality Theory*. Oxford: Oxford University Press.

Bybee, Joan. 1985. *Morphology: a study of the relation between meaning and form*. Amsterdam: John Benjamins.

Carlson, Katy. 1997. Sonority and reduplication in Nakanai and Nuxalk (Bella Coola). Available online from the Rutgers Optimality Archive, ROA# ROA 230-1197.

Carrier-Duncan, Jill. 1984. Some problems with prosodic accounts of reduplication. In Mark Aronoff and Richard Oehrle (eds.), *Language sound structure*. Cambridge, MA: MIT Press, 260–86.

Cho, Young-mee Yu. In press. Derived environment effects in Korean. In Kristin Hanson and Sharon Inkelas (eds.), *The nature of the word: essays in honor of Paul Kiparsky*. Cambridge, MA: MIT Press.

Chomsky, Noam. 1995. *The minimalist program*. Cambridge, MA: MIT Press.

Chomsky, Noam. 2000. Minimalist inquiries: the framework. In Roger Martin, David Michaels, and Juan Uriagereka (eds.), *Essays on minimalist syntax in honor of Howard Lasnik*. Cambridge, MA: MIT Press, 89–155.

Chomsky, Noam and Morris Halle. 1968. *The sound pattern of English*. New York: Harper and Row.

Clements, G. N. 1985. The problem of transfer in nonlinear morphology. *Cornell Working Papers in Linguistics* 7:38–73.

Clements, G. N. and Samuel J. Keyser, 1983. *CV Phonology: a generative theory of the syllable*. Cambridge, MA: MIT Press.

Cohn, Abigail. 1989. Stress in Indonesian and bracketing paradoxes. *Natural Language and Linguistic Theory* 7:167–216.

Cohn, Abigail. 1990. Phonetic and phonological rules of nasalization. PhD thesis, UCLA.

Cohn, Abigail and John McCarthy. 1998. Alignment and parallelism in Indonesian phonology. *Working papers of the Cornell Phonetics Laboratory* 12:53–137.

Cole, Jennifer. 1994. A prosodic theory of reduplication. PhD thesis, Stanford University.

Collins, Chris. 1994. The factive construction in Kwa. *Travaux de recherche sur le créole haïtien* 23:31–65.

Comrie, Bernard. 2000. Morphophonological alternations: typology and diachrony. In S. Bendjaballah, W. U. Dressler, O. E. Pfeiffer, and M. D. Voeikova (eds.), *Morphology 2000: selected papers from the ninth morphology meeting, Vienna, 24–28 February 2000*. Amsterdam: John Benjamins, 73–89.

Conathan, Lisa and Jeffrey Good. 2000. Morphosyntactic reduplication in Chechen and Ingush. In Arike Okrent and John P. Boyle (eds.), *Proceedings of the Chicago Linguistic Society 36–2: the panels*. Chicago: Chicago Linguistic Society, 49–61.

Conathan, Lisa and Esther Wood. 2003. Repetitive reduplication in Yurok and Karuk: semantic effects of contact. In H. C. Wolfart (ed.), *Papers of the thirty-fourth Algonquian Conference*. Winnipeg: University of Manitoba, 19–33.

Conteh, Patrick, Elizabeth Cowper, and Keren Rice. 1985. The environment for consonant mutation in Mende. In G. J. Dimmendaal (ed.), *Current Approaches to African Linguistics*, vol. III. Dordrecht: Foris Publications, 107–16.

Corston-Oliver, Simon. 2002. Roviana. In John Lynch, Malcolm Ross, and Terry Crowley (eds.), *The Oceanic languages*. Richmond: Curzon Press, 467–97.

Crosswhite, Katherine. 1997. Avoidance of homophony in Trigrad Bulgarian vowel reduction. Paper presented at Southwest Workshop on Optimality Theory, University of California, Los Angeles.

Crosswhite, Katherine. 1999. Intra-paradigmatic homophony avoidance in two dialects of Slavic. In Matthew K. Gordon (ed.), *UCLA working papers in linguistics*, vol. I. *Papers in phonology 2*. Los Angeles: UCLA Department of Linguistics, 48–67.

Crowley, Terry. 1982. *The Paamese language of Vanuatu*. Pacific Linguistics Series B-87. Canberra: Australian National University.

Crowley, Terry. 1991. Parallel development and shared innovation: some developments in Central Vanuatu inflectional morphology. *Oceanic Linguistics* 30:179–222.

Crowley, Terry. 1998. *An Erromangan (Sye) grammar*. Oceanic linguistics special publication, no. 27. Honolulu: University of Hawaii Press.

Crowley, Terry. 2002a. Raga. In John Lynch, Malcolm Ross, and Terry Crowley (eds.), *The Oceanic languages*. Richmond: Curzon Press, 626–37.

Crowley, Terry. 2002b. *Serial verbs in Oceanic: a descriptive typology*. Oxford: Oxford University Press.

Crowley, Terry. 2002c. Southeast Ambrym. In John Lynch, Malcolm Ross, and Terry Crowley (eds.), *The Oceanic languages*. Richmond: Curzon Press, 660–70.

Crowley, Terry. 2002d. Sye. In John Lynch, Malcolm Ross, and Terry Crowley (eds.), *The Oceanic languages*. Richmond: Curzon Press, 694–722.

Dahlstrom, Amy. 1997. Fox (Mesquakie) reduplication. *International Journal of American Linguistics* 63:205–26.

DeLacy, Paul. 2002. The formal expression of markedness. PhD thesis, University of Massachusetts, Amherst.

Delancey, Scott. 1991. Chronological strata of suffix classes in the Klamath verb. *International Journal of American Linguistics* 57:426–45.

Delancey, Scott. 1999. Lexical prefixes and the bipartite stem construction in Klamath. *International Journal of American Linguistics* 65:56–83.

Dixon, Robert. 1972. *The Dyirbal language of North Queensland*. Cambridge: Cambridge University Press.

Dixon, Robert. 1988. *A grammar of Boumaa Fijian*. Chicago: University of Chicago Press.

Dobrin, Lise M. 1998. The morphosyntactic reality of phonological form. *Yearbook of Morphology 1997*:59–81.

Dobrin, Lise M. 1999. Phonological form, morphological class, and syntactic gender: the noun class systems of Papua New Guinea Arapeshan. PhD thesis, University of Chicago.

Dolbey, Andrew. 1996. Output optimization and cyclic allomorph selection. In Brian Agbayani and Sze-Wing Tang (eds.), *Proceedings of the fifteenth West Coast Conference on Formal Linguistics*. Stanford: CSLI Publications, 97–112.

Downing, Laura. 1997. Correspondence effects in Siswati reduplication. *Studies in the Linguistic Sciences* 25:81–95.

Downing, Laura. 1998a. Morphological correspondence constraints on Kikerewe reduplication. In Emily Curtis, James Lyle, and Gabriel Webster (eds.), *Proceedings of the sixteenth West Coast Conference* on Formal Linguistics. Stanford: CSLI Publications, 161–75.

Downing, Laura. 1998b. Onset motivated overcopy in reduplication. In E. van Gelderen and V. Samiian (eds.), *Proceedings of WECOL*. Fresno, CA: California State University Press, 81–96.

Downing, Laura. 1998c. On the prosodic misalignment of onsetless syllables. *Natural Language and Linguistic Theory* 16:1–52.

Downing, Laura. 1998d. Prosodic misalignment and reduplication. *Yearbook of Morphology 1997*:83–120.

Downing, Laura. 1998e. Prosodic stem ≠ prosodic word in Bantu. In Tracy Hall and Ursula Kleinhenz (eds.), *Studies on the phonological word*. Current Studies in Linguistic Theory. Amsterdam: John Benjamins, 73–98.

Downing, Laura. 1999a. Morphological constraints on Bantu reduplication. *Linguistic Analysis* 29:6–46.

Downing, Laura. 1999b. Verbal reduplication in three Bantu languages. In Harry van der Hulst, René Kager, and Wim Zonneveld (eds.), *The prosody-morphology interface*. Cambridge: Cambridge University Press, 62–89.

Downing, Laura. 2000a. Morphological and prosodic constraints on Kinande verbal reduplication. *Phonology* 17:1–38.

Downing, Laura. 2000b. Morphological correspondence in Kinande reduplication. *Proceedings of the Berkeley Linguistics Society 23*. Berkeley, CA: Berkeley Linguistics Society.

Downing, Laura. 2001. Ungeneralizable minimality in Ndebele. *Studies in African Linguistics* 30:33–58.

Downing, Laura. 2004. The emergence of the marked: tone in some African reduplicative systems. In Bernhard Hurch (ed.), *Studies in reduplication*. Berlin: Mouton.

Dressler, Wolfgang. 1985. *Morphonology, the dynamics of derivation*, ed. Kenneth C. Hill. Ann Arbor: Karoma Publishers.

Dudas, Karen Marie. 1976. The phonology and morphology of modern Javanese. PhD thesis, University of Illinois.

Durie, Mark. 1985. *A grammar of Acehnese: on the basis of a dialect of North Aceh*. Dordrecht: Foris.

Early, Robert. 2002. Niuafo'ou. In John Lynch, Malcolm Ross, and Terry Crowley (eds.), *The Oceanic languages*. Richmond: Curzon Press, 848–64.

Egbokhare, Francis O. 2001. Phonosemantic correspondences in Emai attributive ideophones. In F. K. Erhard Voeltz and Kilian-Hats (eds.), *Ideophones*. Amsterdam: John Benjamins, 87–96.

Elbert, Samuel H. 1988. *Echo of a culture: a grammar of Rennell and Bellona*. Oceanic Linguistics Special Publication, No. 22. Honolulu: University of Hawaii Press.

Emeneau, Murray. 1955. *Kolami: a Dravidian language*. Berkeley: University of California Press.

English, Leo J. 1986. *Tagalog–English dictionary*. Manila: Congregation of the Most Holy Redeemer.

Ezard, Bryan. 1980. Reduplication in Tawala. *Kivung* 12:145–60.

Ezard, Bryan. 1997. *A grammar of Tawala*. Pacific Linguistics Series C-137. Canberra: Research School for Pacific and Asian Studies, Australian National University.

Fabb, Nigel. 2002. *Language and literary structure: the linguistic analysis of form in verse and narrative*. Cambridge: Cambridge University Press.

Feinstein, Mark H. and Robert M. Vago. 1981. Non-evidence for the segmental cycle in Klamath. In Didier L. Goyvaerts (ed.), *Phonology in the 1980s*. Ghent: Story-Scientia, 119–45.

Fillmore, Charles, Paul Kay, and Mary Catherine O'Connor. 1988. Regularity and idiomaticity in grammatical constructions. *Language* 64:501–38.

Fitzgerald, Colleen M. 1999. Loanwords and stress in Tohono O'odham. *Anthropological Linguistics* 41:193–208.

Fitzgerald, Colleen M. 2000. Vowel hiatus and faithfulness in Tohono O'odham reduplication. *Linguistic Inquiry* 31:713–22.

Fitzgerald, Colleen M. 2001. The Morpheme-to-Stress principle in Tohono O'odham. *Linguistics* 39:941–72.

Fitzgerald, Colleen M. 2002. Tohono O'odham stress in a single ranking. *Phonology* 19:253–71.

Ford, Alan and Rajendra Singh. 1983. On the status of morphophonology. In John F. Richardson, Mitchell Marks, and Amy Chukerman (eds.), *Papers from the parasession on the interplay of phonology, morphology and syntax.* Chicago: Chicago Linguistic Society, 63–78.

Fortune, R. F. 1942. *Arapesh.* Publications of the American Ethnological Society, no. 19. New York: J. Augustin.

Frampton, John. 2003. Root vowel syncope and reduplication in Sanskrit. Paper presented at the thirty-ninth meeting of the Chicago Linguistics Society, University of Chicago.

French, Koleen. 1988. *Insights into Tagalog: reduplication, infixation and stress from nonlinear phonology.* Dallas: SIL and University of Texas at Arlington.

Gafos, Diamandis. 1998a. Eliminating long-distance consonantal spreading. *Natural Language and Linguistic Theory* 16:223–78.

Gafos, Diamandis. 1998b. A-templatic reduplication. *Linguistic Inquiry:* 515–25.

Geraghty, Paul. 2002. Nadrogā. In John Lynch, Malcolm Ross, and Terry Crowley (eds.), *The Oceanic languages.* Richmond: Curzon Press, 833–47.

Gerdts, Donna. 1998. Incorporation. In Andrew Spencer and Arnold Zwicky (eds.), *The handbook of morphology.* Oxford: Blackwell, 84–100.

Goldberg, Adele. 1995. *Constructions.* Chicago: Chicago University Press.

Goodenough, Ward H. 1963. The long or double consonants of Trukese. *Proceedings of the ninth Pacific Science Congress, 1957* 3:77–86.

Gorgoniev, Yu. A. 1976. The relationship between reduplication and some other grammatical means in Khmer. In Stanley Starosta (ed.), *Austroasiatic studies, part 1.* Honolulu: University Press of Hawaii, 309–21.

Green, Antony Dubach. 2002. Word, foot and syllable structure in Burmese. Available online from the Rutgers Optimality Archive, ROA# 551-1002.

Gurevich, Naomi. 2000. Reduplication in Southern Paiute and Correspondence Theory. In Roger Billerey and Brook Lillehaugen (eds.), *Proceedings of the nineteenth West Coast Conference on Formal Linguistics.* Somerville: Cascadilla Press, 167–77.

Haiman, John. 1980. *Hua: a Papuan language of the Eastern Highlands of New Guinea.* Studies in Language Companion Series, vol. 5. Amsterdam: John Benjamins.

Haiman, John. 1998. Repetition and identity. *Lingua* 100:57–70.

Hanson, Kristin and Paul Kiparsky. 1996. A parametric theory of poetic meter. *Language* 72:287–335.

Hansson, Gunnar. 2001. Theoretical and typological issues in consonant harmony. PhD thesis, University of California, Berkeley.

Haraguchi, Shosuke. 1977. *The tone pattern of Japanese.* Tokyo: Kaitakusha.

Hardman, M. J. 2000. *Jaqaru.* Languages of the world/materials 183. Munich: Lincom Europa.

Hargus, Sharon. 1988. *The lexical phonology of Sekani.* Outstanding dissertations in linguistics series. New York: Garland.

Hargus, Sharon. 1995. The first person plural subject prefix in Babine/Witsuwit'en. Available online from the Rutgers Optimality Archive, ROA# 108-0000.

Harris, B. P. and G. N. O'Grady. 1976. An analysis of the progressive morpheme in Umpila verbs. In P. Sutton (ed.), *Languages of Cape York.* Canberra: Australian Institute of Aboriginal Studies, 165–212.

Harrison, Sheldon P. 1973. Reduplication in Micronesian languages. *Oceanic Linguistics* 12:407–54.

Harrison, Sheldon P. 1976. *Mokilese Reference grammar*. Honolulu: University Press of Hawaii.

Hayes, Bruce. 1981. *A metrical theory of stress rules*. Bloomington: Indiana University Linguistics Club.

Healey, Alan, Ambrose Isoroembo, and Martin Chittleborough. 1969. Preliminary notes on Orokaiva grammar. *Papers in New Guinea Linguistics* 9:33–64.

Hendricks, Sean Q. 1999. Reduplication without template constraints: a study in bare-consonant reduplication. PhD thesis, University of Arizona.

Hess, T. M. and V. Hilbert. 1978. *Lushootseed*. Seattle: Daybreak Star Press.

Hess, Thom. 1977. Lushootseed dialects. *Anthropological Linguistics* 19:403–19.

Hess, Thom. 1993. A schema for the presentation of Lushootseed verb stem. In A. Mattina and T. Montler (eds.), *American Indian linguistics and ethnography in honor of Laurence C. Thompson*. University of Montana Occasional Papers in Linguistics No. 10, 113–25.

Hess, Thom. 1995. *Lushootseed reader with introductory grammar: volume 1: Four Stories by Edward Sam*. University of Montana Occasional Papers in Linguistics II.

Hill, Jane H. and Ofelia Zepeda. 1992. Derived words in Tohono O'odham. *International Journal of American Linguistics* 58:355–404.

Hill, Jane H. and Ofelia Zepeda. 1998. Tohono O'odham (Papago) plurals. *Anthropological Linguistics* 40:1–42.

Hockett, Charles. 1954. Two models of grammatical description. *Word* 10:210–31.

Holtman, Astrid. 1996. *A generative theory of rhyme: an Optimality approach*. OTS Dissertation Series Utrecht: LEd.

Horne, Elinor. 1961. *Beginning Javanese*. New Haven: Yale University Press.

Hualde, José. 1988. A lexical phonology of Basque. PhD thesis, University of Southern California.

Hurlbut, Hope M. 1988. *Verb morphology in Eastern Kadazan*. Pacific Linguistics Series B-97. Canberra: Department of Linguistics, Research School of Pacific Studies, Australian National University.

Hyman, Larry M., Sharon Inkelas, and Galen Sibanda. To appear. Morphosyntactic correspondence in Bantu reduplication. In Kristin Hanson and Sharon Inkelas (eds.), *The Nature of the Word: Essays in Honor of Paul Kiparsky*. Cambridge, MA: MIT Press.

Hyman, Larry M. and Al Mtenje. 1999. Prosodic morphology and tone: the case of Chichewa. In Rene Kager, Harry van der Hulst, and Wim Zonneveld (eds.), *The prosody-morphology interface*. Cambridge: Cambridge University Press, 90–133.

Inkelas, Sharon. 1990. *Prosodic constituency in the lexicon*. New York: Garland.

Inkelas, Sharon. 1995. The consequences of optimization for underspecification. In Jill Beckman (ed.), *Proceedings of the Northeastern Linguistics Society* 25: Amherst, MA: GLSA, 287–302.

Inkelas, Sharon. 1998. The theoretical status of morphologically conditioned phonology: a case study from dominance. *Yearbook of Morphology 1997*:121–55.

Inkelas, Sharon. 2000. Phonotactic blocking through structural immunity. In Barbara Stiebels and Dieter Wunderlich (eds.), *Lexicon in focus*. Studia Grammatica 45. Berlin: Akademie Verlag, 7–40.

Inkelas, Sharon and Cemil Orhan Orgun. 1995. Level ordering and economy in the lexical phonology of Turkish. *Language* 71:763–93.

Inkelas, Sharon and Cemil Orhan Orgun. 1998. Level (non)ordering in recursive morphology: evidence from Turkish. In Steven Lapointe, Diane Brentari, and Patrick Farrell (eds.), *Morphology and its relation to phonology and syntax.* Stanford, CA: CSLI Publications, 360–92.

Inkelas, Sharon, Cemil Orhan Orgun, and Cheryl Zoll. 1997. Implications of lexical exceptions for the nature of grammar. In Iggy Roca (ed.), *Constraints and derivations in phonology.* Oxford: Clarendon Press, 393–418.

Inkelas, Sharon and Cheryl Zoll. 2003. Is grammar dependence real? Unpublished ms., UC Berkeley and MIT. Available online from the Rutgers Optimality Archive, ROA# 587-0303.

Innes, G. 1971. *A practical introduction to Mende.* London: School of Oriental and African Studies.

Itô, Junko. 1990. Prosodic minimality in Japanese. In Michael Ziolkowski, Manuela Noske, and Karen Deaton (eds.), *Papers from the twenty-sixth regional meeting of the Chicago Linguistics Society,* vol. II: *The parasession on the syllable in phonetics and phonology.* Chicago: Chicago Linguistics Society, 213–39.

Itô, Junko and Armin Mester. 1986. The phonology of voicing in Japanese: theoretical consequences for morphological accessibility. *Linguistic Inquiry* 17:49–73.

Itô, Junko and Armin Mester. 1995a. *The core-periphery structure of the lexicon and constraints on reranking.* University of Massachussetts Occasional Papers in Linguistics 18. Amherst, MA: GLSA.

Itô, Junko and Armin Mester. 1995b. Japanese phonology: constraint domains and structure preservation. In John Goldsmith (ed.), *The handbook of phonological theory.* Blackwell Handbooks in Linguistics Series Cambridge, MA: Blackwell, 817–38.

Itô, Junko and Armin Mester. 1996a. Rendaku 1: constraint conjunction and the OCP. Available online from the Rutgers Optimality Archive, ROA# 144-0996.

Itô, Junko and Armin Mester. 1996b. Structural economy and OCP interactions in local domains. Paper presented at the Western Conference on Linguistics (WECOL). University of California, Santa Cruz.

Itô, Junko and Armin Mester. 1997. Correspondence and compositionality: the Ga-gyo variation in Japanese phonology. In Iggy Roca (ed.), *Derivations and constraints in phonology.* Oxford: Clarendon Press, 419–62.

Itô, Junko and Armin Mester. 1999. The phonological lexicon. In N. Tsujimura (ed.), *The handbook of Japanese linguistics.* Malden, MA: Blackwell, 62–100.

Itô, Junko, Armin Mester, and Jaye Padgett. 1995. Licensing and underspecification in Optimality Theory. *Linguistic Inquiry* 26:571–613.

Jeanne, LaVerne Masayesua. 1982. Some phonological rules of Hopi. *IJAL* 48: 245–70.

Johanson, Lars and Eva Csato, eds. 1998. *The Turkic languages.* New York: Routledge.

Jones, William. 1919. *Ojibwa Texts, Part 2.* New York: G. E. Stechert.

Kager, Rene. 1996. On affix allomorphy and syllable counting. In Ursula Kleinhenz (ed.), *Interfaces in phonology.* Studia grammatica 41. Berlin: Akademie Verlag, 155–71.

Kager, Rene. 1999. *Optimality Theory*. Cambridge: Cambridge University Press.

Kaisse, Ellen and Patricia Shaw. 1985. On the theory of Lexical Phonology. *Phonology Yearbook* 2:1–30.

Kanerva, Jonni. 1989. Focus and phrasing in Chichewa phonology. PhD thesis, Stanford University.

Kawu, Ahmadu Ndanusa. 1998. The emergence of the unmarked in Niger-Congo verb reduplication. Unpublished ms., Rutgers University.

Kay, Paul. 2002. English subjectless tagged sentences. *Language* 78:453–81.

Kean, Mary-Louise. 1973. Non-global rules in Klamath Phonology. *Quarterly Progress Report, MIT Research Laboratory in Electronics* 108:288–310.

Kelepir, Meltem. 2000. To be or not to be faithful. In Aslı Göksel and Celia Kerslake (eds.), *Proceedings of the ninth International Conference of Turkish Linguistics*. Wiesbaden: Otto Harrassowitz, 11–18.

Kenstowicz, Michael. 1981. Functional explanations in generative phonology. In Didier L. Goyvaerts (ed.), *Phonology in the 1980s*. Ghent: E. Story-Scientia, 431–44.

Kenstowicz, Michael. 1995. Cyclic vs. non-cyclic constraint evaluation. *Phonology* 12:397–436.

Kenstowicz, Michael. 1996. Base identity and uniform exponence: alternatives to cyclicity. In Jacques Durand and Bernard Laks (eds.), *Current trends in phonology: models and methods*. Salford: ESRI, 363–94.

Kenstowicz, Michael. 1997. Uniform exponence: extension and exemplification. In Viola Miglio and Bruce Moren (eds.), *University of Maryland working papers in linguistics: selected phonology papers from the Johns Hopkins Optimality Theory Workshop/Maryland Mayfest*. Baltimore: Department of Linguistics, University of Maryland, 139–55. Available electronically from the Rutgers Optimality Archive, ROA# 218-0997.

Kenstowicz, Michael and Charles Kisseberth. 1979. *Generative phonology*. New York: Academic Press.

Kenstowicz, Michael and Degif Petros Banksira 1999. Reduplicative identity in Chaha. *Linguistic Inquiry* 30:573–86.

Kim, Eun-Sook. 2003. Patterns of reduplication in Nuu-chah-nulth. In M. Kadowaki and Shigeto Kawahara (eds.), *Proceedings of the Northeastern Linguistics Society 33*. Amherst, MA: GLSA, 127–46.

Kiparsky, Paul. 1973a. Phonological representations: abstractness, opacity and global rules. In Osamu Fujimura (ed.), *Three dimensions in linguistic theory*. Tokyo: TEC, 56–86.

Kiparsky, Paul. 1973b. The role of linguistics in a theory of poetry. *Proceedings of the American Academy of Arts and Sciences* 102:231–44.

Kiparsky, Paul. 1982a. From cyclic phonology to lexical phonology. In Harry van der Hulst and Norval Smith (eds.), *The structure of phonological representations, part I*. Dordrecht: Foris, 131–75.

Kiparsky, Paul. 1982b. Lexical morphology and phonology. In I.-S. Yang (ed.), *Linguistics in the morning calm*. Linguistics Society of Korea. Seoul: Hanshin, 3–91.

Kiparsky, Paul. 1982c. Word-formation and the lexicon. In Frances Ingemann (ed.), *1982 Mid-America linguistics conference papers*. Lawrence, KS: University of Kansas, 3–29.

Kiparsky, Paul. 1986. The phonology of reduplication. Unpublished ms., Stanford University.

Kiparsky, Paul. 1993. Blocking in non-derived environments. In Sharon Hargus and Ellen Kaisse (eds.), *Phonetics and phonology 4: studies in lexical phonology*. San Diego: Academic Press, 277–313.

Kiparsky, Paul. 1994. Remarks on markedness. Paper presented at TREND, University of California, Santa Cruz.

Kiparsky, Paul. 1997. Templatic morphology: Base-reduplication Identity constraints vs. cyclicity. Class handout from Scandinavian Summer School in Generative Phonology, Hvalfjardarströnd, Iceland, June 1997.

Kiparsky, Paul. 2000. Opacity and cyclicity. *The Linguistic Review* 17:351–67.

Kisseberth, Charles W. 1972, Cyclical rules in Klamath Phonology. *Linguistic Inquiry* 3:3–33.

Kiyomi, Setsuko. 1993. A typological study of reduplication as a morpho-semantic process: evidence from five language families (Bantu, Australian, Papuan, Austroasiatic and Malayo-Polynesian). PhD thesis, Indiana University.

Klein, Thomas B. 1997. Output constraints and prosodic correspondence in Chamorro reduplication. *Linguistic Inquiry* 28:707–16.

Koenig, Jean-Pierre. 1992. Shared structure vs. constructional autonomy in construction grammar. Proceedings of the fifteenth International Congress of Linguistics, 356–59.

Koenig, Jean-Pierre and Daniel Jurafsky. 1995. Type underspecification and on-line type construction in the lexicon. In Raul Aranovich, William Byrne, Susanne Preuss, and Martha Senturia (eds.), *Proceedings of the thirteenth West Coast Conference on Formal Linguistics*. Stanford: CSLI Publications, 270–85.

Kornfilt, Jaklin. 1997. *Turkish*. London: Routledge.

Krause, Scott. 1980. Topics in Chukchee Phonology and Morphology. PhD thesis, University of Illinois Urbana-Champaign.

Kroeger, Paul. 1990. Discontinuous reduplication in vernacular Malay. *Proceedings of the Berkeley Linguistics Society 15*. Berkeley: Berkeley Linguistics Society, 193–202.

Kurisu, Kazutaka. 2001. The phonology of morpheme realization. PhD thesis, UC Santa Cruz.

Landau, Idan. 2003. Modular recoverability: chain resolution in Hebrew VP-fronting. Unpublished ms., Ben Gurion University of the Negev and Tel Aviv University.

Lathroum, Amanda. 1991. Resolving the disparity between linear and structural order in words: a study of reduplication in Austronesian. PhD thesis, Harvard University.

Lefebvre, Claire and A. M. Brousseau. 2002. *A grammar of Fongbe*. Berlin: Mouton de Gruyter.

Levin, Juliette. 1985a. A metrical theory of syllabicity. PhD thesis, Massachusetts Institute of Technology.

Levin, Juliette. 1985b. Reduplication in Umpila. In Diana Archangeli, Andrew Barrss, and Richard Sproat (eds.), *MIT working papers in linguistics*, vol. VI: *papers in theoretical and applied linguistics*. Cambridge: Massachusetts Institute of Technology, 133–59.

Lewis, Geoffrey. 1967. *Turkish grammar*. Oxford: Oxford University Press.

Li, Charles and Sandra Thompson. 1981. *Mandarin Chinese: a functional reference grammar*. Berkeley: University of California Press.

Lieber, Rochelle. 1980. On the organization of the lexicon. PhD thesis, Masachusetts Institute of Technology.

Lombardi, Linda and John McCarthy. 1991. Prosodic circumscription in Choctaw morphology. *Phonology* 8:37–71.

Longtau, Selbut R. 1993. A formal Tarok phonology. *Afrika und Übersee* 76:15–40.

Lubowicz, Anna. 1999. Derived environment effects in OT. In Kimary Shahin, Susan Blake, and Eun-Sook Kim (eds.), *Proceedings of the seventeenth West Coast Conference on Formal Linguistics*. Stanford: CSLI Publications, 451–65. Available electronically from the Rutgers Optimality Archive, ROA# 239-0198.

Lynch, John. 2002a. Niuafo'ou. In John Lynch, Malcolm Ross, and Terry Crowley (eds.), *The Oceanic languages*. Richmond: Curzon Press, 865–76.

Lynch, John. 2002b. Ulithian. In John Lynch, Malcolm Ross, and Terry Crowley (eds.), *The Oceanic languages*. Richmond: Curzon Press, 792–803.

Lynch, John and Rex Horoi. 2002. Arosi. In John Lynch, Malcolm Ross, and Terry Crowley (eds.), *The Oceanic languages*. Richmond: Curzon Press, 562–72.

Lynch, John and Malcolm Ross. 2002. Banoni. In John Lynch, Malcolm Ross, and Terry Crowley (eds.), *The Oceanic languages*. Richmond: Curzon Press, 440–55.

Lynch, John, Malcolm Ross, and Terry Crowley. 2002. *The Oceanic languages*. Richmond: Curzon Press.

Malkiel, Yakov. 1959. Studies in irreversible binomials. *Lingua* 8.

Marantz, Alec. 1982. Re reduplication. *Linguistic Inquiry* 13:483–545.

Marantz, Alec and Caroline Wiltshire. 2000. Reduplication. In Geert Booij, Christian Lehmann, and Joachim Mugdan (eds.), *Morphologie – morphology*. Berlin: Walter de Gruyter, 557–66.

Mascaró, Joan. 1976. *Catalan phonology and the phonological cycle*. Bloomington: Indiana University Linguistics Club.

Matteson, Esther. 1965. *The Piro (Arawakan) language*. University of California publications in linguistics, vol. 42. Berkeley, CA: University of California Press.

McCarthy, John. 1986. OCP effects: gemination and antigemination. *Linguistic Inquiry* 17:207–63.

McCarthy, John. 1993. The parallel advantage. Paper presented at Rutgers Optimality Workshop 1, Rutgers University.

McCarthy, John. 1996. Remarks on phonological opacity in Optimality Theory. In J. Lecarme, J. Lowenstamm, and U. Shlonsky (eds.), *Studies in Afroasiatic grammar: papers from the second Conference on Afroasiatic Linguistics, Sophia Antipolis, 1994*. The Hague: Holland Academic Graphics, 215–43.

McCarthy, John. 1999. Sympathy and phonological opacity. *Phonology* 16:331–99.

McCarthy, John. 2002a. Against gradience. Available online from the Rutgers Optimality Archive, ROA# 510-0302.

McCarthy, John. 2002b. *A thematic guide to Optimality Theory*. Cambridge: Cambridge University Press.

McCarthy, John and Alan Prince. 1986. Prosodic morphology. Unpublished ms., University of Massachusetts, Amherst and Brandeis University.

McCarthy, John and Alan Prince. 1990. Foot and word in Prosodic Morphology: the Arabic broken plural. *Natural Language and Linguistic Theory* 8:209–83.

McCarthy, John and Alan Prince. 1993. Prosodic Morphology I: constraint interaction and satisfaction. Unpublished ms., University of Massachusetts, Amherst and Rutgers University.

McCarthy, John and Alan Prince. 1994a. The emergence of the unmarked. In Mercè Gonzàlez (ed.), *Proceedings of the Northeastern Linguistic Society* 24. Amherst, MA: GLSA, 333–79.

McCarthy, John and Alan Prince. 1994b. Generalized alignment. In Geert Booij and Jaap van Marle (eds.), *Yearbook of Morphology 1993*. Dordrecht: Kluwer, 79–153.

McCarthy, John and Alan Prince. 1994c. An overview of Prosodic Morphology part I: templatic form in reduplication. Paper presented at Workshop on Prosodic Morphology, Utrecht University.

McCarthy, John and Alan Prince. 1994d. An overview of Prosodic Morphology part II: Template satisfaction. Paper presented at Workshop on Prosodic Morphology, Utrecht University.

McCarthy, John and Alan Prince. 1995a. Faithfulness and reduplicative identity. In Jill Beckman, Laura Dickey, and Suzanne Urbanczyk (eds.), *University of Massachusetts Occasional Papers in Linguistics 18: Papers in Optimality Theory*. Amherst, MA: GLSA, 249–384.

McCarthy, John and Alan Prince. 1995b. Prosodic Morphology. In John Goldsmith (ed.), *Handbook of phonological theory*. Cambridge, MA: Blackwell, 318–66.

McCarthy, John and Alan Prince. 1999a. Faithfulness and identity in Prosodic Morphology. In Rene Kager, Harry van der Hulst, and Wim Zonneveld (eds.), *The prosody-morphology interface*. Cambridge: Cambridge University Press, 218–309.

McCarthy, John and Alan Prince. 1999b. Prosodic Morphology (1986). In John Goldsmith (ed.), *Phonological theory: the essential readings*. Malden, MA: Blackwell, 238–88.

McCawley, J. D. 1968. *The phonological component of a grammar of Japanese*. The Hague: Mouton.

McDonough, Joyce. 1990. *Topics in the phonology and morphology of Navajo verbs*. Amherst: GLSA.

McGuckin, Catherine. 2002. Gapapaiwa. In John Lynch, Malcolm Ross, and Terry Crowley (eds.), *The Oceanic languages*. Richmond: Curzon Press, 297–321.

McLaughlin, Fiona. 2000. Consonant mutation and reduplication in Seereer-Siin. *Phonology* 17:333–63.

Menn, Lise and Brian MacWhinney. 1984. The repeated morph constraint: toward an explanation. *Language* 60:519–41.

Mester, Armin. 1986. Studies in tier structure. PhD thesis, University of Massachusetts, Amherst.

Mester, Armin and Junko Itô. 1995. *The core-periphery structure of the lexicon and constraints on reranking*: University of Massachussets Occasional Papers in Linguistics 18. Amherst, MA: GLSA.

Mintz, Malcolm W. 1994. *A student's grammar of Malay and Indonesian*. Singapore: EPB Publishers Pte Ltd.

Mithun, Marianne. 1984. The evolution of noun incorporation. *Language* 60:847–94.

Mithun, Marianne. 2000. Incorporation. In Geert Booij, Christian Lehmann, and Joachim Mugdan (eds.), *Morphologie – morphology*. Berlin: Walter de Gruyter, 916–28.

Mohanan, K. P. 1986. *Lexical phonology*. Dordrecht: Kluwer.

Mohanan, K. P. 1995. The organization of the grammar. In John Goldsmith (ed.), *The handbook of phonological theory*. Cambridge, MA: Blackwell, 24–69.

Moravcsik, Edith. 1978. Reduplicative constructions. In Joseph Greenberg (ed.), *Universals of human language*. Stanford: Stanford University Press, 297–334.

Mtenje, Al. 1988. On tone and transfer in Chichewa reduplication. *Linguistics* 26:125–55.

Mutaka, Ngessimo and Larry M. Hyman. 1990. Syllable and morpheme integrity in Kinande reduplication. *Phonology* 7:73–120.

Nagaraja, K. S. 1979. Contraction of Khasi nouns in compounds. *Indian Linguistics* 40:18–23.

Nash, David. 1986. *Topics in Warlpiri grammar*. New York: Garland.

Nater, Henry. 1984. *The Bella Coola language*: Canadian Ethnology Service Paper 92. Ottawa: Museum of Man.

Nater, Henry. 1990. *A concise Nuxalk–English dictionary*: Canadian Ethnology Paper 115. Ottawa: Museum of Civilization.

Nespor, Marina and Irene Vogel. 1986. *Prosodic phonology*. Dordrecht: Foris.

Newman, Paul. 1986. Tone and affixation in Hausa. *Studies in African Linguistics* 17:249–67.

Newman, Paul. 1989a. The historical change from suffixal to prefixal reduplication in Hausa pluractional verbs. *Journal of African Languages and Linguistics* 11:37–44.

Newman, Paul. 1989b. Reduplication and tone in Hausa ideophones. In Kira Hall, Michael Meacham, and Richard Shapiro (eds.), *Proceedings of the fifteenth annual meeting of the Berkeley Linguistics Society*. Berkeley: Berkeley Linguistics Society, 248–55.

Newman, Paul. 2000. *The Hausa language: an encyclopedic reference grammar*. New Haven: Yale University Press.

Newman, Stanley. 1971. Bella Coola reduplication. *International Journal of American Linguistics* 37:34–38.

Nguyen, Dình-hoà. 1997. *Vietnamese: Tieng Viet Khong Son Phan*. Amsterdam: John Benjamins.

Niepokuj, Mary Katherine. 1997. *The development of verbal reduplication in Indo-European*. Washington: Institute for the Study of Man.

Noonan, Michael. 1992. *A grammar of Lango*. Berlin: Mouton de Gruyter.

Nunberg, Geoffrey, Ivan A. Sag, and Thomas Wasow. 1994. Idioms. *Language* 70:491–538.

Onn, Farid M. 1976. Aspects of Malay phonology and morphology: a generative approach. PhD thesis, University of Illinois.

Orgun, Cemil Orhan. 1994. Monotonic cyclicity and Optimality Theory. In Mercè Gonzàlez (ed.), *Proceedings of the Northeastern Linguistic Society* 24. Amherst, MA: GLSA, 461–74.

Orgun, Cemil Orhan. 1996. Sign-based morphology and phonology: with special attention to Optimality Theory. PhD thesis, University of California, Berkeley.

Orgun, Cemil Orhan. 1997. Cyclic and noncyclic effects in a declarative grammar. *Yearbook of morphology 1997*:179–218.

Orgun, Cemil Orhan. 1999. Sign-based morphology: a declarative theory of phonology-morphology interleaving. In Ben Hermans and Marc van Oostendorp (eds.), *The derivational residue in phonological Optimality Theory*. Amsterdam: John Benjamins, 247–67.

Orgun, Cemil Orhan. 2002. Phonology-morphology interaction in a constraint-based framework. Unpublished ms., University of California, Davis.

Orgun, Cemil Orhan and Sharon Inkelas. 2002. Reconsidering bracket erasure. *Yearbook of Morphology* 2001:115–46.

Ourn, Noeurng and John Haiman. 2000. Symmetrical compounds in Khmer. *Studies in Language* 24:483–514.

Park, Miae. 2000. Surface opacity and phonological issues in Klamath and Lushootseed. PhD thesis, University of Wisconsin-Madison.

Parker, G. J. 1968. Southeast Ambrym verb inflection and morphophonemics. *Papers in Linguistics of Melanesia*. Pacific Linguistics Series A-15:27–40.

Patterson, Trudi Alice. 1990. Theoretical aspects of Dakota morphology and phonology. PhD thesis, University of Illinois.

Payne, David. 1981. *The phonology and morphology of Axininca Campa*. Arlington, TX: Summer Institute of Linguistics.

Pesetsky, David. 1979. Russian morphology and lexical theory. Unpublished ms., Massachusetts Institute of Technology.

Peterson, David. 2001. The Ingush clitic ʔa: the elusive type 5 clitic? *Language* 77:144–55.

Piñon, Chris. 1991. Falling in paradise: verbs, preverbs and reduplication in Hungarian. Handout from talk delivered at Syntax Workshop, 5/21/91, Stanford University.

Poser, William J. 1984. The phonetics and phonology of tone and intonation in Japanese. PhD thesis, Massachusetts Institute of Technology.

Poser, William J. 1989. The metrical foot in Diyari. *Phonology* 6:117–48.

Prince, Alan and Paul Smolensky. 1993. Optimality theory: constraint interaction in generative grammar. Cognitive Science Center Technical report TR-2, Rutgers University.

Pulleyblank, Douglas. 1986. *Tone in lexical phonology*. Dordrecht: D. Reidel.

Pulleyblank, Douglas. 1988. Vocalic underspecification in Yoruba. *Linguistic Inquiry* 19:233–70.

Pulleyblank, Douglas. 1998. Yoruba vowel patterns: deriving asymmetries by the tension between opposing constraints. Available online from the Rutgers Optimality Archive, ROA# 270-0798.

Pulleyblank, Douglas. To appear. Patterns of reduplication in Yoruba. In Kristin Hanson and Sharon Inkelas (eds.), *The nature of the word: essays in honor of Paul Kiparsky*. Cambridge, MA: MIT Press.

Pykllänen, Liina. 1999. On base-reduplicant identity. In P. Norquest (ed.), *Proceedings of the eighteenth West Coast Conference on Formal Linguistics*. Somerville: Cascadilla Press, 448–61.

Radhakrishnan, R. 1981. *The Nancowry word: phonology, affixal morphology and roots of a Nicobarese language*. Edmonton: Linguistic Research, Inc.

Raimy, Eric. 2000. *The phonology and morphology of reduplication*. Berlin: Mouton.

Raimy, Eric and William Idsardi. 1997. A minimalist approach to reduplication in Optimality Theory. In Kiyomi Kusumoto (ed.), *Proceedings of the Northeastern Linguistic Society* 27. Amherst, MA: GLSA, 369–82.

Ramos, Teresita V. and Resty M. Caena. 1990. *Modern Tagalog: Grammatical explanations and exercises for non-native speakers*. Honolulu: University of Hawaii Press.

Rehg, Kenneth L. and Damian G. Sohl. 1981. *Ponapean Reference Grammar*. Honolulu: University of Hawaii Press.

Rice, Keren. 1989. *A grammar of Slave*. Berlin: Mouton de Gruyter.

Riehemann, Susanne. 2001. A constructional approach to idioms and word formation. PhD thesis, Stanford University.

Roberts, John. 1987. *Amele*. London: Croom Helm.

Roberts, John. 1991. Reduplication in Amele. *Papers in Papuan Linguistics* 1:115–46.

Robins, R. H. 1959. Nominal and verbal derivation in Sundanese. *Lingua* 8:337–69.

Robinson, J. O. 1976. His and hers morphology: the strange case of Tarok possessives. In Larry Hyman, L. Jacobson, and Russell Schuh (eds.), *Studies in African Linguistics, Supplement 6*. Los Angeles: Department of Linguistics, UCLA, 201–09.

Rose, Sharon. 1999. The (non)interaction of lenition and reduplication. *Papers from the Regional Meetings, Chicago Linguistic Society* 35:277–92.

Rose, Sharon and Rachel Walker. 2001. A typology of consonant agreement as correspondence. Unpublished ms., University of California, San Diego; and University of Southern California. Available online from the Rutgers Optimality Archive, ROA# 405–0800.

Rosen, Sara. 1989. Two types of noun incorporation. *Language* 65:294–317.

Ross, Malcolm. 2002. Kaulong. In John Lynch, Malcolm Ross, and Terry Crowley (eds.), *The Oceanic languages*. Richmond: Curzon Press, 387–409.

Rubino, Carl. 2001. Iconic morphology and word formation in Ilocano. In F. K. Erhard Voeltz and Christa Kilian-Hatz (eds.), *Ideophones*. Amsterdam: John Benjamins, 303–20.

Sag, Ivan and Thomas Wasow. 1999. *Syntactic theory: a formal introduction*. Stanford: CSLI Publications.

Saperstein, Andrew. 1997. A word-and-paradigm approach to reduplication. PhD thesis, Ohio State University.

Sapir, Edward. 1930. Southern Paiute, A Shoshonean language. *Proceedings of the American Academy of Arts and Sciences* 65, no. 1, Cambridge, MA.

Schachter, Paul and Fe Otanes. 1972. *Tagalog reference grammar*. Berkeley: University of California Press.

Schmidt, Hans. 2002. Rotuman. In John Lynch, Malcolm Ross, and Terry Crowley (eds.), *The Oceanic languages*. Richmond: Curzon Press, 815–32.

Schuh, Russell. 1998. *A grammar of Miya*. University of California Publications in Linguistics 130. Berkeley: University of California Press.

Selkirk, Elisabeth. 1982. *The syntax of words*. Cambridge, MA: MIT Press.

Sezer, Engin. 1981. The k/Ø alternation in Turkish. In George N. Clements (ed.), *Harvard Studies in phonology*. Bloomington: Indiana University Linguistics Club, 354–82.

Shaw, Patricia A. 1980. *Theoretical issues in Dakota phonology and morphology*: Outstanding dissertations in linguistics. New York: Garland.

Shaw, Patricia A. 1985. Modularisation and substantive constraints in Dakota Lexical Phonology. *Phonology* 2:173–202.

Sherrard, Nicholas. 2001. Blending and reduplication. PhD thesis, University of Essex.

Sibanda, Galen. 2004. Issues in the phonology and morphology of Ndebele. PhD thesis, University of California, Berkeley.

Sibomana, Leo. 1980. Grundzüge der Phonologie des Tarok (Yergam). *Afrika und Übsersee* 63:199–206.

Sibomana, Leo. 1981. Tarok II: Das Nominalklassensystem. *Afrika und Übersee* 64:25–34.

Sietsema, Brian M. 1988. Reduplications in Dakota. In *Papers from the regional meeting, Chicago Linguistic Society*. Chicago: Chicago Linguistic Society, 337–52.

Singh, Rajendra. 1982. On some "redundant compounds" in Modern Hindi. *Lingua* 56:345–51.

Smith, Jennifer. 1997. Noun faithfulness: on the privileged status of nouns in phonology. Available online from the Rutgers Optimality Archive, ROA# 242-1098.

Smith, Jennifer. 1998. Noun faithfulness and word stress in Tuyuca. In Jennifer Austin and Aaron Lawson (eds.), *Proceedings of ESCOL 97*. Ithaca: CLC Publications, 180–91.

Smolensky, Paul. 1993. Harmony, markedness and phonological activity. Rutgers University: Rutgers Optimality Workshop 1.

Soltész, Katalin J. 1959. *As ösi magyar igekötök [The ancient Hungarian preverbs]*. Budapest: Akadémia Kiadó.

Sommer, Bruce. 1981, The shape of Kenjen syllables. In Didier L. Goyvaerts (ed.), *Phonology in the 1980s*. Ghent: E. Story-Scientia, 231–44.

Spaelti, Philip. 1997. Dimensions of variation in multi-pattern reduplication. PhD thesis, University of California, Santa Cruz.

Spencer, Andrew. 1998. Morphophonological operations. In Andrew Spencer and Arnold Zwicky (eds.), *Handbook of morphology*. Oxford: Blackwell, 123–43.

Spring, Cari. 1990. Implications of Axininca Campa for Prosodic Morphology and reduplication. PhD thesis, University of Arizona.

Sproat, Richard. 1986. Malayalam compounding: a non-stratum ordered account. In Mary Dalrymple, Jeffrey Goldberg, Kristin Hanson et al. (eds.), *Proceedings of the fifth West Coast Conference on Formal Linguistics*. Stanford: Stanford Linguistics Association, 268–88.

Sprouse, Ronald. 1997. A case for enriched inputs. Available online from the Rutgers Optimality Archive, ROA# 193–0597.

Sprouse, Ronald. In preparation. Allomorphy in the lexicon: blocking, opacity, and ungrammaticality. PhD thesis, University of California, Berkeley.

Srichampa, Sophana. 2002. Vietnamese verbal reduplication. In Robert S. Bauer (ed.), *Collected papers on Southeast Asian and Pacific languages*. Canberra: Pacific

Linguistics, Research School of Pacific and Asian Studies, Australian National University, 37–47.

Steriade, Donca. 1988. Reduplication and syllable transfer in Sanskrit. *Phonology* 5:73–155.

Steriade, Donca. 1997. Lexical conservatism and its analysis. *Selected papers from SICOL 1997*. Seoul: Hanshin, 157–79.

Steriade, Donca. 1999. Lexical conservatism in French adjectival liaison. In Marc Authier, Barbara Bullock, and Lisa Reed (eds.), *Formal perspectives on Romance linguistics*. Amsterdam: John Benjamins, 243–70.

Stevens, Alan M. 1985. Reduplication in Madurese. In *Proceedings of the Second Eastern States Conference on Linguistics*. Columbus: Linguistics Department, the Ohio State University, 232–42.

Steyaert, Marcia. 1976. Verb reduplication in Dakota. *Minnesota working papers in linguistics and philosophy of language*. Minneapolis, MI: University of Minnesota Linguistics Department, 127–43.

Struijke, Caro. 1998. Reduplicant and output TETU in Kwakwala. In H. Fukazawa, F. Morelli, C. Struijke, and Y. Su (eds.), *University of Maryland working papers, vol. 7: Papers in phonology*. College Park: University of Maryland, 150–78.

Struijke, Caro. 2000a. Existential Faithfulness: a study of reduplicative TETU, feature movement, and dissimilation. PhD thesis, University of Maryland.

Struijke, Caro. 2000b. Why constraint conflict can disappear in reduplication. In Mako Hirotani (ed.), *Proceedings of the Northeastern Linguistics Society* 30. Amherst, MA: CLSA, 613–26.

Stump, Gregory. 1998. Comments on the paper by Inkelas and Orgun. In Steven Lapointe, Diane Brentari, and Patrick Farrell (eds.), *Morphology and its interaction with syntax and phonology*. Stanford, CA: CSLI Publications, 393–405.

Sumukti, Rukmantoro Hadi. 1971. Javanese morphology and phonology. PhD thesis, Cornell University.

Suzuki, Keiichiro. 1999. Identity avoidance vs. identity preference: the case of Sundanese. Paper presented at annual meeting of the Linguistic Society of America, Los Angeles.

Tauli, V. 1966. *Structural tendencies in Uralic languages*. London: Mouton.

Thomas, Linda May Kopp. 1975. Klamath vowel alternations and the segmental cycle. PhD thesis, University of Massachusetts, Amherst: GLSA.

Topping, Donald. 1973. *Chamorro reference grammar*. Honolulu: University of Hawaii Press.

Uhlenbeck, E. M. 1953. Word duplication in Javanese. *Bijdragen tot de Taal-, Land- en Volkenkunde* 109:52–61. Reprinted in Uhlenbeck, 1978, *Studies in Javanese morphology*. The Hague: Martinus Nijhoff, pp. 89–97.

Uhlenbeck, E. M. 1954. Duplication in the morphology of the Javanese verb. *Bijdragen tot de Taal-, Land- en Volkenkunde* 110:369–87. Reprinted in E. M. Uhlenbeck (ed.), 1978, *Studies in Javanese morphology*. The Hague: Martinus Nijhoff, pp. 98–115.

Urbanczyk, Suzanne. 1996. *Patterns of reduplication in Lushootseed*. Amherst: GLSA.

Urbanczyk, Suzanne. 1998. A-templatic reduplication in Halq'eméylem. In Kimary Shahin, Susan Blake, and Eun-Sook Kim, (eds.), *Proceedings of the Seventeenth West Coast Conference on Formal Linguistics.* Stanford: CSLI Publications, 655–69.

Vanbik, Kenneth. 2003. Junctural and parasitic voicing in Burmese. Paper presented at Berkeley Linguistics Society 29.

Vaux, Bert. 1996. Abkhaz Mabkhaz: m-reduplication in Abkhaz and the Problem of Melodic Invariance. Unpublished MS, Harvard University.

Vaux, Bert. 1998. *The Phonology of Armenian.* Oxford: Clarendon Press.

Vaux, Bert. Forthcoming. *The Cwyzhy dialect of Abkhaz.* Stanford: CSLI Publications.

Walker, Rachel. 2000a. Long-distance consonantal identity effects. In Roger Billerey and Brook Lillehaugen (eds.), *Proceedings of the nineteenth West Coast Conference on Formal Linguistics.* Somerville: Cascadilla Press, 532–45.

Walker, Rachel. 2000b. Yaka nasal harmony: spreading or segmental correspondence? In Lisa Conathan, Jeff Good, Darya Kavitskaya, Alyssa Wulf, and Alan C.-L. Yu (eds.), *Proceedings of the Berkeley Linguistics Society* 26. Berkeley, CA: Berkeley Linguistics Society, 321–32.

Walker, Rachel. To appear. Consonantal correspondence. *Proceedings of the workshop on the lexicon in phonetics and phonology.* Edmonton: University of Alberta.

Walsh, D. S. 1982. Variation of verb-initial consonants in some Eastern Oceanic languages. *Pacific Linguistics Series C*-74:231–42.

Wash, Barbara. 1995. Productive reduplication in Barbareño Chumash. MA thesis, University of California, Santa Barbara.

Watson, Richard L. 1966. Reduplication in Pacoh. MA thesis, Hartford Seminary Foundation.

Weber, David John. 1989. *A grammar of Huallaga (Huánuco) Quechua.* Berkeley: University of California Press.

Wee, Lionel. 1994. Identifying the reduplicant. Paper presented at Trilateral Phonology Weekend (TREND) II, Stanford University.

Weeda, Donald Stanton. 1992. Word truncation in prosodic morphology. PhD thesis, University of Texas, Austin.

Wells, Margaret. 1979. Siroi grammar. *Pacific Linguistics Series B* 51.

White, Robin Barbara Davis 1973. *Klamath phonology.* Studies in Linguistics and Language Learning, vol. 12. Seattle: University of Washington.

Wierzbicka, Anna. 1986. Italian reduplication: cross-cultural pragmatics and illocutionary semantics. *Linguistics* 24:287–315.

Wiesemann, U. 1972. *Die phonologische und grammatische Struktur der Kaingang Sprache.* The Hague: Mouton.

Wilbur, Ronnie. 1973. *The phonology of reduplication.* Bloomington: Indiana University Linguistics Club.

Wise, Mary Ruth. 1986. Grammatical characteristics of PreAndine Arawakan languages of Peru. In Desmond C. Derbyshire and Geoffrey K. Pullum (eds.), *Handbook of Amazonian languages,* vol. I. Berlin: Mouton de Gruyter, 567–642.

Yip, Moira. 1982. Reduplication and CV skeleta in Chinese secret languages. *Linguistic Inquiry* 13:637–61.

Yip, Moira. 1997. Repetition and its avoidance: the case of Javanese. In Keiichiro Suzuki and D. Elzinga (eds.), *Arizona phonology conference Proceedings, vol. V: Proceedings of the South Western Workshop on Optimality Theory (SWOT)*. Tucson: University of Arizona, Department of Linguistics coyote Papers, 238–62. Available electronically from the Rutgers Optimality Archive, ROA# 82-00002.

Yip, Moira. 1996. Lexicon optimization in languages without alternations. In Jacques Durand and Bernard Laks (eds.), *Current trends in phonology: models and methods*. Salford: University of Salford Publications, 757–88.

Yip, Moira. 1998. Identity avoidance in phonology and morphology. In Steven LaPointe, Diane Brentari, and Patrick Farrell (eds.), *Morphology and its relations to phonology and syntax*. Stanford: CSLI Publications, 216–46.

Yip, Moira. 1999. Reduplication as alliteration and rhyme. *GLOT International* 4:1–7.

Yoquelet, Corey. 2004. Grammaticalization and the epiphenomenon of the so-called repeated morpheme constraint. Unpublished ms., University of California, Berkeley.

Yu, Alan C.-L. 2000. Stress assignment in Tohono O'odham. *Phonology* 17:117–35.

Yu, Alan C.-L. 2003. The phonology and morphology of infixation. PhD thesis, University of California, Berkeley.

Zepeda, Ofelia. 1983. *A Papago grammar*. Tucson: University of Arizona Press.

Zepeda, Ofelia. 1984. Topics in Papago morphology. PhD thesis, University of Arizona.

Zigmond, Maurice L., Curtis G. Booth, and Pamela Munro. 1990. *Kawaiisu: a grammar and Dictionary with Texts*. Berkeley: University of California Press.

Zimmer, Karl and Barbara Abbott. 1978. The k/Ø alternation in Turkish; some experimental evidence for its productivity. *Journal of Psycholinguistic Research* 7:35–46.

Zoll, Cheryl. 2002. Vowel reduction and reduplication in Klamath. *Linguistic Inquiry* 33:520–27.

Zuraw, Kie Ross. 2000. Exceptions and regularities in phonology. PhD thesis, University of California, Los Angeles.

Zuraw, Kie Ross. 2002. Aggressive reduplication. *Phonology* 19:395–439.

Index of languages

Index of names

Abbi, A. 36, 60, 61, 79, 80, 215
Abbott, B. 72
Akinlabi, A. 2–3
Alderete, J. 3, 42, 74, 75, 78, 81, 83, 99, 100, 216, 224
Anderson, S. 12, 18, 31, 158
Anttila, A. 70, 71, 105, 118, 218
Applegate, R. 4, 185–86, 188, 189, 190, 191, 195, 196
Apte, M. 79, 205
Arnott, D. 51
Aronoff, M. 32, 45, 90, 182, 184, 206–09
Austin, P. 79

Bagemihl, B. 204
Barker, M. 113, 114, 116, 118, 218
Barnes, J. 78
Bat-El, O. 215
Bates, D. 21, 98, 119
Benua, L. 65, 74, 75, 157, 158
Bhaskararo, P. 42
Bissell, T. 202
Black, D. 21
Blevins, James 45, 90
Blevins, Juliette (= Levin, J.) 96, 97, 156, 203
Bloomfield, L. 214, 222
Blust, R. 213
Boas, F. 100
Bochner, H. 12, 215
Booij, G. 67, 140, 182, 184
Booth, C. 48
Bosson, J. 42
Bowen, D. 78
Breen, G. 37
Broselow, E. 119, 127
Brousseau, A. 5
Bruening, B. 42, 80
Burkhardt, P. 124, 221

Burzio, L. 218
Bybee, J. 165

Caena, R. 78
Carlson, K. 21, 127
Carrier-Duncan, J. 182
Chittleborough, M. 93
Cho, Y. 70, 218
Chomsky, N. 3
Clements, G. 4, 135
Cohn, A. 98–103, 104, 108, 110–11, 112, 157, 158, 218
Cole, J. 140, 145, 182, 184, 185
Collins, C. 5
Comrie, B. 67
Conathan, L. 8–9, 166
Conteh, P. 51
Corston-Oliver, S. 94, 130, 200
Cowper, E. 51
Crosswhite, K. 211, 224
Crowley, T. 9, 10, 49, 50–51, 52–53, 54, 55–57, 58, 215
Csato, E. 42, 80

Dahlstrom, A. 124, 165–67, 168–70, 171, 172
DeLacy, P. 124
Delancey, S. 114
Deloria, E. 100
Dixon, R. 27, 28, 29, 30
Dobrin, L. 206–09
Dolbey, A. 34
Downing, L. 6, 10, 11, 31, 33, 38, 39, 41, 65, 83, 89, 132, 140, 145, 184, 185, 188, 191, 216
Dressler, W. 67
Dudas, K. 137, 138, 139, 144–45, 147–48, 150, 173
Durie, M. 63–64, 67

Index of subjects

ablaut 17
affix reduplication 27–31
'Aggressive Reduplication' 221
alliteration (see also rhyme, consonance) 204
  'alliterative concord' 205–09
allomorphy in Optimality Theory 34
A-morphous Morphology 31
anti-identity effects 210–11
  in reduplication (see also
    dissimilation) 79–80
antonym constructions (see also synonym
    constructions, near-synonym
    constructions) 47, 61–62, 63, 64
a-templatic reduplication 213

backcopying 24, 113–14, 174–75, 182,
  186–87
  in morphological reduplication 114–18,
    175–76, 182–85, 193
  in phonological assimilation 177–79
'base-dependence' in reduplication 92–97
'base-priority' in Optimality Theory 74
Base-Reduplicant Correspondence Theory
    (BRCT) (see also backcopying, Coerced
    Identity theories, Kager–Hamilton
    problem) 4, 8, 23, 24, 26, 41, 65, 68, 77,
    80, 82, 85–86, 88–89, 99, 102–03
  opacity in 104, 106, 107–08, 109–12,
    113–14, 115–16, 135, 138, 149, 158–60,
    161, 165

Coerced Identity theories 18, 23, 24, 68, 77,
    81, 104, 107–08, 149
consonance (vs. reduplication) 204
constructions (morphological) 7, 11–20, 25,
    45, 61, 201
  in reduplication 7–11, 15–16, 19–20, 34,
    37, 44, 46, 57–59, 60–62, 68, 185, 188

meta-constructions 12, 118
  phonology of: see cophonologies
  semantics of 13–16, 28
cophonologies 16–18, 19–20, 24, 69, 70–88,
    89, 97, 99, 100, 102, 103–04, 106, 115,
    117–18, 120, 123, 124, 127, 129–30, 133
  cyclic/layered nature of 103, 136, 148–49,
    151–52, 154–56
  inside-out nature of (see also cyclicity) 74,
    75
  Master Ranking of 71
  of daughter nodes in reduplication (see also
    the Independent Daughter Prediction) 18,
    19, 25, 69, 75–97, 140, 161
  of mother node in reduplication (see also
    the Mother Node Prediction) 19, 25, 69,
    70, 71, 75–77, 95, 96, 98, 155, 161
  scope of 74, 75, 100, 133, 162–73
  vs. constraint indexation 74–75, 100, 106
Copy and Association theory of reduplication
    (see also templates in reduplication) 3–4,
    68
Correspondence Theory: see Optimality
    Theory
cyclicity (see also layering) 16, 20, 51, 70, 75,
    99, 110, 133, 136
  as source for opacity 135–36, 138–43,
    146–47, 148–50, 153–55, 156–58, 161,
    169, 172, 173

derived environment effects 105, 129–30
dissimilation, input–output (see also Melodic
    Overwriting) 78, 80–81, 211
divergent allomorphy in reduplication 8–11,
    40
  semantically empty morphs 10–11, 27, 31,
    36
  (see also Melodic Overwriting)

251